Calling Cards

Calling Cards

Theory and Practice in the Study of Race, Gender, and Culture

Edited by

Jacqueline Jones Royster

and

Ann Marie Mann Simpkins

STATE UNIVERSITY OF NEW YORK PRESS

Published by
State University of New York Press, Albany

Printed in the United States of America

For information, address State University of New York Press,
90 State Street, Suite 700, Albany, NY 12207

Production by Kelli Williams
Marketing by Susan M. Petrie

Library of Congress Cataloging-in-Publication Data

Calling cards : theory and practice in the study of race, gender, and culture / edited by Jacqueline Jones Royster and Ann Marie Mann Simpkins.
p. c.m.
Includes bibliographical references and index.
ISBN 0-7914-6375-3 (alk. paper) — ISBN 0-7914-6376-1 (pbk.: alk. paper)
1. Rhetoric—Social aspects. I. Royster, Jacqueline Jones. II. Simpkins, Ann Marie, Mann

P301.5.S63C35 2005
808—dc22 2004048166

10 9 8 7 6 5 4 3 2 1

Contents

Illustrations

Preface

In the nineteenth century in both Europe and the United States, there was a firmly established and highly developed social ritual of presenting oneself to others within elite social circles by means of a small, often elegantly decorated, card. Calling cards, as they came to be called, became a primary instrument by which social overtures were made, invitations were extended, and social acceptance (or rejection) in these circles was negotiated. This tradition harkened back to an earlier habit in the eighteenth century of the use of cards by tradesmen to advertise their wares and services, and it resonates today with our contemporary use of business cards and now web pages for both social and professional purposes.

We chose the image of "calling cards" as an appropriate symbol in the academic arena to suggest the ways and means by which professional roles and identities are encoded and symbolically deployed in the negotiation of acceptance (or rejection) in the academic world as well. In textual studies (rhetoric, literacy, composition, literature, etc.), as the focus of this publication, race, gender, and culture have become for many of us the "cards" by which we have participated more boldly than ever before in the social and political processes of academe. Using such terms, we have entered disciplinary discourses and engaged actively in research, scholarship, and teaching. In both the making and transmission of knowledge, race, gender, and culture have animated a critical questioning of agency, identity, and authority, and brought attention to the workings across time of power, privilege, and entitlement in many of our professional enterprises, including the operational systems of the academy itself. The body of scholarship shaped by such focal points continues to grow, invigorating multiple discourses and generating strategies for using this enhanced knowledge base to address complex contemporary issues.

Such efforts have pushed and indeed shifted the boundaries of place and purpose, reframing, often provocatively, what we can do in textual studies with license and how we can do it. Certainly, we have extended the range of subjects deemed appropriate for scholarship, identified a broader array of terms of engagement by which we can interrogate subjects, and established a wide range of disciplinary and interdisciplinary methodologies by which to critique, analyze, and interpret data. Boundaries have, in fact, become more fluid, and the fluidity has given rise to an escalating value for knowledge making that transcends traditional disciplinary frameworks in order to account more generatively for human experience and achievement.

Colleagues in mainstream and not so mainstream academic circles have learned to focus more acutely on what it actually means to carry out a research agenda that is defined and substantively directed by schemata (race, gender, culture) that have traditionally been marginalized and disregarded. We have learned to adapt and invent research and teaching strategies, and we have also struggled to negotiate the social and political dynamics of academic lives that are so clearly tied to traditionally devalued interests. In the main, there have not been road maps by which to determine appropriate and worthy pathways, since these interests actually go against the grain of many traditional practices. We hear the tales of colleagues who have worked without advocates, mentors, or champions to run interference or to keep resources and enabling structures in place. Personally and professionally, many of us have felt on our own, isolated, and struggling against the odds. These are the facts of many lives.

Most pertinent for this collection is not so much a focus on personal career histories, as it is on using such perspectives and the work produced to create clearer occasions for critical dialogue. The opportunity to engage in discourse is compelling, permitting an interrogation of the impacts and consequences of the work and the features and circumstances that mark and sustain its credibility and value. While scholars who centralize race, gender, and culture are certainly developing and refining theoretical frameworks and methodologies, what remains, in our view, is a need to dedicate more time to critical reflection, not just one by one but in the company of others. The goal is to engage an active metadiscussion of what we are discovering, how these discoveries help to shape and signal excellence, and what such insights enable in terms of theories, methodologies, and practices. How are we thinking about what we do? What are explicit and tacit dimensions of our work? How do race, gender, culture, and other related terms enable sense-making strategies and permit more generative interpretive frameworks?

A persistent challenge has been the terms and categories themselves—race, gender, culture. Such concepts have emerged via socially determined frameworks and remain ambiguous and contentious. They are definable most vibrantly within specific contexts that vary in material conditions and circumstances. Such variability and indeterminacy pose multiple challenges, as suggested by the essays in this collection, and exacerbate the need to articulate approaches, theories, and practices as we bring both substance and flexibility to the professional integrity of this work. We respond to a mandate to develop ways of working that are just as capable of making room for race, gender, and culture in the discourses of our field as they are of garnering respect and regard for us as the purveyors of this scholarly expertise. We search for ways to do the work and for ways to intervene in the tradition-bound discourses that surround the work. The imperative is to mark what we do, not just as exotic, provocative, or interesting, but as excellent and worthy.

In conceptualizing this collection, Ann Marie and I started with our own interests in African American women in rhetorical studies and the need to bring more critical attention to the dynamics of power, privilege, authority, and entitlement in the disciplinary practices of this field. We quickly realized, however, the range of interesting work that colleagues across related fields in English studies are doing, as well as the need to see this work as whole cloth, as part of a common effort to situate these concepts authoritatively and instructively in academic enterprises.

In extending the call for papers, our goal was twofold: to invite colleagues in rhetoric, literacy, composition, language, and literature to share their work and also their reflections about it—methodologically, ideologically. We wanted to keep central a concern, as suggested by Toni Morrison (1991), about fluidity, the gendering of race and culture, as well as the racing and acculturation of gender, especially as we examine particular groups within specific contexts. We invited contributors to reflect deliberately on their own work and to consider the convergences of race, gender, and culture. We invited them to think about theoretical frameworks, processes, and methodologies and about the quality of the knowledge and understanding that such approaches generate.

We asked the contributors questions: How do we take this work seriously as intellectual work and set the terms of engagement flexibly and clearly enough to engender excellence? What assumptions, theories, and methodologies have enabled current work and seem viable in an ongoing evolutionary process? What makes it possible to do the work well? How do we name or talk about the work? What kind of work is it?

In other words, we asked contributors to consider what they do, how they do it, why, and with what benefits. We did not prescribe a framework for how a contributor might address any of the questions.

We asked them instead to share their work as an enactment or illustration of whatever they deem important. In addition, we expressed our desire to have an on-line conversation at the end of the drafting process in which contributors would read the entire collection and engage in a short discussion of the implications and consequences of seeing their work in the company of similar work by others. For this part of the process, we asked contributors to consider: the range of work represented by this collection; whether they saw patterns of any kind; whether a meta-view suggested missing voices and views; how they saw strengths, ongoing challenges, and implications.

In deliberately establishing an opportunity for both scholarly productivity and critical reflection, our intent was to set in motion a process that would function organically to acknowledge individual experiences while simultaneously positioning those experiences within and perhaps against the contours of institutionalized practices. Moreover, our hope was that the inclusion of colleagues from several areas in textual studies would underscore that both a collective view and individual views are important, not comprehensive necessarily, nor representative, but certainly suggestive. As indeed the volume actually demonstrates, the individual arguments are compelling at the same time that the collective implications of those arguments raise issues that resonate in patterned ways related to theory, methodology, and practice, but most instructively also in terms of what it actually means to perform this type of work both professionally and personally, especially with a clearer view of the ways in which we are all always raced, gendered, and acculturated.

At the outset of this project, of course, we could not have predicted a particular outcome for our goals and expectations, so we were content to leave the question of "calling cards" open. After the submissions were in place, we found that those who had indeed accepted the invitation presented chapters that were both affirming and instructive. We discovered that patterns are discernable but also that they are gelatinous with a capacity to shape and contextualize issues in multifaceted ways. Consequently, we found no one obviously perfect arrangement that might reveal and enlighten. There were several. We were not surprised, for example, that the collection could not actually be defined, as is typical of several collections, by method, theory, or practice, and certainly not by the separation of theory and practice. Instead, we found such boundaries to be fluid, with the various chapters offering insights that are relevant across academic work, rather than in just one area.

With a range of choices for how individual pieces might be arranged or rearranged, we were drawn toward constructing a case for how race, gender, and culture disrupt discourses, encourage invention, and provocatively suggest often dramatic renovations to knowledge and interpretation. We chose to center the collection around the idea that "calling cards" function as both occasion and instrument for rethinking, refiguring, and reforming. We clustered the chapters to bring attention to the need to adjust interpretive frameworks and language; to extend substantially our thinking about experiences and achievements; to showcase particular methodological practices with culturally specific sites; and to face provocative issues of presentation and representation.

The collection is divided into three sections: Part I: "Rethinking Race, Whiteness, Gender, and Class," with chapters that bring one or several of these concepts to critical view in research, scholarship, and teaching. Part II: "Refiguring Culture, History, and Methodology," with the authors taking various approaches that are grounded in studies of race, gender, and culture in engaging both professional and personal issues related to research, scholarship, and teaching. Part III: "(Re)Forming Analytical Paradigms," with chapters that use race, gender, and culture as analytical frames for textual renderings and interpretation. We close the collection with an extrapolation from our on-line conversation. In "Last Words," each of us had the opportunity to look back at our individual contributions within the context of the whole and to have a "last word."

As we come now to the moment of completing the project, we are grateful to the contributors for offering such a sterling array of insights about race, gender, and culture and for helping us to create a collective "calling card," an instrument by which we can invite others into critical conversation. We are also grateful to SUNY Press for being willing to consider this idea a worthy one and to all of our colleagues there who worked with us to bring the project to fruition. Ultimately, we hope that the collection adds meaningfully to escalating dialogues in academe generally, but most particularly to the discourses that are ever evolving in our own areas in textual studies as well.

Jacqueline Jones Royster, The Ohio State University

Introduction

Marking Trails in Studies of Race, Gender, and Culture

Jacqueline Jones Royster

> Only the Black Woman can say "when and where I enter, in the quiet, undisputed dignity of my womanhood, without violence and without suing or special patronage, then and there the whole *Negro race enters with me.*"
>
> —Anna Julia Cooper, *A Voice from the South*

A HISTORY OF RESISTANCE AND STRUGGLE

In 1892 Anna Julia Cooper issued a bold challenge when she invited her audience to imagine African American women as trailblazers for their race, as intellectual scouts audaciously dedicated to carving out pathways to full participation in American society. Moreover, she invited all to consider that, as those held in lowest esteem, African American women inevitably foretell the entry of their ethnic group as a whole into "civilized" conversations and onto the world's stage. She envisioned a place where her talents and the talents of those like her (i.e., African American women and men) could have equal authority and agency in the human enterprise of making a better world.

Since Cooper's publication of *A Voice from the South,* there have indeed been increased educational opportunities for African Americans and other marginalized groups as well. These opportunities have enabled formerly disfranchised people of various identities to enter academic circles and participate more actively as well-trained researchers and scholars. We have worked for and claimed the authority to acquire and use academic credentials, and even harder in many ways to do so as ourselves—as racialized, gendered, sexualized, and culturally distinctive human beings, rather than as mirrors, imitators, shadows, or other categorizations that might suggest apparently prescribed models of "academic professional" and indeed "academic work." Entering this world, however, has not been simple. As evidenced by this volume, over the generations, we have faced challenges on several fronts in the effort to operate with agency, autonomy, authority, professional respect, and also to get the work done that we feel impassioned to do.

One hundred years ago, William E. B. DuBois, a contemporary of Cooper's, articulated the basic dilemma in his often-quoted statement about the peculiar sensation of "double-consciousness," "this sense of always looking at one's self through the eyes of others, of measuring one's soul by the tape of a world that looks on in amused contempt and pity" (*The Souls of Black Folk*, 5). DuBois brought to bolder relief the longing of African American men for "self-conscious manhood" and the persistent barriers they faced in their desires to exhibit a sense of agency and authority "without being cursed and spit upon by his fellows, without having the doors of opportunity closed roughly in his face" (5).

While DuBois's focus was on African American men and the social order more generally, the message is no less meaningful for a full range of individuals in academe (African American scholars included) who have faced the pulls and tares of being both scholar and Other—racialized, gendered, acculturated beings amid discourses where dominant social and political forces are privileged to ignore and disregard us and our work with the same type of amused contempt and pity articulated by DuBois in 1903. Being different with regard to race, gender, and culture, and/or choosing focal points for research, scholarship, and teaching that go against the grain of academic traditions with regard to these same types of factors has been and continues to be a story of resistance and struggle.

In 1984, eighty-one years after *Souls of Black Folk*, bell hooks rearticulated the dilemma for yet another generation as she sought to make a place for the full participation of people who continue to be deemed marginal:

> To be in the margin is to be part of the whole but outside the main body. . . . Living as we did–on the edge—we devel-

> oped a particular way of seeing reality. We looked both from the outside in and from the inside out. We focused our attention on the center as well as on the margin. We understood both. This mode of seeing reminded us of the existence of a whole universe, a main body made up of both margin and center. Our survival depended on an ongoing public awareness of the separation between margin and center and an ongoing private acknowledgment that we were a necessary, vital part of that whole. (*Feminist Theory*, Preface)

Profiting from well over a century of experience, hooks focused on the distinctive variety of agency and authority that marginality enables rather than constrains. She provided a springboard for seeing the two-ness as both challenge and opportunity, making more visible yet another challenge that remained unacknowledged, the need for an ongoing "public" awareness of an ongoing "private" understanding.

Typically, we have positioned academic discourses in the realm of public discourses, highlighting abstracted, objectified, and dispassionate voices as most valuable. In the schema of private, social, and institutional discourses, academic work operates most vibrantly within the institutional realm, relegating the individual and even social experience of academic work as private—not institutional, not public, not scholarly. The peculiarities of either personal or social experience, therefore, are typically cast as not academically salient, interesting, or consequential, and thereby institutionally inappropriate. Traditionally, personal and social peculiarities exist below the waterline, with only the sanitized tip of the iceberg viewable or valuable. Out of sight, out of the purview of a more deliberately "public" awareness, the desire to incorporate such views and experiences into knowledge-making or policy-making schemata poses a challenge.

In the ongoing evolution of resistance and struggle, with this volume we join those who want to recognize, not only the artificiality of public-private dichotomies as demonstrated, for example, through feminist analyses of public and private spheres (Fraser 1989 and 1997; Ryan 1990), but also to recognize that dualities (two-ness, double-consciousness, margin-center relationships) are more often than not multiplicities. Our sociocultural environment is endowed by the impacts and consequences of complex histories, including the implications of race, gender, culture, sexuality, etc. This type of contemporary scholarship embraces the value added in an accounting of differences in specific contexts, and particularly the intersection of differences (see, for example, the work of Kimberle Crenshaw (1995) and others in critical race theory). Theoretical perspectives have evolved, in fact, in ways that permit a reimagining, not simply of when and where we might enter disciplinary space, but how.

Using the idea of "calling cards" as a metaphor (see the explanation in the preface), we have the option of presenting ourselves in terms of disciplinary values (as the "Americans" in DuBois's terms), as people with politicized interests (by our focus on race, gender, class, culture, sexuality, and other intersections), and also as participants in academic circles who, given the merging of public and private discourses, assert more forthrightly that none of us, regardless of our personal identities, set aside ideological assumptions when we participate in academic enterprises. None of us are really objective in our knowledge-making work; all of us are stakeholders of one sort or another in the work; all have beliefs, presumptions, and alliances that shape and direct the work; and the knowledge that we make has potential for social and political consequences. What has become more visible, therefore, is that in the case of traditional academic values where ideologies are naturalized, ideology goes unnoticed and uninterrogated. In contrast, when ideologies are against the grain of traditional values, they are deemed problematic, contentious, or even "un"-natural. Studies of race, gender, and culture have emerged from value sets that were not traditionally naturalized within academic constructs, such that engaging in such studies politicizes both the work done and the people who do it.

This ability of researchers and scholars to acknowledge disciplinary values, politicized interests, and ideological assumptions as part of public academic engagement represents a paradigmatic shift in scholarly practices. The change not only shifts who enters the conversation when and how, but also the qualities of the discourse itself as the conversations make room for participation in more inclusive terms. This latter shift is toward dialogues that operate more freely as a process of interchange rather than as a core process for acculturation or indoctrination. The task, however, is still the task of joining ongoing worldly conversations. The twist, as suggested by this volume as one example, is in having the privilege of envisioning such conversations as dynamic rather than static. As Kenneth Burke suggests in *A Grammar of Motives* (1969), we reset the fidelity of the scene, modifying the arrangements and the terms of engagement in order to make a more accommodating space for qualitative differences.

In *Calling Cards,* a volume deliberately and explicitly centered in studies of race, gender, and culture, the mandate is to claim the authority to enter worldly conversations and to claim an equal authority to bring in with us by whatever pathways we have followed the interests and concerns that have formed along the way. We claim the right to narrate our peculiar experiences, to situate them within larger social frameworks, and to enter by these terms into institutionalized discourses, whether those discourses have been designed with our viewpoints in mind or not. The ongoing need is for a public acknowledgment that individual and social experiences are necessary and vital dimensions of the wholeness of academic enterprises. We present our various perspectives, therefore, in this textured way, understanding that our own ability to thrive as productive academic professionals and the capacity of academics in general to sustain excellence depend on an ongoing public awareness of the multidimensional realities of our work and the separations that continue to exist between margin and center.

MAPPING A PROFESSIONAL TRAJECTORY

In my own work, I view forbears such as Cooper and DuBois, and a legion of others, as having established a legacy of trailblazing, entering uncharted spaces and raising voices of resistance to hegemonic practices. As those of us in this volume move forward with our own work, my view is that we must learn from prior experiences and insights just as those after us may learn from us. Learning well, however, is tied to recovering more fully articulated accounts of the work and from the privilege of thinking about these stories of achievement in the company of others, not just by ourselves in isolated private ways, with the goal of contextualizing this intellectual ancestry and determining our own relationships to these legacies.

This collection affords me a fairly rare opportunity to account for the research that I have done over the last two decades in rhetorical studies within this historical framework. In mapping my experiences below, my intention is twofold, to:

1. trace the development of my concern that researchers and scholars need to interrogate critically the goals, nature, and processes of knowledge making in rhetorical studies in light of shifts in who researchers and scholars are these days, what their focal points are, the contexts in which we exist, and the hegemonic ways that quality and value have been established for both the focus and the process of knowledge making;

2. situate my interests in the rhetorical practices of African American women within a call for a transformative vision of rhetoric

> by asserting the need to extend disciplinary parameters for what counts as knowledge, as well as to actually use these extended boundaries to rethink aesthetics and integrity.

In 1995 in my CCCC Chair's address, I spoke publicly for the first time about challenges that I saw in knowledge-making processes in rhetorical studies. I placed myself within the tradition of DuBois and others of his generation and claimed that I was dedicated, as I said then, "to raising this veil [as he had tried to do], to overriding these systems of insulation by raising another voice, my voice in the interest of clarity and accuracy" (CCC 34). In the article in *CCC* that followed the address, I tried to make clear that the type of work that I do, in its being so thoroughly informed by a viewpoint that centralizes race, class, gender, and culture, just did not fit neatly into traditional knowledge-making paradigms in our field and that this fact of scholarly life dictated a need for transformation. I asserted the following:

> In discussing nineteenth century African American women's work, I bring tales of difference and adventure. I bring cultural proofs and instructive examples, all of which invariably must serve as rites of passage to credibility. I also bring the power of storytelling. These tales of adventure in odd places are the transitions by which to historicize and theorize anew with these writers re-inscribed in a rightful place. Such a process respects long-standing practices in African-based cultures of theorizing in narrative form. As Barbara Christian says, we theorize "in the stories we create, in riddles and proverbs, in the play with language, since dynamic rather than fixed ideas seem more to our liking" ("The Race for Theory," 336). The problem is that in order to construct new histories and theories such stories must be perceived not just as "simple stories" to delight and entertain, but as vital layers of a transformative process. (35)

I have been consumed actually since then with the effort to carry out in historically sanctioned arenas, rather than marginalized ones, the mandate that I created for myself that day, with three examples serving as landmarks along this path. The first marker is in my co-authored article with Jean C. Williams, "History in the Spaces Left: African American Presence and Narratives of Composition Studies." In this article, we sought to broaden the information base in histories of composition with a more fully textured view of the presence of African

Americans in higher education in terms of both student participation and achievement, and the long history of contributions in research, scholarship, and disciplinary practices by African American scholars. At the end of the article, we stated the need for a paradigmatic shift along three basic fault lines. We called for:

> 1. A systematic commitment to resist the primacy of "officialized" narratives;
> 2. A search for better interpretive frames that are capable of accounting more richly for the participation and achievements of the many rather than the few, and;
> 3. A renewed interest in using the knowledge and understanding acquired through suggestions one and two in order to help a broader range of students to perform at higher levels of achievement. (582–83)

The second and most substantive trail marker actually addressed item number 2 from this article in searching for a better interpretive frame. In chapter 6 of my book, *Traces of a Stream,* which I titled "A View from a Bridge: Afrafeminist Ideologies and Rhetorical Studies," I sought to write in a more direct, deliberate, and metaconscious way about knowledge-making and interpretive practice along two planes: to discuss what I had previously named in my CCCC address as "the systems of deep disbelief as contending forces, as prevailing winds that push against scholarly proactivity and toward a continual re-inscription of the status quo" (254); and to draw attention to the nature of scholarly ethos and how it informs research and practice. I was particularly interested in the intersections of these two planes, and I proposed a model for action for those who participate in knowledge-making processes in which race, class, gender, culture, and other such values matter. I explained that my approach embodied the notion that mind, heart, body, and soul operate collectively, rather than separately, even in scholarship, and that this view of collectivity requires intellectual work to include, from my point of view, at least four sites of what I called "critical regard": careful analysis, an acknowledgment of passionate attachments, attention to ethical action, and a commitment to social responsibility (279).

At the end of the chapter, I sought to reconnect this approach to my own work, and I ended with this paragraph:

> These women's stories suggest that, as users of language, we construct ways of being, seeing, and doing in recognition of

> the materiality of the world around us and of who and how we are in our sundry relationships to it. Their work suggests that we should not automatically discount the discordant, revolutionary, or evolutionary voices of the unsanctioned or un-institutionally authorized. It also suggests that, in order to be generative in our interpretations of contemporary language practices, we need analytical models of discourse that are flexible enough to see the variability of the participants and their worlds, to draw meaning from the shifting contours of rhetorical negotiation across and within material relationships, and to imagine the possibility of building bridges . . . we can see how connections are merging between private, social, and public space. We can understand the simultaneity of competing and conflicting agenda . . . we can imagine, as African American women have traditionally done, that the "public" arena is a place where negotiation can be with words rather than with weapons, and we can commit ourselves, as African American women writers have done, to turning our thoughts toward action in making a better world for us all. (285)

A third and most recent marker on this trajectory is "Disciplinary Landscaping, or Contemporary Challenges in the History of Rhetoric" (*Philosophy and Rhetoric,* 148–67). In this article I take up the argument where I left off in *Traces of a Stream* and propose the need to understand knowledge as an interpretive enterprise and thereby a social construction; to articulate the limitations of historical and current knowledge-making practices and the scholarship produced by such practices; to sustain perspectives in the history of rhetoric that assume, rather than minimize the view that the terrain of rhetorical experiences is much fuller than we have documented and embraced in our scholarship; to reform disciplinary practices. Moreover, I assert that the legacies of rhetorical scholarship demonstrate the extent to which theories and practices have operated hegemonically and tended to function with a heavy and relentlessly constraining hand. Even a cursory survey demonstrates that we have privileged Western territories and elite male experiences within those territories, and in the article I raise this question:

> What if I started a rhetorical interrogation with a consideration of more southern territories, with a focus on women, and with the possibility that eliteness may or may not hold its viability across variations in rhetorical performance? How,

> after all, might the concept of eliteness shift when the focus of interrogation or the site of interrogation shifts? (150)

My goal in this essay was to draw attention to the complexity of the rhetorical landscape as variable and dynamic, a terrain that we are just beginning to envision in more global (as compared with more Western) terms. Further, I underscored the idea that much work remains to be done if we are to understand more fully the potential of human beings as "symbol-using animals," to use Burke's (1966) term and I raised the idea that we can benefit greatly by showcasing other areas, reframing and foregrounding different features, and becoming more attuned to the aesthetic values of other views. Basically, I proposed that there are values added when we start with the notion that the history of Western rhetorics is indeed what we *know* best, but with an understanding that such a distinction does not suggest that this record automatically constitutes what *is* best. I proposed in the article that there is plenty of room in knowledge-making enterprises to celebrate what we know while still extending those parameters in dynamic and generative ways.

SITUATING A SCHOLARLY SELF

I have taken time in this rather ego-centered way to trace the development of my own concerns about knowledge-making processes in order to assert two points that I consider to be critical to my own academic calling cards. First, I claim that as a scholar in the history of rhetoric I have not been operating arbitrarily but well within the scope of theories and methodologies in the field. Second, I claim that my interests in race, gender, class, and culture are not shaped by a series of random or opportunistic events but by the application of critical apparatuses to focal points that have not always garnered central attention in the past. By these terms, I present myself as a scholar who sustains an abiding professional commitment to the rhetorical history of African American women but who also understands that the context for critical engagement requires a transformative vision, one that imagines the possibility of things currently unseen.

Further, I might frame my editing of this volume as a fourth marker along this trajectory since I expect this collection to deepen the critique of disciplinary habits and to serve as a concrete display by which we can reconfigure what counts as knowledge, recognizing, of course, that knowledge is indeed socially constructed. While the chapters in this volume certainly do not constitute the fullness of the rhetorical landscape with regard to race, gender, and culture, they do bring texture to the need to rethink interpretive frames; to assess continuities and discontinuities with regard to both terms of engagement and terms of credibility and excellence.

In situating my own work within this historical context, my central points of inquiry have included: What difference did education, particularly higher education, specifically literacy education/rhetorical education, make in African American women's lives? How did it function? What conditions made it possible for such women in such a time, place, and context to believe in their own agency, despite contending messages that dominated in their sociocultural environment, and not only to believe in their own agency, but to act so defiantly and so courageously? What made them think that they had the capacity to do anything at all, but particularly to speak and to write in the interest of social, political, economic, educational reform? As this series of questions suggests, I have developed a habit of critical questioning, of speculating in order to make visible unnoticed possibilities, to pose and articulate what we see now, what's missing, and what we might see instead.

In the process of gathering data about nineteenth-century African American women, I began to realize that I had been aware of many of the *facts* of African American women's lives, conditions, and contributions intellectually for a long time, but through my own scholarly efforts I came to understand in a more visceral way the importance of the transformation of *facts* into *knowledge.* I began to see how important it is to understand that, certainly, I had *seen* before, I had *known* before, but in so many ways I had not *noticed* before not just what has been happening with this group but what has been going on with them. For example, strangely, it was not that I didn't know that nineteenth-century African American women went to school. I actually knew that. It was that their being there had not operated in my mind and imagination with consequence. My knowing had not been transformed into knowledge or understanding until my head, my heart, my backbone, and my stomach had also become more fully engaged. During that moment of more holistic awareness, I was drawn to a quotation from Audre Lorde that came to be very instructive, and I have referred to it often in my writing since then. Lorde says:

> It's not that we haven't always been here, since there was a here. It is that the letters of our names have been scrambled when they were not totally erased, and our fingerprints upon the handles of history have been called the random brushings of birds. (Foreword, *Wild Women in the Whirlwind,* xi)

Coming to this distinction between facts and knowledge constituted a moment of scholarly growth in that I came to understand both intellectually *and* viscerally that knowledge making is sense making, and sense making is an interpretive process.

A general challenge for me continues to be to build, balance, and harmonize experience in the making of a common ground in which knowledge related to African American women's practices can be made and have the capacity to operate persuasively, with impact and with consequence. I recognize, especially in cross-disciplinary work, the importance of mechanisms, including narratives, that permit knowledge to be amplified. With amplification, knowledge can be perceived as significant, understandable, *and* believable across multiple audiences. We see the sea of information. We understand the claims. We occupy a common space that permits an opportunity for substantive interaction and for persuasion.

With these two frameworks—the use of speculation in critical inquiry and the viewing of knowledge as a persuasive process of interpretation, I return to the example of *Traces of a Stream.* I wrote *Traces of a Stream* with an eye toward demonstrating appropriate places for storytelling as a process that helps to reset the conditions for engagement; for history telling as a process for enriching the conceptual base through experience building; and for theory making as a process throughout sense making that in the case of African American women not only enables the creation of a usable past, but also amplifies knowledge in ways that help to make that knowledge more persuasive and help, thereby, to make it recognizable as *news.*

In general, my goal in *Traces* was to account for the systematic ways literacy has functioned in the lives of African American women in support of sociopolitical action. I wanted to shift analytical paradigms that have habitually marked the historical presence of African American women at 1619, rather than acknowledging a much longer historical trajectory that considers cultural continuities as African women were transformed into African American women through the bizarre circumstances of the rise of chattel slavery. I wanted to use this shifted view to look again at their survival of these oppressive conditions and at their persistent uses of their talents as speakers and writers to bring about social changes. I sought to make a distinction between what we know in finely drawn detail about African American women's heritage and what we know with much less detail from a more landscape view, a distinction that mirrors the difference between looking at a digital image that seems seamless and knowing that the image is made of pixels.

There is a truth in broad/long range scope. There is a truth at closer ranges. I talk about this interpretive distance in terms of both time and space through the use of two Swahili terms, *sasa* and *zamani*. I raise, at that point, the question of a place in scholarship for what I call the "critical imagination," a term that encodes the need to engage in a reconstruction process that includes what might be called "educated guesses." I chose "critical imagination" as the operational term, however, because I wanted to underscore this concept as a skill to be consciously developed and strategically used relative to seeing, analyzing, and interpreting data. In my view, such speculation begins with a mindset, a willingness to imagine the possibility of truth in order to develop an ability to recognize small pieces of a puzzle as meaningful.

Ultimately, what I think that my work demonstrates most clearly, as suggested by *Traces of a Stream*, is that I have been engaging in a disciplinary ground-clearing process in terms of theoretical, historical, and ideological practices in the field. The imperative has been to enable not just my own work but also to encourage more generally scholarship that commands greater interpretive and persuasive power. My basic goal, therefore, has been to acquire a better understanding, certainly, of the ways and means of African American women's writing, as a racialized, gendered, and culturally distinctive group, but also to understand human creativity in the exercise of language well used. I have labeled this imperative the search for a transformative vision in the history of rhetoric, and I see it as responsive to a very practical interest, one that I attach historically to long-standing intellectual habits among African American women.

In *Freedom Dreams: The Black Radical Imagination*, Robin D. G. Kelley speaks similarly of the role of imagination in revolutionary movements. He cites the example of his mother's ability to "dream out loud" (1) as a springboard for understanding the extent to which revolutionary movements use imagination to inspire passion and to enable change. He says:

> Sometimes I think the conditions of daily life, of everyday oppressions, of survival, not to mention the temporary pleasures accessible to most of us, render much of our imagination inert. We are constantly putting out fires, responding to emergencies, finding temporary refuge, all of which make it difficult to see anything other than the present. As the great poet Keorapetse Kgositsile put it, "When the clouds clear / We shall know the colour of the sky." When movements have been unable to clear the clouds, it has been the

> poets—no matter the medium—who have succeeded in imagining the color of the sky, in rendering the kinds of dreams and futures social movements are capable of producing. Knowing the color of the sky is far more important than counting clouds. Or to put it another way, the most radical art is not protest art but works that take us to another place, envision a different way of seeing, perhaps a different way of feeling. (11)

In reinvoking the spirit of Anna Julia Cooper as a woman with a radicalizing imagination, we need to imagine a world for rhetorical studies that is global, flexible, and specifically aware of its own complicity in the deploying of systems of domination and oppression. By resetting the parameters by which we engage in rhetorical work, we open new possibilities for sense making and for mediating the gaps between what we know and rightly celebrate and what we might see more insightfully if we developed the habit of looking again and looking with different eyes. Such commitments to encouraging paradigmatic shifts will, no doubt, disrupt longstanding hegemonic practices and likely reconfigure what constitutes knowledge. The question that remains, then, is one of imagination. Can we clear the clouds that currently engulf us in studies of race gender, and culture and discover the color of the sky?

PARLOR TALK

When Ann Marie Simpkins and I distributed the call for this collection, we were drawn to an image in Kenneth Burke's *The Philosophy of Literary Form* (1973):

> Imagine that you enter a parlor. You come late. When you arrive, others have long preceded you, and they are engaged in a heated discussion, a discussion too heated for them to pause and tell you exactly what it is about. In fact, the discussion had already begun long before any of them got there, so that no one present is qualified to retrace for you all the steps that had gone before. You listen for a while until you decide that you have caught the tenor of the argument; then you put in your oar. (94–95)

We wished for an opportunity for the contributors to engage in a collective conversation after we all had the chance to see what each other had written. Our thinking was that too often we engage in this type of work alone, crossing paths and exchanging ideas in meetings and conferences, using articles and books that we find evocative in teaching and research, but not typically having the chance to think about and talk about what our work together suggests. Opportunities are rare for eighteen professionals who have engaged in the exact same task to think about what they have done together, how we see it individually and collectively, and even more rarely writing about these metaperspectives in public.

As explained in the preface, we decided to make the effort to have such a moment of reflection and conversation by setting up an online exchange. We didn't have the time or space in the collection for it to function as a full and substantive dialogue in the way suggested by the quotation above from Burke, but we did take the time to read, to think, and to put forth some last words. That section of this collection, like the articles that we have contributed, does not represent all that we might say. What it does, as we hope the full volume does, is to use our professional "calling cards" as a signal that the dialogue remains open and that indeed it is an important one.

Part I

Rethinking Race, Whiteness, Gender, and Class

Chapter 1

The More Things Change . . . Or, Why I Teach Whiteness

Valerie Babb

For most of my scholarly life I have considered myself an Americanist and dedicated much of my research to the study of race, gender, and culture, precisely because so much of what is embodied in the term *American* arises from contestations between these categories and their representations. Who has the right to call himself or herself American has been part of national discourse from the framing of treaties, to the crafting of constitutional amendments, and currently to debates surrounding the public policy of racial profiling. That race continues to be the problem of the twenty-first century, to paraphrase W. E. B. DuBois, suggests that we have not learned our lessons on race very well, that rather than change the hegemony of race we simply change the position of different groups within it. This consistency of practice stems from a cultural tendency to view the experience of race more from the position of those victimized by it and not, until recently, those who benefit from it. Such a perspective allows unstated privilege to masquerade as a "level playing field" and makes meaningful, lasting changes to the often unfair racial dynamics of the United States impossible to achieve.

It is precisely this state of affairs that has made me turn my attention to the impact of whiteness within the culture of the United States. I have come to realize that through its obvious yet unstated presence it impinges upon all discussions of American identity.[1] I should mention here that by whiteness I am not referring to a phenotypic classification; rather, I am referring to an invented ideological construct that blended the histories, cultures, and traditions of various European nationals into a hegemonically privileged race category. Its content is a wholly manufactured one developing unevenly over a period of time and responding to a variety of historical events and social conditions: among them, the need to create historical antecedents for a European polyglot that had none, the need to crystallize national identity, and the need to minimize class warfare. At different cultural moments various icons and institutions were mobilized to sustain this ideology of whiteness, and cultural rhetoric solidified its identity. Examination of its evolution offers clear illustration of why discussions of race are so complicated today and seem to accomplish little.

To quote Richard Slotkin, "A people unaware of its myths is likely to continue living by them. . . . The voluminous reports of presidential commissions on violence, racism, and civil disorder have recently begun to say to us . . . that myths reach out of the past to cripple, incapacitate, or strike down the living" (4–5). One myth that certainly incapacitates many modern engagements of race because it continues to reinvent itself and continues to shape representations of a pluralistic society is that of white primacy. Not to interrogate it dooms us to repetitive voluminous reports, conferences, panels, and commissions that all seem to tread already-trod ground. The continuing clashes over affirmative action, over immigration policy, over academic curricula, and over remedies to the increasing isolation of segments of American culture from the larger culture, are just some examples of the noxious effects of an ideology whose values equate Americanness with whiteness.

Whiteness studies must go hand in hand with any inquiry into race and gender so that a comprehensive understanding of the sociocultural dynamics that give these categories their potency is fully understood. What I hope to present in this chapter is an overview of sites where the emergence of whiteness is evidenced and where its analysis might provide an understanding of hegemonically sustained traditions, practices, and beliefs that privilege some over many and make a culture of varied peoples vulnerable to increased divisiveness.[2]

To illuminate the deleterious effects of white ideology, one need only examine its ironic construction amidst a nation of many peoples, and perhaps the best venue for beginning such an inquiry are documents of the pre-national period. No set of works has been so misread or so narrowly read. Because they are canonized as texts of national heritage, these exciting documents of first contact are often relegated to the status of historical artifacts or paeans to nation formation; yet, within them are the first instances of imaginative content that became the cornerstones for abiding American notions of race and gender. As they chronicled English colonialist expansion, tensions over Native American removals, responses to an increasing African presence in North America, early American writings evidenced the gradual creation of a racial consciousness that conformed the many races, ethnicities, classes, and genders that populated pre-national America to a cultural hierarchy privileging whiteness and masculinity.

It is important to remember that in seventeenth-century North America there was no single racial or cultural majority. The eastern seaboard colonies in particular were a stew of Native American nations, African and Arab nationals, and European ethnics. The idea of a white race emerged when propertied English settlers with strong ties to Calvinist traditions sought to forge ties among English, Welsh, Irish, Scots, and other European ethnics drawn to the North American continent for various reasons—obscene land rents, desire to better their lives, desire for their own religious state. As these settlers' need for land necessitated incursions into Native American space, as plantations grew dependent on unpaid labor, and as the pre-Revolutionary period posed the question who was to be considered American, a discourse developed to balkanize an English Puritan elite from those they sought to dominate. Within this discourse, loosely strung historical events were interpreted to tell the story of "pilgrims" who conquered a sometimes unforgiving landscape and built a promised land that would subsequently incorporate many "huddled masses." The contribution of an imagined whiteness to this effort was to smooth the fragmentation that characterized a European polyglot that had not yet surmounted distinctions of ethnicity and class to become a single white race.

A constructed whiteness becomes identifiable in the genres that would constitute the nascent American written canon—travel narratives, narratives of captivity, execution narratives, maps, religious tracts, legal statutes.[3] For example, captivity narratives systematized the values of patriarchy and white racial purity that would shape American understandings of race and gender. Written against the backdrop of a time when cultural rhetoric proffered the persistent image of a virginal North America awaiting its chosen ones "flying from the Depravations of Europe, to the American Strand . . . wherewith His Divine Providence hath Irradiated an Indian Wilderness" (Mather 89), these works assert an English and subsequently white right to North America. As the "chosen ones," their land acquisition in America and the subordination of other races and ethnicities that this acquisition necessitated were justified as divine destiny. Through contrasting white captives to Native Americans, savagery to civility, Christian to heathen, early American texts dramatized what an ideal whiteness was by juxtaposing it to images of what is was not.

Figure 1.1 "Indians Gambling for the Possession of a Captive," *Harper's Weekly* (26 March 1870), 197. Courtesy of Hargrett Rare Book and Manuscript Library/University of Georgia Libraries. Even as late as 1870 images of a victimized whiteness persisted, as this sketch by M. W. Cary illustrates.

When Mary Rowlandson's 1682 narrative cast Native Americans as rapacious predators and the English as hapless martyrs, she rendered racial difference as intrinsic and immutable, a vision typical in many captivity narratives designed to demarcate the difference between "us" and "them" and allow an increasingly fragmenting European populace to envision themselves as part of a unified white identity.[4]

At the turn of the seventeenth to eighteenth century, narratives of crime and execution equaled the captivity narratives in their power to fix notions of idealized whiteness. Acts of confession, testimonial, and execution were part of a cultural performance in which immense crowds, numbering three to five thousand by some estimates, became voyeurs to the sins of the criminal and, via the sermons at these events, were encouraged to see themselves in those condemned to die. The reprinting of the executed's narratives disseminated the racial and gender content within these performances to an audience beyond actual viewers, and the published characterizations of the condemned became the parameters by which racial and social acceptability were defined. While many of the qualities decried at executions were general human failings, the narratives attached them to specific class, gender, ethnic, and racial groups. Criminal narratives of the 1780s and 1790s exhibited consistent tropes in which women were too weak to surmount moral temptation; criminals were from the lower classes; and sexual deviation was marked as "black."[5]

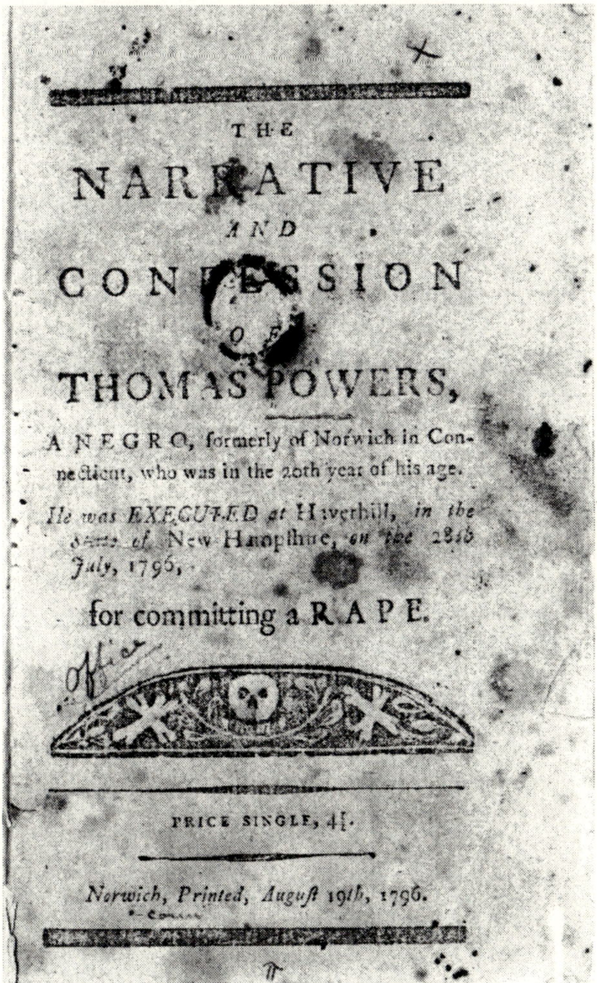

THE

NARRATIVE

AND

CONFESSION

OF

THOMAS POWERS,

A NEGRO, formerly of Norwich in Connecticut, who was in the 20th year of his age.

He was EXECUTED at Haverhill, *in the State of* New Hampshire, *on the 28th July*, 1796,

for committing a RAPE.

PRICE SINGLE, 4d.

Norwich, Printed, August 19th, 1796.

Figure 1.2 Title page, *The Narrative and Confession of Thomas Powers.* Library of Congress Rare Book Reading Room. Execution narratives of black criminals condemned for sexual crimes often contained title pages highlighting race while those of white criminals rarely did.

Joseph Mountain's narrative, subtitled *Sketches of the Life of Joseph Mountain,* A NEGRO, Who was executed at New-Haven, on the 20th Day of October, 1790, For a Rape, details the events that led to his arrest. Though he denies the rape, he is condemned to die and he closes his narrative with the following lines:

> If the reader of this story can acquiesce in my fate and view me "stumbling on the *dark* mountains of the shadow of death," with composure he will yet compassionate a soul *stained* with the foulest crimes, just about to appear unimbodied before a God of infinite *purity.*" (qtd. in Williams 300–301; italics mine).

Terms such as "dark" and "stained" in reference to Mountain and his soul contrast with the infinite "purity" of God. That this symbolic contrast is transposed to a living black being invites a color ideology of black and white in which black is inherently evil and white inherently good to become a racial one in which blacks are inherently depraved while whites are the moral norm.

Through both the captivity and criminal narratives, white readers became connected to one another, and through the medium of the written word a common identity of whiteness solidified. The sustained demonization of Native Americans, Africans and African Americans, and believers in non-Christian faiths allowed a nascent white identity to cohere around representations of racial and religious differences; while the sustained demonization of women implied that the ideal white identity was masculine. Universal human characteristics—hard work, piousness, honesty, cognitive ability, physical beauty—were increasingly associated with whites, and other racial groups were used to symbolize deviance from these parameters. The Revolutionary period would build upon these representations and add to them an implicit equating of American identity with white racial identity.

In Hector St. John de Crevecoeur's answer to his own question, who is an American? the equation of Americanness and white European antecedents that characterized the Revolutionary period and beyond is evident. Crevecoeur opines that an American is "either an European, or the descendant of an European" (49). His musings reflect sentiments expressed as the question of who should benefit from American resources was heatedly debated by "founding fathers." John Jay in the *Federalist Papers* supplants the plurality of races and cultures that was the American actuality with his own monocultural vision:

> Providence has been pleased to give this one connected country to one united people—people descended from the

> same ancestors, speaking the same language, professing the same religion, attached to the same principles of government, very similar in their manners and customs. (Hamilton, Jay, and Madison 8–9)

Benjamin Franklin, who saw distinctions among those we would today categorize as white—"in Europe, the Spaniards, Italians, French, Russians and Swedes are generally of what we call a swarthy Complexion; as are the Germans also, the Saxons only excepted"—expresses his desire for a white America in the following terms:

> The Number of purely White People in the World is proportionably very small. All Africa is black or tawny. Asia chiefly tawny. America (exclusive of the new Comers) wholly so. And I could wish their Numbers were increased. (Labaree, 234)

The existence of these sentiments amidst the liberatory rhetoric of the Revolutionary period, along with the growing presence of enslaved Africans and the continued removal of Native Americans created ironic tensions which a white racial classification remedied. Conceiving of the authentic American identity as white provided a rationale for the disenfranchisement of some within an emerging democracy.

While the documents of the Revolutionary period in many ways provide the opportunity for observing the equating of whiteness and Americanness, the effective dissemination of this equation was not accomplished through documents written by propertied English men, in essence, for propertied English men. The hegemonic nature of this ideology could only be achieved through a consistent mass marketing of ideas, a mass marketing aided by the industrialization of the nineteenth century.

Daniel Walker Howe describes the nineteenth century in the United States as "a time of industrialization, knowledge explosion, immigration and vast population growth, urbanization, geographical expansion, changing race relationships, and the greatest armed conflict on American soil" (3). One cultural response to these conditions was, as Howe goes on to observe, an "increased sensitivity to culture" and "an intense preoccupation with national identity" (7). These preoccupations manifested themselves in many ways, among them the urge to create a national literature, the urge to systematize American identity through the exposition culture of worlds fairs and the emerging everyday entertainment venues of dime museums, circuses, and slumming tours through which Americans increasingly defining themselves as white could have their identities validated against constructions of racial others.

The combination of this cultural activity achieved a systematizing of racial portraiture in which a white norm acted as a measuring stick against which other racial groups were evaluated. This period in many ways can be seen as taking what went before, the ideas and representations, the content if you will of the pre-national and Revolutionary periods and shaping them for mass consumption during an era increasingly concerned with classification and quantification. The result was a packaged bag of race and gender "goods" made formulaic for a twentieth century on the fast break.

Certainly, literary texts of the nineteenth century offer ample illustrations of creating whiteness by creating myths of the racial other. Novels such as James Fenimore Cooper's *The Last of the Mohicans* (1826) or Lydia Maria Child's *Hobomok* (1824) are examples offering two different engagements of racial identity beyond the racial classification of white that still manage to emphasize native exoticness against the backdrop of a white norm. Cooper creates a character descending from the frontiersman persona popularized by Daniel Boone. Natty Bumpo throws off the trappings of an English-inspired definition of Americanness, taking his conceptions instead from his Mohican counterparts and the woods around him; but even though he is dressed in a hunting shirt and is renowned for his knowledge of the forest, he continually asserts that he is "a man without a cross," thereby dispelling any danger of racial slippage and ensuring the purity of a white identity. He may mask as a racial other, but he is still one of the dominant group. Child's *Hobomok* fathers a son with a white Englishwoman, but by novel's end, he has headed for a wilderness away from New England. His child is renamed, raised by his English mother and her white, English husband and subsequently attends Cambridge. What these examples illustrate is that even while white American writers are rightly sensing the multiplicity of American identities, they are also, despite their best efforts, presenting this multiplicity as ultimately giving way to the white norm. The Native Americans in these works "naturally" cede to the advent of a superior race that has ascended to its historical time. Though they may be romanticized for their connection to the diminishing frontier and their antithesis to the dehumanization that is part of civilization's progress, they are nostalgic relics in a nation that is clearly establishing itself as white.

Literary works were not the only products of the nineteenth century contributing to constructions of whiteness and its ability to shape conceptions of other racial identities. Exposition culture, dime museums, and the new vogue of slumming tours all aided in creating white hegemony. The racial imaginings showcased at Chicago's 1893 World's Columbian Exposition, for example, included "Daily ethnographicical exhibitions illustrating the customs of nations "savage and civilized."[6]

Figure 1.3 Coin purse showing Columbus's American landing. Chicago Historical Society. This souvenir from the Chicago World's Fair is an example of the many items of material culture promulgating white mythohistory at the exposition. Columbus stands laying claim to the New world while its indigenous inhabitants bow down before him.

As attendees of the exposition strolled along the Midway Plaisance, the carnivalesque area of the fair devoted to popular forms of entertainment, they could view "natives" in reproductions of a Dahomey Village, Cairo Egypt, or an Igorrote Village of the Philippines. These along with the Bureau of Indian Affairs exhibits on Indian life in which viewers could contrast "the red man as a savage wrapped in a blanket, and his child in the dress of civilization" (Badger 105) were framed against a backdrop of Beaux-Arts buildings such as the Art Palace where painting after painting commemorated American "high" art (works whose subjects and techniques valorized European traditions), or the Transportation Building among other where American technological progress was validated. These contrasting tableaus of "high" and "low" reinforced notions of racial hierarchy and cemented associations of whiteness to ideas of advancement, civilization, and privilege. They provided edifying content that taught the American populace how to *read* race and centralized whiteness as the American ideal while doing so.

Along with exposition culture, a growing museum industry contributed to the work of cementing representations of whiteness. While museums designed to be centers of scientific and artistic studies were evolving, also evolving were their popular counterparts. Generally termed "dime" museums these institutions offered inexpensive displays of the "wonders of the world." For a small fee viewers could be "edified" by stuffed animals, menageries, theatrical performances, and dioramas of all manner of content.[7] This genre of museum took on particularly racial tones when Phineas Taylor Barnum opened his Chinese Museum in which mostly white onlookers could gaze at actual Chinese as living objects while having their own whiteness reinforced against a background of distanced exotica.

Barnum developed this idea in an even wider global context in 1882 with his traveling circus. Called the Ethnological Congress it paraded representatives of the "uncivilized races" Cannibals, Nubians, Zulus, Mohammedans, Pagans, Indians, Wild Men—in gilded chariots. A flyer describes his desire in its creation as seeking to form "a collection, in pairs or otherwise of all the uncivilized races in existence." He goes on to add, "My aim is to exhibit to the American public not only human beings of different races, but also, when practicable, those who possess extraordinary peculiarities" (qtd. in Adams 181–82). The objectification of races not considered white as "uncivilized" allowed white viewers to imagine white identity as an implicit civilized standard. This equation leaves no room for other cultural interpretations. If whiteness were the unspoken standard, then all values must be measured against its values; all cultural practices must be compared to its practices; and what deviates from its ever-shifting parameters is exoticized or demonized.[8]

The "museumfication" of human beings would continue into the early twentieth century as entrepreneurs such as Chuck Connors, the Irish ex-boxer and self-proclaimed "mayor of Chinatown," hosted a Chinatown vice tour. In 1906 white New Yorkers could tour Chinatown and be enthralled by stories of white slavery. They could call on an opium den (really the tricked out apartment of Connors's friends George Yee and his white wife Blonde Lulu) to see "degraded" humans in an opium stupor (really George Yee and Blonde Lulu performing an opium stupor). At the end of the viewing they could close the evening with a meal at what was commonly called a "chop suey" restaurant. Slumming parties were so much the vogue that a writer observed in *Theatre Magazine*, "Even New Yorkers to whom Broadway is a twice-told tale, and whose jaded appetites a Delmonico, Sherry, or a Martin scarce can tempt, surprise themselves with new sensations when they saunter through this populous but clean and orderly Chinatown, peering into its weird shops and stores, buying souvenirs from the rich and gorgeous stock of its bazaars, and dining on mo goey chop suey with snow-like rice and tea that is a blissful revelation in the "Chinese Delmonico's or the Celestial Sherry's" (Tyrrell 170).

A reportorial from *Munsey's Magazine* describes a staged opium den, quite likely that of Chuck Connors:

> [A] Chinaman is lying to the left of the sputtering lights and to the right is a shell of a white woman, with hollow cheeks and bare, bony arms. The eyes of the Chinaman and the woman—she is his wife—seem to burst from their heads. The pair go through the motions of opium-smoking . . . the holding of the canted bowl against the flame; and then the long guttural inhalations; and a burst of smoke from the nostrils. (Meloney 820)

The description again evokes the white voyeur using constructed images of the exotic to crystallize conceptions of white normalcy. Also symbolized in this tableau is the figure of the white female implicitly lured to victimization by her nonwhite husband and the evil habit of opium smoking. This female figure who transgresses racial lines helps to construct the myth of white sexual restraint. Her intercourse with a man from another race creates a subtext of sexual violation that threatens visible race difference and reinforces conceptions that differentiate white identity not only along lines of skin color, nationality, or cultural practices, but also along lines of sexual morality.

Popular performances of the early twentieth century continued to erase the overt presence of whiteness as a racial construct. The ability to attach the concepts implied in terms such as *uncivilized, heathen, exotic, immoral* to actual humans allowed those claiming the privilege of whiteness to imagine themselves as more highly evolved specimens of humanity deserving to be rulers of lesser races. To see encased in glass or paraded on chariots peoples who were so displayed because of their difference increasingly allowed whites from diverse ethnic and class backgrounds to solidify a group identity that would constantly need perceptions of difference to give it significance. The result is a steady fabrication of racial and class stereotypes to sustain a manufactured white identity needing nonwhiteness to give it form.

Figure 1.4 "Uncle Sam's Thanksgiving Dinner," *Harper's Weekly* (20 November 1869): 745. Courtesy of Hargrett Rare Book and Manuscript Library/University of Georgia Libraries. While a commendable multicultural impulse is evident in this illustration, also evident is a presumed white stewardship represented through Uncle and "Mrs." Sam as welcoming hosts; the statuary of the Goddess Columbia and Justice as a blindfolded white female; and the portraits of Lincoln, Washington, and Grant adorning the walls.

In the contemporary cultural moment whiteness continues to exert its unstated privilege, and meaningful discussions of race must engage how this privilege came to be constructed throughout the history of the United States. Cultural materials reveal the ways in which the idea of whiteness allowed European nationals who had no natural ties to invent a mythohistory. Indentured servants, merchants, and propertied English men with often conflicting interests became pilgrims coming to the New World to practice their religion freely; the land inhabited by native Americans became an unforgiving wilderness tamed by pioneers; and industrial cities that exploited immigrant group after immigrant group became refuges for the huddled masses. This mythohistory defined an American as one who possesses white skin, thereby tacitly asserting that those who do not possess this racial trait are not "real" Americans and should not expect full access to American resources. Thus, whiteness is privileged while its privileging is masked.

The instances in which white privilege went unnamed are numerous. For example, unlike Native American and African Americans white working-class laborers were granted special access when their race did not prohibit them from gaining land during the 1862 Homestead Act; however, cultural history records this not as a race privilege but as expanding the nation's frontier for hardworking and eager settlers. Unlike African American men and women, white men who owned property (and eventually even those who did not) were granted special access when their race did not prohibit them from voting, running for public office, or serving on juries; however, cultural perceptions view this privilege merely as men exercising their rights as participants in a democracy. Over time in media representations of the '20s, '30s, '40s, and '50s whites were allowed roles that were not servile or sexually exoticized; they could be woman, wife, husband, father, educator, scientist, child. The did not have to argue that their physical beauty could serve as an inspiration to art, their imaginativeness as an inspiration to literature; nor did they have to catalog their unrecognized contributions to larger American society. Not all participants in this multiracial society benefited from such affirmative actions. These few illustrations of the unspoken privilege accorded white identity offer a sense of why attempts at racial equality often meet with fierce resistance. It is difficult to argue for parity when those who benefit from privilege do not realize they do.

So much of our dialogue centers around making an existing ideology, one that presumes the primacy of whiteness, amenable to the needs of a diverse populace (how do we extend the privileges of whiteness to others?) rather than around considering why we hold on to a system that privileges one racial group over others. This hegemonic inertia deepens social stratification because it feeds on the idea of difference as something against which a bulwark must be constructed rather than as something that characterizes the nature of a pluralistic nation.

What I hope this overview suggests are possible points along which an enhanced understanding of the operations of race within American culture can be divined. The aforementioned periods constitute just some of the many opportunities to view the values that begin to codify an American hierarchy privileging whiteness. By examining the ways in which such an ideology enlists newspapers, novels, stage productions, songs, and material objects; by considering how it appropriates universal human characteristics such as hard work, piousness, civility, cognitive ability, physical beauty for one racial group only; we achieve a greater understanding of the vast hegemony that accomplishes implicit exclusion without explicit rationales of racial superiority.

We need to understand the construction of whiteness in order to understand how our modern assumptions and presumptions about race are based upon it and why these presumptions should be reevaluated. The study and teaching of whiteness is a challenge, yet one worth undertaking because it combines with other approaches to offer a more self-conscious awareness of the foundations of racial and social categories. To consider race, gender, and culture without considering the often invisible hegemony that produces these constructs is to doom ourselves continually to "reinventing the wheel." Over and over the social, political, and economic damage enabled by cultural representations will be identified, their impact felt and studied; however, without clear deconstruction of the mechanism that fortifies them, their presence will remain an unchangeable fact of cultural interaction. Ultimately, the invisibility of whiteness poses the greatest "homeland" threat to a diverse nation.

NOTES

1. This chapter reflects upon work begun in *Whiteness Visible.* See Babb.

2. When whiteness studies emerged during the culture wars of the 1980s, it was greeted with skepticism that viewed it as yet another quirk of "political correctness." Over the course of the 1990s and into the twenty-first century, however, many cultural critics have come to see an understanding of whiteness as crucial to rethinking social systems within the United States. Though an exhaustive review of the literature in this area would be impossible here, worth mentioning briefly are some of the texts that have shaped the field.

Perhaps no work explores with greater historical breadth the formation of whiteness in both the European and American contexts than Theodore W. Allen's opus, *The Invention of the White Race* (1994). Allen argues persuasively that "the 'white race,' . . . is no part of genetic evolution. It is rather a political act" (22). Using English treatment of the Irish as an example, he demonstrates how acts of legal and social subjugation defined peoples with common phenotypes as distinct races. David Roedigger and Alexander Saxton explore the intertwining of race and class that gave rise to whiteness in the United States. In *The Wages of Whiteness* (1991) Roedigger observes that, "the pleasures of whiteness could function as a 'wage' for white workers. That is, status and privileges conferred by race could be used to make up for alienating and exploitative class relationships" (13). Saxton observes in *The Rise and Fall of the White Republic* (1990) how the class tensions between Whig republicanism and Jacksonian democracy influenced manipulations of whiteness through the political upheavals of the Civil War, Reconstruction, and the Jacksonian era. With an emphasis on the intertwining of gender and race, Peggy McIntosh in her essay, "White Privilege and Male Privilege" discusses how work in women's studies helped her to conceive of whiteness as "an invisible package of unearned assets that [she] can count on cashing in each day, but about which [she] was 'meant' to remain oblivious." In *White by Law* (1996), Ian F. Haney-Lopez explores the "central role law plays as both a coercive and ideological force in the construction of race" (202). A collection considering similar subject matter is *Critical White Studies: Looking Behind the Mirror*, edited by Richard Delgado and Jean Stefancic (1997), in which law review articles as well as essays explore the meaning of whiteness to American law and the meaning of American law to whiteness. A work that contemplates whiteness within the area of American literature is Toni Morrison's study *Playing in the Dark* (1992). In reflecting upon the effect of what she terms an Africanist presence on American creativity Morrison investigates "the impact of notions of racial hierarchy, racial exclusion, and racial vulnerability and availability on non-blacks who held, resisted, explored, or altered those notions" (11). A view of Hollywood's contribution to constructions of whiteness can be found in *Classic Hollywood, Classic Whiteness*, edited by Daniel Bernardi (2001). This collection views films from the 1920s through the 1960s and the ways in which they represented and perpetuated racial values creating a hierarchical system giving whiteness primacy. Lastly, Mason Stokes's *The Color of Sex* (2001) addresses the links between whiteness and heterosexuality. Other studies of whiteness to consider include the following: F. James Davis, *Who Is Black?: One Nation's Definition* (1991); Virginia Dominguez, *White by Definition* (1986); Ruth Frankenburg, *White Women: Race Matters* (1993) and *Displacing Whiteness* (1998); Maurice Berger, *White Lies* (1999); and *The Making and Unmaking of Whiteness*, edited by Birgit Brander Rasmussen, Irene J. Nexica, Eric Klinenberg, and Matt Wray (2001).

3. For a more detailed analysis of these materials, see Babb, chapter 2.

4. For more information on the use of race content within captivity narratives, see Slotkin.

5. For more information on the criminal narratives' potential to fix racial type, see Williams 1993.

6. For more information of the Chicago World Columbian Exposition see Carr.

7. For more information on the advent and decline of the dime museum, see Dennett.

8. For further information on Barnum see Adams.

Chapter 2

Bombs and Bullshit

Interventions in a Very Dangerous Time

Renee M. Moreno

> If we had only known
> that we could make
> chemicals, fertilizer?
> Bombs from bullshit?
> We would have blown up
> with the first lie . . .
>
> —Sekou Sundiata, "Bombs from Bullshit"

A question at the heart of *Calling Cards* deals with why race, gender, and culture, as compounding factors, are central to research agendas and how those agendas can be used to understand and challenge dominant power structures. In the poem that opens this essay, Sekou Sundiata's prophetic voice invites reflection in a similar way. Written in response to the Oklahoma City bombing, Sundiata places hate and rage in the same category as chemicals and fertilizer, the ingredients used by Timothy McVeigh to blow up the Murrah Federal Building, as well as names so many other "unstable compounds" with explosive potential. He suggests that we might do well to remember the many other combinations of things: the war on terror, killing of innocents, tattered social contracts, that have the capacity, in combination with hate and rage, to explode. All beg questions about shaping a different direction for where we might go as a society.

In 1963, James Baldwin expressed a similar idea when he wrote, "We are living through a very dangerous time," describing a "revolutionary situation," where society "is desperately menaced, not by Khruschev, but from within" (3). Baldwin also wrote that education creates an informed citizenry who question the society in which they live. Certainly, in our own time, the events of September 11 and our post-9/11 world and the real and imagined holy wars waged against the United States and its citizens have emphasized that an informed and mindful citizenry is essential to safety and survival. Baldwin noted a problem, however. In a nation that operates so persistently from the point of view of an oppressive dominant culture, the United States educational system has a way of robbing people of their most precious resources, replacing intact structures of identity with misperceptions, self-doubts, and a predilection for nonconscious, uninterrogated viewpoints. Both Baldwin and Sundiata suggest the need for corrective measures that can yield more creative outcomes, ones that make possible a more inclusive participation. Baldwin argues that, with corrective measures, teachers can undo some of the more damaging effects of education, and Sundiata locates change in a different consciousness when he states:

> If I had to qualify it at all, I would say that I am a ritual poet. That I have been trying to work the ancient roots of poetry in myth and drama, chant, ritual and dance. Only my ritual chant is usually the stage, and the mythology is our life and times as I see it.
> (http://www.grdodge.org/poetry/content_Sundiata.htm)

I agree with these views. We must help ourselves, as teachers and students, to see through the assumptions and lies that govern our lives and to make ourselves consciously aware of our interconnectedness and mutual dependences in the world. Even though difference is often cast, discursively at least, as what divides us, we must face the basic classroom challenge of developing critical strategies to combat the explosive forces that surround us. One of the ways to combat those forces is through the creation of counterdiscourses and counterknowledge that corrects, as Baldwin suggests, "so many generations of bad faith and cruelty, when it is operating not only in the classroom but in society . . ." (Baldwin 3).

In this chapter, my focus is on critical understanding—critical consciousness—providing opportunities for students to develop and hone a critical perspective of their experiences as racial, ethnic, gendered subjects in U.S. society. I teach in California, a distinctive state both demographically and economically, one that I believe can be instructive to the nation. A recent C-SPAN discussion, "The California Recall and the Future of Democracy," described California as the nation's "experiment in [new forms of] democracy" (21 Aug. 2003). The panelists described California's 2003 recall of the governor as "democratic distemper" and ongoing referendum processes as "a systematic transformation of conventional democratic orthodoxy," which they said was both good and bad. The discussion was framed around several assumptions, primarily that the nation is in the midst of great demographic changes, which California reflects; for example, California's growth of Latino and Asian populations was described as an important shift suggesting, among other things, a shrinking middle class, a situation that creates misplaced resentments and gives rise to "wedge issues," such as propositions 187, 209, 227, and 21 (discussed below). Indeed, during a recent conversation with my Faculty Mentor Group at CSUN, we discussed the uniqueness of our campus as it reflects California's large diverse population. Interestingly, we reached some consensus that discussions of multiculturalism such as those from the '90s do not necessarily provide us with a concise language to describe all we face—especially the fact that white students rarely see their stake in conversations about diversity or that white people's growing fear is their own status as minorities in the state. In my view, how California frames these discussions may very well impact the nation.

Similarly, a recent "Talk of the Nation" (a call-in talk show on the National Public Radio network) also referred to California as "our nation's experiment," *but* where the strains of U.S. diversity are tested. Los Angeles Unified School District (LAUSD), for example, serves a number of students who speak approximately seventy-five different languages and language varieties. LAUSD is, therefore, a large and diverse system, reflecting the state's demographics. It is no surprise that some of the more interesting (and deeply problematic) developments with education have been going on in California—prominent among them, the financial woes that plague the state; Band-Aid measures to support (and educate) a large, diverse school-age population; the extraordinary numbers of immigrants needing to learn English.

California voters, moreover, have passed reactionary social policies (ironically, aimed at education) that penalize immigrants, who are among our most vulnerable citizens. Of note are propositions to the state's constitution that have whittled away the rights of immigrants (both legal and illegal) in the form of Proposition 187[1]; that have done away with affirmative action (especially at the state's most prestigious public institutions of higher education) in the form of Proposition 209; that have eliminated bilingual education (insidiously referred to as English for the children) in the form of Proposition 227; that have continued to vilify juvenile offenders as threats to society, increasing funding for prisons instead of schools, in the form of Proposition 21.

In addressing these concerns, in this chapter I have chosen to tell a story, namely, to use narrative as exemplary evidence, in order to examine how such policies impact individuals. In the fall semester 1999, Adriana (a pseudonym), a first-year student enrolled in a basic writing course, recounted a story to me about a memory that she connected to her own literacy development. Adriana's story shows the effects of feeling erased when she should have been acknowledged. Sadly, I do not think that Adriana is unique. In many ways, she is quite representative of the students CSU serves—second language learners, immigrants, first generation college students, along with the race, ethnicity, gender, and class issues our students represent.

In a writing assignment adapted from William Condon's "literacy autobiography" (2000), I ask students to write about the role of literacy in their own lives. In this assignment, much like Condon's original assignment, I ask students to define literacy, both in terms of a common definition (usually based on articles that we examine together as a class) and their own recollections of the role literacy plays in their lives. I ask them to focus specifically on instances and moments when they are aware of learning to read, write, or interpret the world. Adriana chose a moment of triumph.

When Adriana was in the sixth grade, she entered a writing contest, which invited all sixth graders in the state of California to define the word *justice.* Winning the contest would garner them a trip to Sacramento to meet then governor Pete Wilson[2]; an opportunity to read the paper to the state assembly; an interview with a local television station; and the awarding of a resolution ("which is like a big diploma," Adriana remembered) by a local assemblywoman. As a first-generation immigrant student, "justice" had special significance for Adriana. Her parents, like many Latino immigrant parents, struggled to carve out a life for themselves in their newly adopted country and to provide their children with the education that they did not receive in their homelands. In writing about her parents, Adriana states,

> My parents didn't have much of an education because they had to go out and work to take care of me, my brother and sister. Although they were young[,] they learned to take care

> of us, work[ed], and learn[ed] lessons the hard way. People would say that my parents are illiterate because they didn't finish school, but if they knew who my parents are and what they have gone through and have done[, t]hose people would realize that my parents know more about life than they ever would[,] and to me that [is being] literate.

Adriana won the contest and took her trip to Sacramento with her parents. She met many state legislators, but the meeting with Governor Wilson and the interview with the local television station never took place.

Reflecting on this incident in a conversation with me, Adriana recalled her disappointment and explained that she always felt perplexed about why the local assemblywoman had evaded the question about why the meeting with Governor Wilson did not take place, despite this woman's repeated earlier promises that Adriana and her family would be able to meet him during their time in Sacramento. In the conversation with me, Adriana ventured a hypothesis that perhaps the visit didn't happen because she had not fit prevailing notions of what the winner of a writing contest defining the word *justice* was supposed to look like. Adriana is Central American, and what she had come to understand is that her success countered the prevailing discourses of the day that inscribed immigrants as "drains on society"—discourses that in fact fuel California's wedge issue propositions.

As I was listening to this story, bearing witness to an incident that had both perplexed and hurt her and listening to her moment of critical consciousness, I understood that the assignment had given Adriana space to analyze a troubling experience in the context of critiques of race, ethnicity, and socioeconomic conditions. Her analyses were provocative but entirely rational, and I concurred with her sense that, as a dark-skinned, Indio-looking immigrant, she might very well have been a disturbing challenge to Governor Wilson (and others in Sacramento), especially given his anti-immigrant stance at the time. Moreover, as a writing teacher who is teasing out the multilayered, complex issues surrounding students' acquisition of a second language, their literacy development, and their critical consciousness, I add that, in my view, the conversion of Adriana's memory into a moment of critical consciousness makes visible the real consequences of California's political terrain. Minority students who achieve and who might achieve are often left with an incomplete sense of affirmation, many unanswered questions, and an undue sense of doubt about their potential.

My thinking here is influenced by Baldwin's "A Talk to Teachers," where he raised critical issues about the impact and consequences of what happens to students in schools. Adriana came to a new level of critical consciousness in her understanding of this disappointing literacy event in her life. Through the use of race, ethnicity, class, and culture as critical lenses of analysis in this classroom assignment, she was able to reset her view to consider, not just her disappointment, but also the contextual conditions that might have contributed to it. In having the opportunity to think critically about the context of her life, she was in a better position to see, for example, how California propositions, such as 187, are a coalescing point for an ideology of "hate and rage" that can be so easily directed toward marginalized immigrants and directed toward them with such explosive consequences. A narrative moment helped Adriana to recharge her thinking and remedy the impact of damaging educational experiences, and not only that, it also helped her to understand in a different light equal opportunity for education as a deeply challenging ongoing experiment for U.S. society.

Indeed, as the state's school-aged population grows and as more demands are put on an already stressed school system—whose student body is becoming more ethnically, racially, and linguistically diverse and where this growth has outpaced building new schools—educational measures often exacerbate rather than help the problem. An example is the twenty-five-year-old Concept 6 calendar, a multitrack, year-round school calendar that reduces the time that K-12 students in California actually spend in school. The long-standing existence of this calendar, of course, begs the question of how prepared for higher education the immigrant students who are among those subjected to this calendar can be.[3] Concept 6 purports to alleviate overcrowding in Los Angeles schools, but as Hector Villagra (9 Nov 2001), Los Angeles Regional Counsel for the Mexican American Legal Defense and Educational Fund (MALDEF) states,

> At the outset, it's important to understand a few things about the Concept 6 calendar: one, it is not a calendar used for purposes of providing quality education; it is supposed to be a temporary way to deal with severe overcrowding without building new schools and classrooms; two, it has many significant disadvantages that impede teaching and learning; and three, it is used only out of desperation; no one would choose to do it if other options were available. . . . Indeed, State Superintendent of Schools Delaine Eastin recently put it very succinctly: "I would love to get rid of Concept 6. But schools didn't move to it because they were trying out some educational innovations. It was out of desperation" (Giese 26 Oct. 2001). (3)

MALDEF is pursuing legal means to reverse the Concept 6 calendar and seeking instead to funnel more monies into building schools.

By all measures, these mandates are often a reaction to the state's changing demographics, which include a majority of Latinos, both citizen and noncitizen, and their language, Spanish. As Gutierrez, Baquedano-Lopez, and Asato note, "The extraordinary numbers of English-language learners, predominately Latino, have created a new educational challenge that has been met with resistance from educators, politicians, and the general populace. The collective response [especially with proposition 227, the anti-bilingual education measure], however, has become more exclusionary and more overtly racialized . . . and employed a language of reform that both devalued the Spanish language (and other home languages), its utility, and thus, its community" (8). In California, U.S. Latinos and other Latino groups living in the United States have become the targets of backlash policies, and as evidenced, for example, by propositions 187 to 227, language is the crucial battleground.

Adriana's story, the MALDEF's challenges to Concept 6, and Gutierrez's observations all underscore a need for critical consciousness generally, but most pointedly in the context of the classroom. We encounter students in our classrooms with real lives who are affected by the sociopolitical landscape in which they reside, in this case, the contested terrain of California. As professional educators, we must be critically conscious of: Who inhabits our classrooms; what circumscribes these sites; and how research on race, culture, and gender impact and transform social and educational policy. In my view, classrooms offer opportunities to embrace, not only students, but also to centralize in a useful way critical analyses of the social and political issues that are the inevitable consequence of education that they are receiving. The possibility of a conservative, reactionary governor such as Pete Wilson encountering a high achieving Central American immigrant student like Adriana offers a powerful moment for interrogation and reinterpretation. For all students, and especially for students like Adriana, the classroom can be a space for critical conscious *and* celebration.

Unfortunately, stories such as Adriana's are not only what needs attention. In addition to the propositions previously discussed, the state has also enacted Executive Order 665, which will eliminate remedial math and English course offerings at the California State University system by 2007. The order requires that incoming freshpersons have one year to complete their remedial courses, and their failure to do so results in expulsion from the state system. Students who don't succeed in one year have the option to complete courses at a community college, which enables them to re-enroll. The question, however, is how much stamina does a student who is already greatly marginalized in the society have to have in order to pursue higher education in the face of such a rejection? California State University students are often first generation college students, second language learners, immigrants or recent immigrants, students whose families have completed, maybe, the most basic education.[4] Coming to college the first time is an act of courage and determination. These are not students that I want to dismiss; they are the very students to whom we should be most committed—especially if California, but also the United States more generally, is to honor seriously our claims to educational leadership, democracy, and social justice.[5]

Because I teach basic writing at California State University, Northridge, and have gauged abilities of students coming from LAUSD, I can testify that these students enter into the state university system with all sorts of levels of preparedness and unpreparedness. Years of success stories among them offer evidence that writing, despite their degrees of prior preparation, often helps to maximize their abilities to compete and to succeed. These are not students the state should so readily dismiss as unteachable, as implied by Executive Order 665. The point to be emphasized, as the MALDEF lawsuit suggests, is that when public education can resemble something close to "equal" for all students—regardless of race, class, culture, gender—then perhaps the state can enter a discussion about eliminating measures designed to accomplish what does not exist now without them, an approximation of a level playing field.

The movement to eliminate remedial course offerings (and by extension open enrollment policies, which grants access to university to many students) has gained particular prominence at the City University of New York (CUNY), where, ironically, open enrollment began. Former New York mayor Rudolph Giuliani led the fight to "cleanse CUNY" of its less desirable students (Herbert 29A). These students, he argued, "drain" the resources of educational institutions; "obviously" are not prepared for college, as evident by their need to take remedial courses in English and math; and often take seven years or more to graduate—much like CSUN students. Giuliani cited these examples to justify eliminating remedial course offerings, in effect, denying access to a population of students who are most in need.

As Adriana's story and the California and New York scenes indicate, we *are* living in a very dangerous time. After many, many decades of research and scholarship by Latino/as, African Americans, Asian Americans, and Native Americans in this area, what difference have we been able to make with such challenges? How does our ongoing work on race, ethnicity, class, gender, and culture have an impact on an indifferent and oftentimes hostile academy? More importantly, how might we pursue agendas in the post–affirmative action world capable of greater impact?

One point to be made is that Giuliani's position, and policies such as EO 665 and Concept 6, must be countered by remembering the educational gains experienced a little more than thirty years ago. "Between 1964 and 1970, the number of black college students nearly doubled, from 234,000 to half a million . . ." (Harding, Kelley, and Lewis 532), and one of the main reasons for this jump was the activism of black and Latino parents to enroll their children in college prep classes in high school (533). Indeed, civil rights movements of the '60s and '70s exposed a collective dissatisfaction with the mainstream and status quo in this country and called for a more level playing field that recognized certain rights as important for all citizens of this country.

Further, although college enrollments for Latinos have been lower than those of African Americans, there has been a tradition of Latino scholarship, beginning with scholars such as George I. Sanchez and Julian Samora and continuing with people like Rudolfo Acuña, and more recently, Frances Aparicio, Kris Gutierrez, Victor Villanueva, my colleagues in Chicano studies at CSUN. The early work of Sanchez and Samora sought to undo many of the stereotypes surrounding Latino communities. This important history, a story to counter stereotypical failures, is recounted in a document, "The State of Research on the United States' Latino Population" (2000).

In his introduction to a special edition of *Amerasia Journal*, Warren Furumoto writes, "Ethnic Studies departments were founded on the struggles of people (actually students) of color. . . . A coalition of Black, Latino, and White students closed down the [CSUN] with a series of demonstrations, which culminated in a mass arrest. With support from nearby Afro-American and Mexican-American communities, the students ultimately gained major concessions from the university: a huge expansion of the Educational Opportunity Program and the formation of autonomous Pan African Studies and Chicano Studies departments . . ." (1).

The activism of both students and scholars across minority groups led to policies, such as open enrollment strategies at many state colleges and universities and the many programs that ensured students' educational success, for example, remediation and educational opportunity programs. Over subsequent years, these programs have helped to generate a pipeline of people who are invested in the strengthening of their home communities and who have, thereby, paved the way for subsequent generations of scholars. Current Latino/a students now have available to them Chicano, Puerto Rican, and Latino studies departments and programs and more recently centers focusing on Latino research.

For many activists from this era, "the fight to transform education was merely a small part of a larger revolutionary movement" at this significant point in our nation's history (Kelley and Lewis 533). As Furumoto argues, "Today, to honor the legacy of those students who struggled to create Ethnic Studies, these departments must take a leadership role in the struggle for remolding educational institutions from the bottom up. . . . This means reconnecting education to social justice—equity in the social, cultural, racial and economic realms—and disconnecting education from the reproduction of social inequities" (1). Furumoto's gesture "to honor the legacy" of student protesters and to remember the connection of "education to social justice" is furthered with a call for a paradigm shift in Ethnic Studies. While remembering the power of cooperation among the student protesters from the past, he invites Ethnic Studies departments to lead the way "to adopt the *instructional strategies of constructivism* as powerful tools of learning" (my emphasis). He further states, "The use of cooperative or collaborative learning, critical thinking, multiple intelligences, inquiry and discovery-based learning, and authentic assessment have all proven to stimulate intrinsic motivation to learning" (1).

At this important moment in time, several educators are also thinking forward with an eye toward how to transform existing models into a more substantial set of strategies, partly in response to some of the backlash that I just outlined and partly in response to the need to rethink research agendas for twenty-first-century needs. The questions are: What should these agendas be? Who should be included under the umbrella of Ethnic studies—especially as populations grow through immigration and birth? How can the concept of "remediation" be enriched by critical consciousness and critical literacy? How can teachers help students to move along in their own educational pursuits—to open up their own visions of the world, to transform thinking and being in the world in the way Paulo Freire conceptualized (1987). Baldwin set up the paradox well during the '60s, stating:

> It becomes thoroughly clear, at least to me, that any Negro who is born in this country and undergoes the American educational system runs the risk of becoming schizophrenic. . . . On the one hand he is born in the shadow of the stars and stripes and he is assured it represents a nation

> which has never lost a war. He pledges allegiance to that flag which guarantees "liberty and justice for all." He is part of a country in which anyone can become president, and so forth. But on the other hand he is also assured by his country and his countrymen that he has never contributed anything to civilization—that his past is nothing more than a record of humiliations gladly endured. (4)

Given what I have presented here, with California's backlash legislation and other mandates, many Latino students suffer from the "schizophrenia" Baldwin describes. A pedagogy that embraces questions about race, culture, ethnicity, and gender helps students to interrogate these incongruities and to recontextualize their views and experiences with a clearer critical sense of their own identity, authority, and possibilities.

While we might be tempted to read Baldwin's words as an indictment on educational institutions (and it is!), I would also argue that Baldwin is leading us to consider seriously the real, material consequences of race, ethnicity, and gender constructions particular to U.S. society. In the '60s, he anticipated Guinier and Torres's (2002) recent work that argues for looking to how people on the margins fare as a signal of the political climates in this country; their analogy is to a miner's canary that reacts to a toxic environment long before a miner would. If Latinos, African Americans, Asian Americans, Native Americans, women—historically marginalized groups—are not doing well, then this country couldn't be doing well either, they argue. Their call, moreover, is not to ensconce ourselves in our differences, to balkanize our communities, but to ask questions about to whom we link our fate, which we have to link to one another (10).

Similarly, by paying critical attention to race, gender, and culture, as I try to do in my basic writing classrooms, my effort is to cast eyes toward the human beings in my classroom and to understand how social policies affect them. Individual stories magnify understanding and counter dominant narratives; therefore, my work on race, gender, ethnicity, culture, and class combines paying attention to the present state of affairs, to voices such as Sundiata's, with listening to the past, to voices such as Baldwin's. In this work, I also have always paid attention to story and how stories are told in communities of people of color. Stories of success and failure are important analytical tools. As with Adriana's story, the narratives students choose to share in their writing and speaking in class are instructive. In my view, Adriana's story, as the example at hand, became an important lesson for us both. For me, the story signified the real—not imagined—consequences of California's miseducational policies. For Adriana, it provided an opportunity for her to reveal something she had always known but didn't have the words or the analytical framework to describe. Thinking back now on the way she related the story, I am convinced she knew far more than she gave herself credit for. I suspect that she was doing some of that critical work long before she came to my classroom. In my class she was able to put together the pieces, and the process was a way for her to heal.

Working on the development of a critical consciousness through narrative, telling very personal and at times very particular stories may not be the stuff of "hard" research methodologies. However, the impact of social injustices—racism, sexism, ethnocentrism, economic oppression—has left us wounded—the individuals victimized, as well as the society as a whole. Employing a dialectic of knowing and engaging through narratives offers an effective way to recover. We write and speak ourselves onto the landscape, casting light and understanding on things for which there may be no easy words. We use our stories to push the boundaries of interpretive paradigms so that we can heal and act responsibly—as individuals and as a nation. The impact is that we are left in a better position to decide how we will link our fates and move forward.

NOTES

Special thanks to the Institute for Latino Studies at the University of Notre Dame for a faculty fellowship to work on this chapter. Thanks also to the Critical Literacy Joint Task Force of NCTE and IRA, which gave me the opportunity to present a version of this paper in Quito, Ecuador, Summer 2001, which ILS also funded.

1. Proposition 187 is described by Jorge Bustamante as "the most anti-Mexican law in the history of bilateral (U.S.-Mexico) relations" (20). I should also note that Proposition 187, after being tied up in the courts, never became "law," and eventually, legal pursuits to enforce the law were dropped by Governor Gray Davis, who decided not to pursue appeals. To be recognized is that Proposition 187 was a thinly disguised attempt to overturn *Plyer v. Dole* (1982), a case won by "lawyers hired and paid by Mexican American [civil rights] organizations that were concerned [about] the vulnerability of Mexican migrants as subjects of human and labor rights. In this case [*Plyer v. Dole*] the U.S. Supreme Court upheld a decision of a federal court in Houston that declared it unconstitutional to exclude from public schools the children of undocumented immigrants from Mexico" (16). See also "The Ghost of Proposition 187: Identity Politics Is Once Again the Hot Issue in California Politics" (5 Sept. 2003).

2. Wilson's anti-immigrant stands during his governorship are well known in the state.

3. "But while the Concept 6 calendar may make efficient use of space, it does not provide an education equivalent to that provided by the traditional

calendar. On the Concept 6 calendar, the school year is shortened by four weeks. To make up for the lost weeks, extra minutes are added to daily class periods. By lengthening the school day, the Concept 6 calendar, in theory, provides the same amount of instruction time as the traditional calendar; in practice, however, it does not afford teachers and students the same opportunity to cover the material required by the curriculum as thoroughly as teachers and students on the traditional calendar..." (Villagra, 9 Nov. 2001, 3–4). Citing a 1987 Los Angeles Unified School District study, Villagra reports that teachers "only sometimes used the additional minutes to cover more [classroom] content" (4).

4. I have documented many of my claims in an ongoing research project, entitled, *"A Praxis of Engagement": The Literacy Practices of Basic Writers* (in progress) and " 'The Politics of Location': Text as Opposition" (Dec. 2000). Both projects examine the composing strategies of writers and their literacy development through examination of certain "artifacts" from basic writing courses, especially the assignment of a "literacy autobiography," as discussed in this essay. Students explore their literacy development in this assignment by recounting their histories as learners, readers, and writers as far back as they can remember, and their family histories. Most students report low levels of literacy in their families. Instead of being a liability, many of these students testify to their parent's sacrifices to encourage their children's further educational pursuits.

5. Note the phrase that was echoed during the last presidential election, "Knowledge is the currency in a democracy." I am also thinking about the escalating restrictions on opportunities for foreign students to come to the United States for educational opportunity. The situation of foreign students seems frighteningly similar to that of U.S. youth from inner cities. Escalating policies that constrain the participation of citizens in the United States leave increasingly few options for many students to pursue their educational goals. Certainly, the events of September 2001 have enlightened us all to the blight around the world caused by shortsighted foreign policy and abandonment of whole societies. We must remember also to pay attention to our own national policies as well.

Chapter 3

Transforming Images

The Scholarship of American Indian Women

Susan Applegate Krouse

INTRODUCTION

What is the image of American Indian women that students in our classrooms have? Very likely they have *no* image of Native women—there are only 2.8 million Indian people total in the United States—less than one percent of the total U.S. population. Our students have likely never had an Indian woman as a teacher, or as a professor. Indian women, and Indian people in general, are not well represented in academia. When we come calling in academia, our cards are not even recognizable by most of the people in the college or university setting.

My own research and teaching focus on American Indian women, particularly women in urban Indian communities. I want to draw attention to the lives of Indian women, and to the roles they play in their communities, as mothers, teachers, activists, and leaders. I use narratives of American Indian women in my teaching, to help my students to experience the lives of those women and expand their understanding of the diversity of Native communities and cultures in North America. We need to move beyond just recounting narratives, however, to change the limited perceptions of American Indian women. A small group of Native women academics has begun to undertake the task of critical analysis of the lives and roles of American Indian women in their communities. I want my students to read the narratives of Indian women, but I also want them to recognize and understand the theoretical frameworks in which those narratives are created and examined.

INDIANS IN ACADEMIA

If asked to name an American Indian woman, most students would probably be able to respond with Pocahontas, or possibly Sacajewea. Both are historical figures, from what students probably see as the distant past. They also both acted as intermediaries for Europeans and Americans—Pocahontas interceding for the Jamestown colonists, and Sacajewea guiding Lewis and Clark through territory in what is now the northwest United States. They represent the two images of Indian women that predominate in the larger society, Pocahontas as the "princess" and Sacajewea as the "squaw."

The reality of Indian women in the United States is different from this image, more complex and inherently more interesting. Of the approximately 2.8 million Indians in the United States (as of the 2000 census), some 1.5 million are Indian women. They are from five hundred nations, tribes, bands, communities, and urban areas. There are many more mixed bloods than full bloods. The population is young, with more than one-third under the age of eighteen (Pavel et al. 67). The average Indian family income is lower than that of the general population. In 1990, only 66 percent of Indian people had a high school degree, and only 9 percent had a college degree. Even fewer, only 3 percent, have a graduate or professional degree (Pavel et al. 68). Nonetheless, many Indian people hold positions of tremendous responsibility in their communities, even without advanced degrees or even formal education, serving as tribal chairs, directors of economic development, educational coordinators, language specialists, counselors, and spiritual leaders. Indian people work in the larger society as well, in professional and technical capacities, at skilled and unskilled jobs.

Indian people are an even smaller percentage of the population in academia. According to statistics from the 2001–2 Almanac Issue of *The Chronicle of Higher Education*, Indians make up less than 1 percent of the total number of college students. That number has increased dramatically in the last twenty years, from 83,000 American Indian college students in 1980 to 145,300 in 1999 ("College Enrollment by Racial and Ethnic Group. Selected Years" 20). In 1999, Indians received less than 1 percent of the total number of advanced degrees awarded, most of them in education, the social sciences, or the professions, such as law and medicine ("Characteristics of Recipients of Doctorates, 1999" 24). In 1997, Indians made up less than one-half of 1 percent of the total full-time faculty, and only about one-third of those Indian faculty held ranks above assistant professor ("Number of Full-Time Faculty Members by Sex, Rank, and Racial and Ethnic Group, Fall 1997" 28). At my own university, there are only five American Indian women faculty, including myself, and none of us are tenured—yet. Without a meaningful presence in the academy, American Indian women have not in the past had a significant impact, either as scholars or as subjects of research and inquiry. That neglect is beginning to change.

DEVELOPING A THEORETICAL FRAMEWORK

Over the last twenty-five years, a theoretical framework has begun to develop in which we can examine the lives of American Indian women. The scholarship of American Indian women has been crucial to identifying the lack of attention given to Native women and the roles they play in their communities. We can look at six essays in particular to see areas of concern that American Indian women academics have identified in their research. Rayna Green (1976) pointed out the princess/squaw dichotomy that has formed the most pervasive stereotype of Indian women. Rebecca Tsosie (1988) surveyed literature by and about American Indian women, noting that contemporary Native women's writing provides a more complex and dynamic picture to counter the stereotype. Teresa D. LaFromboise, Anneliese M. Heyle, and Emily J. Ozer (1990) compared traditional and contemporary roles of Indian women, focusing on the importance of the past for Native women today. Clara Sue Kidwell (1992) urged historians and anthropologists to explore the role of Indian women as cultural mediators in the contact between indigenous peoples and colonizers. Beatrice Medicine (1993) explored the effects of conquest and domination on the rights of Native women following contact with Europeans. Devon A. Mihesuah (1996) proposed that histories of Indian women must acknowledge their heterogeneity of culture and experience.

In these essays that examine American Indian women's lives, spanning twenty years, several predominant concerns emerge. First, we need to move beyond the princess/squaw stereotype that has pervaded most depictions of Indian women. Then, we must acknowledge that Indian women have faced overwhelming domination by the larger society, and yet have survived, and we must understand how that domination has affected their lives. For many Indian women, the past, or tradition, informs the present; we now want to look at how the past contributes to the revitalization of Native communities in the present. Next, the role of Indian women as mediators between their communities and the larger society must be documented and analyzed. And finally, in all our work, we need to keep in mind the diversity of cultures, histories, and individuals that make up Native North America. Let us take each of these concerns, with stereotypes, domination, tradition, mediation, and diversity, in turn.

Rayna Green (1976), a mixed blood Cherokee folklorist with the Smithsonian Institution, pointed out the "Pocahontas Perplex," or the idea that Pocahontas, representing all Indian women, is both a princess and a squaw. Pocahontas's princess image began with her status as the daughter of Powhatan, whom Europeans regarded as a king, and grew as she saved the life of John Smith. However, she is at the same time linked to a squaw status because she is part of a Native community, wild and uncivilized. She is the noble savage, caught in a dichotomous stereotype, without links to her real life or her real people. Green documented the pervasiveness of this Pocahontas image in American popular culture, including legends, songs, and jokes.

Rebecca Tsosie (1988), a Yaqui attorney on the faculty at Arizona State University, concurred with the extensiveness of this Pocahontas image, pointing out that it appears even in literature that is sympathetic to Indians, such as in Helen Hunt Jackson's novel *Ramona* (1884) or Oliver LaFarge's *Laughing Boy* (1929). However, Tsosie believes that the work of contemporary American Indian women writers challenges this set of stereotypes, by looking at the real lives of real women through autobiography, such as that of *Mountain Wolf Woman* (Lurie 1966), and fiction written in an autobiographical style, such as Paula Gunn Allen's *The Woman Who Owned the Shadows* (1984).

Beatrice Medicine (1993), a Lakota and the first Indian woman to earn a PhD in anthropology, now professor emeritus at California State University at Northridge, chronicled the effects of conquest and domination on Native women following contact with Europeans, as well as the remarkable record of survival in the face of that onslaught. Moreover, she reminded us that Indian people have maintained their cultural variability, in spite of efforts to assimilate all Indians into the mainstream.

Teresa D. LaFromboise, a descendent of the Miami tribe of Indiana and assistant professor of Counseling Psychology at University of Nebraska—Lincoln, and her co-authors Anneliese M. Heyle and Emily J. Ozer (1990) echoed Medicine's concern with the effects of colonization, as Indian women's power and status declined and they were pressed to navigate between Indian and Anglo worlds. They urged us to consider the examples of contemporary Native women who are leaders in their communities, despite generations of domination by the larger society.

LaFromboise, Heyle, and Ozer also emphasized that drawing on the past, or "retraditionalization . . . represents a major current attempt on the part of Indian women to integrate traditional and contemporary demands in a positive, culturally consistent manner" (469). Traditionally, women fulfilled spiritual, biological, and social roles in their communities as links to the "Spirit Mother," as bearers of children and as transmitters of culture (457). Today, the authors argued, Indian women draw on their own traditional tribal cultures to help them lead economic, political, and social programs. With that traditional base, Indian women differ from non-Indian feminists, emphasizing family and community over self.

In an article adapted from her 1991 presidential address at the American Society for Ethnohistory meetings, Clara Sue Kidwell (1992), Choctaw and Chippewa, director of the Native American Studies Program at University of Oklahoma, challenged historians and anthropologists to explore the roles of Indian women as cultural mediators in the contact between indigenous peoples and colonizers. She used the familiar examples of Pocahontas and Sacajewea, among others, and questioned, "how, if at all, can we ever understand their actions and intentions in what they did?" (Kidwell 98). Kidwell argued that Indian women's roles as cultural mediators were complex, rooted in particular cultures and times, and that their motivations must be examined both historically and ethnographically. Devon Mihesuah (1996), a Choctaw and professor of history at Northern Arizona University, expanded the discussion of mediation to include women of mixed Indian and Euroamerican heritage, urging also that the particular circumstances of their physical appearance, social identity, and individual motivation must be taken into account.

Mihesuah, in her article "Commonality of Difference," brought together the theme found most frequently in all these essays, that "there was and is no such thing as a monolithic, essential Indian woman" (15). While Indian women do share a commonality of gender and oppression by colonizers, they differ substantially in terms of tribal cultures, social classes, political activism, racial heritage, and how much power they hold in their own cultures and in the larger society. Mihesuah pointed out what should be obvious, but often is not: "If writers want to find out what Indian women think, they should ask Indian women" (22). And, we might add, they should listen.

While the scholarship on American Indian women is not large, it does encompass more than these six articles and authors. I have chosen these six for specific reasons. First, the authors are all Native women, working to examine the lives of American Indian women in a larger, critical framework that incorporates discussion of stereotypes, cultural domination, tradition and revitalization, mediation, and diversity of roles, cultures, histories, and individuals. And second, these Native women are working in the scholarly format of conference presentations and peer-reviewed journals. They are publishing in both American Indian Studies journals (*American Indian Culture and Research Journal, American Indian Quarterly*) and in more generalized academic journals (*Ethnohistory, Massachusetts Review, Sex Roles*). The presence of these articles and authors in mainstream journals moves the discussion of American Indian women from the periphery into a larger scholarly sphere. These articles represent just a small sample of the work of these six American Indian women academics. They are well known for their contributions in the fields of anthropology, folklore, history, law, and psychology.

AMERICAN INDIAN WOMEN'S NARRATIVES

With a framework for critical analysis in hand, my students are better prepared to examine the lives of American Indian women, looking at the images and concerns presented in the narratives. Most of my courses are taught in an anthropology department, where the usual course readings would be ethnographies, written descriptions of cultures or certain cultural practices, or ethnohistories, histories of a people, written from that people's point of view. However, very few ethnographies or ethnohistories are available on American Indian women. Consequently, I have expanded my courses to include what I term American Indian women's narratives—autobiography, life history, memoir, and even fiction. Among those narratives are the lives of Buffalo Bird Woman, Hidatsa, born about 1839 (Wilson 1987); Mountain Wolf Woman, Winnebago, born 1884 (Lurie 1966); and Florence Edenshaw Davidson, Haida, born 1896 (Blackman 1995); along with the lives of three generations of Cherokee women chronicled in the novel *Faces in the Moon* (Bell 1994). These narratives represent a variety of time periods, cultures, and adaptations, but in each the women tell an individual story of their lives in their own communities and in interaction with the larger society. They counter the prevailing stereotypes of the princess and the squaw, address cultural domination, include the role of tradition, provide examples of mediation, and present a diversity of American Indian women's lives.

BUFFALO BIRD WOMAN

One of the ethnographies I do use is an unusual one in that it focuses on an American Indian woman, Buffalo Bird Woman (Wilson 1987). She was a Hidatsa woman, born about 1839, who lived with her people along the Knife River in North Dakota. The Hidatsas were agriculturalists, raising a variety of crops, and supplementing cultivated foods by hunting. They were forced to give up their traditional villages in the mid-1880s and move to the Fort Berthold Reservation, which they share today with the Mandans and the Arickaras.

This is Buffalo Bird Woman's story, as told to anthropologist Gilbert L. Wilson. He worked with Buffalo Bird Woman from 1906 to 1918, and was adopted into her Prairie Chicken clan and her Hidatsa tribe. He was interested in describing traditional agriculture, particularly for the insights it might provide into how the Hidatsas practiced farming before contact with Europeans. What is most unusual about Wilson, this early ethnographer, is that he decided to rely on what he termed a "typical informant" and to "let the informant interpret her agricultural experiences in her own way" (3). As Devon Mihesuah has urged (22), Wilson talked to Buffalo Bird Woman, and he endeavored to let Buffalo Bird Woman tell her own story, which he described as

> not, then, an account merely of Indian agriculture. It is an Indian woman's interpretation of economics; the thoughts she gave to her fields; the philosophy of her labors. May the Indian woman's story of her toil be a plea for our better appreciation of her race. (5)

Buffalo Bird Woman's story unfolds, taking us through the agricultural year. She described how she cleared gardens, planted various crops, and then cultivated, harvested, and stored those crops. She described the processing of squashes for storage:

> When the squashes, emptied from the baskets, made a great heap on the floor of the drying stage, the women of the family made a feast, cooking much food for the purpose; some old women were then invited to come cut up the squashes with knives, into slices to dry. We regarded these old women as hired; and I remember that in my father's family we hired sometimes eight, sometimes ten, sometimes only six. I think that at the time I was a young woman, when my mothers made such a feast, about ten old women came (Wilson, 70).

Buffalo Bird Woman also made it clear that not everything is work. She responded to a question from Gilbert Wilson:

> Did young men work in the fields? (laughing heartily.) Certainly not! The young men should be off hunting, or on a war party; and youths not yet young men should be out guarding the horses. Their duties were elsewhere, also they spent a great deal of time dressing up to be seen of the village maidens; they should not be working in the fields!
>
> But old men, too old to go to war, went out into the fields and helped their wives. It was theirs to plant the corn while the women made the hills; and they also helped pull up weeds.
>
> When their sweethearts were working in the fields, young men often came out and talked to them, and maybe worked a little. However, it was not much real work that they did; they were but seeking a chance to talk, each with his sweetheart. (115)

Indians as agriculturists is not often part of the image that students have of Native people. Buffalo Bird Woman's expertise at gardening moves students beyond the image of Indians as only hunters and gatherers, to a more complex understanding of the importance of women in traditional subsistence systems.

From this unique ethnography we get a picture of a Hidatsa woman living in a traditional way for most of her life and being able to retain much of her daily life and customs. Certainly, this is not the only picture we want students to have of Indian life in the past. Rather, we want them to understand, as LaFromboise, Heyle, and Ozer (1990) urged, how Indian people made the transition from traditional ways of life to the present, while retaining ties to their cultural heritage. Two women anthropologists, both of them non-Natives, helped two Native women to tell their life stories, two lives that bridged between those traditional times and today. I have taught both of the stories of these remarkable women many times and they have never failed to delight me and my students.

MOUNTAIN WOLF WOMAN

Mountain Wolf Woman, a Winnebago, told her story to anthropologist Nancy Oestreich Lurie during the winter of 1958, beginning with her early life among her Winnebago people in Wisconsin, still living much as they had for centuries. However, Mountain Wolf Woman was born in

1884, and by the time she was in her teenage years, the Winnebagos were being drawn more and more into non-Indian society. She attended mission school and worked as a wage laborer, but she continued to be engaged in many traditional practices, including the Winnebago Medicine Society and later on in her life, the Native American or Peyote Church.

During World War II, one of her daughters moved with her husband and family to Oregon to do "war work." Mountain Wolf Woman decided to join them, and even though she was in her sixties, she went to work picking and packing berries. Then she received word that one of her sons had been wounded in the war, was coming back to Wisconsin, and wanted her to return as well. Mountain Wolf Woman and one of her granddaughters took the train back east, across the country. Her granddaughter requested that they eat in the dining car. Winnebago grandparents are typically indulgent of their grandchildren, acceding to their wishes. They went to the dining car and Mountain Wolf Woman had this encounter:

> We went to the fifth car; that was the dining car. There were little square tables. Two soldier boys were sitting there and we sat there too. There we sat, four of us. They were wearing khaki uniforms.
>
> "Oh," I said, "I am going to eat with my sons. Whenever I see somebody wearing khaki, I always think that might be my son." I was speaking English.
>
> The boy across from me got up. "My mother died when I was born. I never had a mother. Now I have a mother," he said. Then he shook my hand. He was very pleased that I said to him that he was my son. He was glad, he said, because now he had a mother.—I was glad too because I was feeling unhappy about my boy. "Well, boys, I am happy to know you," I said. "I am glad too, mother," he said. (Lurie 76–77)

Mountain Wolf Woman and other Winnebago people hold warriors in high regard. Her extension of family ties to these young soldiers allowed her to feel closer to her own soldier son. Mountain Wolf Woman's story illustrates this esteem, as well as her own need to connect with her wounded son. Students are not often aware that Native people have served in the United States armed forces, or that warriors are still an integral part of Native communities. Winnebago war mothers, such as Mountain Wolf Woman, continue to be honored today for their part in raising "soldier boys."

FLORENCE EDENSHAW DAVIDSON

In more recent years, other women anthropologists have undertaken the recording of Native women's lives. One notable example is Margaret Blackman's (1996) life history of Florence Edenshaw Davidson, a Haida woman from the small community of Masset, on the Queen Charlotte Islands in northern British Columbia. The Haida have a rich material and ceremonial culture, marked by elaborate ritual giveaways called potlatches. Despite intense missionary activities of the Anglican Church (and others), the Haidas managed to maintain much of their traditional culture.

Florence Edenshaw Davidson was born in 1896, to a highly placed Haida family, including her father, artist Charles Edenshaw. The Haida are a ranked society, with different lineages occupying higher or lower levels on the social scale. Rank is not fixed, and a motivated individual or family can move up in rank by working hard and living according to Haida values. The princess image, examined by Rayna Green (1976) and Rebecca Tsosie (1988), is belied by the real work undertaken by this real Haida woman.

Florence was the last girl in her community to undergo traditional ritual seclusion when she reached puberty, and shortly thereafter she was married, despite her objections, to an older man from an even higher ranked lineage. While she was unhappy at first, she built a strong and lasting relationship with her husband, who was also an artist. They had thirteen children, nine of them still living at the time of Florence's death in 1993. The Davidsons worked hard, not only to provide for their children, but to acquire goods to give away; Florence herself sponsored "four potlatches and more than a dozen feasts" (Blackman 140) in her lifetime. The importance of hard work became especially apparent at one point in Davidson's life:

> In 1952 we lost our home in a fire. I lost everything, even my shoes. No pillows, no blankets, no shoes, no sweaters. All of us lost everything. We had all kinds of clothes and the upstairs was full of groceries we had received from Woodwards in Vancouver. . . .
>
> The fall after our house burned we went fishing with my cousin Douglas Edenshaw on his big seine boat. I cooked for the crew. One day when I was in the galley my husband yelled that they needed me to look after the winch. So I looked after the winch while they were brailling the fish on. I was real proud that I was doing men's work. . . .

> I used to pray that we would get a home. I prayed for my whole family because Claude and Alfred and Victor [Primrose's husband] were going to build houses, too. We all started building at the same time. . . .
>
> My husband and I designed the house. I wanted the front room twenty feet long and twenty feet wide, big enough to invite all the people in. We had lots of girls and when they got married I wanted to use our home for the wedding dinner. Men used to come to my husband and say, "G[e]niy[a], you're making such a big house. What are you going to do in it?" "Son," he used to say, "I know what I'm doing. Where we're staying now, the whole family comes in and they have to stand around having coffee. No room to sit down. [T]hat's why I plan a big house, so they'll be comfortable when they come home and sit around." (121–23)

The Haida people value property and possessions, and the public display of wealth, so for Davidson it was imperative that they get her house rebuilt and made comfortable for her family. This value placed on material possessions is not new among the Haidas; it is part of their traditional culture, along with the concurrent value placed on giving those possessions away. Students have not often encountered the idea of Native people surrounded by material goods, instead picturing a simple tipi with only the barest necessities. Davidson's collection of two hundred teacups, which she used at feasts and potlatches, astounds my students. Haida women such as Florence Edenshaw Davidson work hard and live well, benefiting themselves, their families, and their communities.

LUCIE EVERS

Not all Indian women take pride in their heritage, as these three strong women have been able to do. For many Indian women, their ancestry has meant discrimination, poverty, and abuse, as Beatrice Medicine (1993) discussed in her article on cultural domination. Betty Louise Bell's novel *Faces in the Moon* chronicled three generations of mixed blood Cherokee women and their struggles with their lives and their identities. Bell is herself a mixed blood Cherokee, and used at least some of her own family history in the story. The book is powerful and evocative, ringing so true that in one of my classes, a student interrupted our passionate discussion of the main character's fate to remind us, "It's a novel!" Lucie Evers is that main character, and in the story, she grows up in poverty in Oklahoma, but eventually makes her way to college and graduate school, and marries Melvin, a well-to-do Jewish man from the North Shore area of Chicago. Lucie's mother Gracie comes from Oklahoma to attend the wedding, and creates quite a stir:

> She came to my wedding. She stepped out of the cab dressed for the event, a tea-length multilayered turquoise chiffon, her hair freshly peroxided and tightly permed. Her shoes and purse had, obviously, not taken the first dye and were now in the "anyone's guess" color scheme. And the hat, Lord have mercy, was a wide-brim straw with a sequined turquoise horse in the front. I watched from the picture window as three hundred pounds of turquoise, with gloves, tried to find the front door of my in-laws' North Shore home. Melvin's grandmother, coming in from the back, caught a look at Gracie, shrieked, and had to be rushed into the back room by Melvin's parents. They seated Gracie on the bride's side, along with the black maid, and she sobbed through the entire ceremony. When the guests in cool summer linen stood up to cry *mazel tov*, Momma let go a heart-stopping cry, "My baby!" The black maid patted her on the shoulder.
>
> Passing by the buffet table, I heard a matron in pearls say, "I never met a real Indian before."
>
> Momma was loading her plate with shrimp du jong.
>
> "My momma was a full-blooded Cherokee. She had hair down to her waist. This far." She placed the spoon just above her wide ass. "Indians don't get many shrimps. There ain't nothing I loves better'n shrimps." (Bell, 49–50)

It is not until after her mother's death that Lucie truly begins to recover herself and her heritage, and come into her own as a Cherokee woman who can mediate on behalf of her Indian family, as Clara Sue Kidwell (1992) and Devon Mihesuah (1996) have described. In the last scene in the novel, Lucie has returned to Oklahoma to amend her family's history, and she finds herself confronting an uncooperative librarian at the Oklahoma Historical Society, who questions her identify. She grabs the librarian by the collar and responds:

> "I ain't asking you to tell me who I *think* I am. I am the great-granddaughter of Robert Henry Evers, I am the granddaughter of Hellen Evers Jeeters, I am the daughter of Gracie Evers, the niece of Rozella Evers, and the grandniece of Lizzie Sixkiller Evers." . . .

> "Let me put it to you this way. I am a follower of stories, a negotiator of histories, a wild dog of many lives. I am Quanah Parker swooping down from the hills into your bedroom in the middle of the night. And I am centuries of Indian women who lost their husbands, their children, their minds so you could sit there and grin your shit-eating grin."
>
> I eased him back against his chair and took a pen from my pocket.
>
> I said, waving the pen, "I am your worst nightmare: I am an Indian with a pen." (192)

An Indian with a pen, an Indian *woman* with a pen, presents a powerful image of women capable of resistance to domination and mediation with the dominant society. Through these narratives, we can introduce our students to American Indian women whose lives are more than the same tired stereotypes. The theoretical framework for understanding the complexity of American Indian women, their lives, and their narratives has only begun to be built. That framework is being constructed largely through the work of Native women academics who are choosing to take their scholarship to the larger arena of academic conferences and peer-reviewed journals. My own work draws on the efforts of scholars before me, who have challenged the limited images of American Indian women and by their work have transformed those images.

Chapter 4

Men as Cautious Feminists

Reading, Responding, Role-Modeling as a Man

Patrick Bizzaro

In his provocative essay "Teaching and Learning as a Man," Robert Connors notes what many men in the academy have seen for themselves: male students often reach out to their male teachers as mentors (138). Connors wants to "assert [his] own hierarchical place, construct [his] own manhood" in an effort "to provide a role model" for his male students (139). In her strong critique of Connors's essay, Laura Micciche makes clear why someone now needs to offer an answer to the question Connors deliberated on several years ago: What kind of role model should a male teacher be to younger men in the academy? I think Connors wants to answer this question by saying that men should unify in the profession in a fashion similar to the way women have. In this way, argues Connors, male teachers may develop a truly masculine method for mentoring young men, a method predicted by the profession's historical reliance on agonistic encounters

---

This chapter is dedicated to my sons, Jason and Antonio.

in the classroom. I want to consider what this method will require of older men. What will be its costs? These are the questions Connors does not address.

According to Micciche, rather than going ahead and satisfying this "desire" by examining the role(s) men might play in mentoring male students, Connors "turns to historical accounts of rhetoric in order to expose the agonistic nature of the discipline in which his desire is embedded" (22), suggesting by doing so that a model has long existed for men mentoring men in English studies. My indebtedness to Connors should be clear, though I need to stress that in what follows I depart from his apparent conclusion; nonetheless, Bob's work makes me reconsider the possibility for a male feminism in composition studies—the basis for a different way of mentoring young men than Connors had in mind—by observing how men have thus far theorized issues of gender. Further, I am interested in how as a male I might model for younger men a kind of maleness in my dealings not only with them, but with women as well. In this essay, then, I make an effort to understand how men over the past fifteen years, during a time marked by the growing influence of feminism in composition studies, have dealt with matters related to gender.

To hollow out the space in which I will work, let me place Connors's essay on one side and Tania Modleski's *Feminism Without Women* on the other. Connors stakes out his territory in the following terms: "[T]he shift from a male-dominated rhetoric to a feminized and feminist composition studies has illuminated women's issues in writing while leaving many male teachers uncertain of how or whether they fit in" (143). Modleski claims her territory, by contrast, by expressing concern over liberal feminism's emphasis on equality and postmodern feminism's tendency to eliminate the meaningfulness of the category of *woman*. Elizabeth Flynn interprets Modleski's view as follows: "If the critique of essentialist approaches to feminism is pushed too hard, women disappear almost completely and are replaced by men" (357).

While Connors, according to Micciche, "seems most intent not on complementing feminist work, but on the displacement of feminism by men's studies" (27), Modleski criticizes the emphasis on "male feminism" which places attention once again on men, taking us back, Modleski argues, to a "pregendered" past. There are some difficulties here, to be certain. For one, Micciche seems most concerned over Connors's "displacement of feminism by men's studies." But it seems to me that Connors seeks something far less troubling and, from my vantage point as a man, more important: a viable role model for young men, a topic worthy of my best efforts not only in this chapter but in my day-to-day life as well, both on campus and off. No doubt, though, in his pursuit of a man's role in mentoring younger men, Connors argues that men have been systematically excluded from feminism, which he sees as a well-defined and fully articulated position in English studies. For Connors, as a result, feminism does not offer a viable identity to men for their efforts in working with other men. Modleski is concerned about men's appropriation of the political power women have amassed in the profession and the potential disappearance of women from feminism altogether. As I read him, Connors works from the premise that men have no place in feminism (have not, thus, been invited in) and should, in response to this exclusion, implement what we might generally describe as male studies approaches in their dealings with younger men. As I read her, Modleski assumes, by contrast, that men *are* interested in feminism and that their interest is not only unhealthy, but may also predict women's exclusion from it. I work from the premise that this middle space BETWEEN Connors and Modleski is well suited to a male feminism. It is the space, then, I want to explore in this chapter in an effort to reach some tentative conclusions about how feminism can guide men in their efforts to mentor other men, specifically their male students.

In negotiating this difficult territory, I would like to begin by exploring a fundamental difference in my task from the tasks Connors and Modleski have undertaken. In "The Other 'F' Word: The Feminist in the Classroom," Dale Bauer writes: "[T]he classroom is a place to explore resistances and identifications, a place also to explore the ambiguous and often ambivalent space of values and ethics" (387). I will not hold Bauer (or anyone, for that matter, including myself) to something said years ago, in what might seem a prior life. But I do want to understand Bauer's statement and statements like it as descriptions of one way many *women* have negotiated the composition classroom. This understanding arises from my belief—and clearly Connors's and probably Modleski's—that men have a slightly different problem to solve in attempting to negotiate classrooms and the profession as a whole in becoming feminists in composition studies, in the profession, and even in the community. This problem is for me uniquely linked to my belief that most men also want to maintain credibility with the younger generations of men whom we teach and with whom we interact (not to mention with our fathers), many of whom may not be in the academy at all. One might argue that both feminist men and feminist women start in the same place; that is, both must fight through the system that has taught them to read, write, and even teach as men.

So what, as a man, do I hope to accomplish by writing this chapter? My issues are both professional and personal, though the driving force, and where I end this essay, is in the personal. On the one hand, I want to further orient myself to feminist theory both as a male in the academy, one who teaches writing courses, and as a teacher who would like to employ feminist theory and do it authentically, as I attempt to accomplish (can I say *complete*?) what I believe Connors set out to do in his effort to "provide a role model" for male students. But I am also a man who works in an institution of higher learning that is bordered by a community of mostly blue-collar workers: factory workers, farmers, and fishermen. This is a difficult issue for me to address since I also want to be accepted in the community by *these* men, men like my father. This desire to be accepted by other men in my community only superficially seems divorced from the theoretical pieces I read, study, and especially those I write.

Needing to start somewhere, I have begun my personal deliberations on male feminism in composition studies with concerns well expressed by Bernard Duyfhuizen. I cannot stress enough that, to mean much to me at all, theoretical pieces must be applicable equally to the day-to-day world in which I live as well as to my life in the academy. "Feminist criticism," writes Duyfhuizen, "often asserts that reading is both a learned and a gender-oriented activity that male readers have long controlled by expounding, consciously or unconsciously, a masculine perspective on literary value and interpretive significance" (411). At the same time, many feminist critics call for revisions of readings that have long privileged certain literary texts and espoused certain cultural values. Duyfhuizen, writing in 1988, continues: "[D]espite some gains in the last fifteen to twenty years, feminist approaches are still only slowly reaching classrooms" (411). No doubt, this statement is especially true of classrooms where composition is taught (see Bauer, E. Flynn "Composing"). But in some ways it is even more appropriate to an understanding of the off-campus community in which I live where men do not debate who is responsible for the oppression of women. These men are unwilling to give up privileges they receive simply by being men. In fact, they would want to argue that they too are trapped by social and economic expectations and, thus, that the activities of their day-to-day lives are likewise dictated to them.

I am interested, at least at first, in how men have already constructed themselves in the published literature (even when they do so unsuccessfully) as men who are in the process of unlearning privilege or, to use Connors's phrase and to pick up on this idea where he left off, "to provide a role model" for other men to follow. When we look in the published literature, we see in men's discussions of gender conscious use of principles widely associated with various feminisms. Still, there is a difference between the way men apply these principles personally in their individual classrooms and in the way they apply these same principles in critiques of the profession as a whole (not to mention differences in the way women in composition studies employ these same principles). But let's not stop there. I am even more concerned with the way men apply these principles in the communities in which they live. And I believe there is a place along a virtual continuum—or, perhaps, it might be better envisioned as a kind of bridge—where feminist principles are the foundation for other concerns such as ecology where many men, including the factory workers, farmers, and fishermen in my community, argue, perhaps unknowingly, for positions that have feminism as their hidden foundation or those that share certain beliefs with a kind of feminism. In any event, what interests me in this topic is that it provides me with an opportunity to isolate and, thus, focus upon the kind of relationship(s) men might have with other men, including their students, by beginning with what has already been done, using published works in composition studies as a starting point, and then considering my behavior in light of those efforts.

The question I ask, then, echoing Connors's concern, is simple enough: How might I best mentor my male students, especially those who look to me, as an older male, to mentor them (and especially, in this context, my graduate students who want to enter the profession)? Let me provide the framework for one solution, the solution as I now see it, by beginning with published literature by men who, perhaps even unknowingly, addressed this problem.

READING AND WRITING AS MEN IN COMPOSITION STUDIES

How have men in composition studies addressed questions of gender, including their own efforts to attend to gender and, on some occasions, to be feminists? I believe they have attempted thus far to solve the problem of gender issues in the composition classroom in three ways: by avoiding feminist issues entirely (see essays by Connors and Catano), by oversimplifying complex issues associated with gender (see Lynn), and by critiquing their own privileged position as teachers, members of the community, and as readers (see Murphy and Flynn). Only the third of these efforts advance the cause of a male feminism.

This third response by men to their uses of feminist principles can be seen in an exchange that involves Jonathan Culler. In "Reading as a Woman," Culler offers a brief history of feminist criticism in which he locates "moments" central to its development. While Culler's account logically hypothesizes that male and female readers might construct the gender of their reading positions for themselves, he does not cite examples of men reading and, worse yet, nowhere refers to himself as a reader. In short, Culler does not establish the much-needed ethos I believe is essential if men read literary and student texts from a feminist critical perspective.

More recently, men who believe that gender issues must be addressed in the classroom have taken time to critique their habits as male readers and, in so doing, to establish ethos with the students in their classrooms and with the members of the profession who have read their work. Clearly, to be believed, to be an authentic, trustworthy, and credible feminist in dealings with students as well as with others in the professional community, men have found it necessary to define themselves as readers.

Take as an example of what I mean John Flynn's effort at establishing ethos in his essay "Learning to Read Student Papers from a Feminine Perspective, II." The most curious identifier is the "II" at the end of his title, since John's wife, Elizabeth Flynn, entitles her article "Learning to Read Student Papers from a Feminine Perspective, I" in the same collection of essays. Then John locates himself further:

> I would claim that even if we admit gender as a first principle, an essential attribute of being, my view of reality, and my perspective as a reader of student texts, needs to be elaborated by counting other qualifiers. So I would describe myself as a male, working-class, Brooklyn Irish Catholic, social-democrat, feminist, environmentalist, conservative, antifascist, disabled Vietnam veteran, peace activist, and recovered cancer patient. (131)

Once so identified (after admitting gender to be a first principle in his reading of student texts), John becomes, if not less threatening, more authentic in his application of feminist principles in his reading of student essays. He continues: "[I]f we accept gender as experienced by an upwardly mobile, working-class male during the 1960s as a condition of my reading of student texts, then I wish to claim my pedagogy as feminine and women as my teachers" (132). We might say, of course, to avoid oversimplification, that we all read as members of different communities, that ethnicity, for one example, also influences our readings of various texts. My point here, however, is that by so identifying himself, John Flynn provides men with a model for how they might employ feminist principles in their encounters with others, both professionally and privately.

Though Patrick D. Murphy does not take the extreme measures taken by John Flynn in identifying the position from which he uses feminist criticism, he does advocate doing so. Murphy posits: "[W]e need to find ways to break down the position of authority awarded us as teachers from the outset, not in some pseudo-egalitarian way limited to just rearranging seats in a circle while simultaneously keeping the grade firmly in our grasp, but in ways that clarify the importance of each student's developing her or his own self-conscious critical posture" (173). To do so, Murphy advocates establishing ethos: "[L]et the students in on the 'secrets' of why the teacher is doing what she or he is doing (thereby performing a meta-criticism of the pedagogy in process), and engage in self-critique and group evaluation of the pedagogy and the subject matter. . . ." Only then, continues Murphy, "can [we] break down the myth of 'competence equals patriarchy.' " To more fully describe this myth, Murphy quotes Paula Treichler, who summarizes: "Thus behaviors judged as traditionally male—a lecture format, little student give and take, the transmission of a given body of content, little attention to process—seem also to signal professional competence" (qtd in Murphy 173). Murphy concludes that to be truly competent teachers, men need to teach differently by overcoming what they have learned from the culture in which they work and live.

One model male teachers might employ in mentoring male students requires that men actively critique the privileges and cultural assumptions such privileges seem to make. Many young men do not recognize privileges that have always been theirs; they do not know any other way, and it is not their fault, in my estimation, that they don't. It is the fault of their male mentors. Thus, what we learn from a simple survey of approaches to gender in articles about teachers teaching in individual classrooms is this: *A man must consider what it means to read and teach as a man and, in a classroom dialogue with his students or in an essay intended for other members of the professional community or if necessary in the public sphere, explore the patriarchal biases he has been taught by culture.* Without the care and pain of such a critique, men may use feminist theory irresponsibly by masquerading as women and appropriating the feminine voice and fail to establish the credibility necessary if they hope to explore a text from a feminist perspective. At the same time, I want to stress that men run the risk that they will be disrespected by other men, including male students and even male counterparts. One solution, the one offered by Donald McAndrew discussed below, links male feminism with another cause, for some an overriding one, ecology.

NEGOTIATING IDENTITY THROUGH A HYBRID MODE OF ARGUMENTATION IN THE ACADEMY

Naturally, if we view a male feminism as an evolutionary process, there must be more to it than simple classroom change—men must carry these beliefs with them when they leave the classroom, and even when they leave campus, and I believe they *inevitably* will and should. In my experience, it is one thing to make changes in the privacy of our classrooms but quite another matter to advocate these beliefs at the institutional level—in faculty meetings, at public gatherings, in informal conversations with others, some of whom may be friends, others not. Somewhere along the evolutionary trail, men have tended to align themselves with causes that, when analyzed further, have at their foundation certain feminist principles. One such cause is ecology.

Elizabeth Flynn, in "Feminism and Scientism," helps us understand at least one way men have unlearned privilege and, thus, critiqued the profession as a whole. According to Flynn, "The concept of feminization is powerful because it suggests that feminist analyses of the situation of women can be usefully applied analogously to academic fields. If women can be abused and undervalued, fields of study can be as well" (354). Flynn's words provide a thesis, as it were, supported by the work of a range of men in the academy. Works discussed here by Donald McAndrew and James Sosnoski demonstrate how the evolution of such thinking has found its way into the published literature.

In "Ecofeminism and the Teaching of Literacy," McAndrew writes of the way feminism may shape our view of institutional concerns. McAndrew begins by locating his topic: "Ecofeminism is the intersection of two critical perspectives—ecology and feminism—creating a libratory political and social construction for those who deplore the denigration of nature and women" (367). Ecofeminism offers an opportunity for men, such as McAndrew, to see an analogy between the oppression of women and violations of nature and, by acknowledging his indebtedness to feminism, in general, to advocate institutional change as a male feminist.

Both women and nature, as McAndrew argues, are exploited, and for the same reason: "the masculinist and patriarchal drive for dominance" (368). McAndrew restates his position in these very clear terms: "[I]t is patriarchy's domination that is the problem for both women and the environment." Both women and nature have been treated in the patriarchal scheme of things as "others," something that, from the masculinist view reflected in science and technology, must "be mastered or conquered" (371). The solution for McAndrew and other ecofeminists is clear: "Only a revaluing that restores the feminine to a balanced place with the masculine can supply humans with the wholeness of personhood necessary to end the exploitation of nature and other peoples." Can this, in fact, happen? McAndrew answers this question by quoting Ariel Sallek: this will not happen "'until men are brave enough to rediscover and to love the woman inside themselves' " (373).

No doubt McAndrew has made changes in the way he teaches writing in his classroom, but in this essay he calls for reform in the way we teach composition generally:

> In our thinking about literacy, ecofeminism points the way to new issues and focuses, in addition to reinforcing many... parallels to current composition theory.... Most importantly, theory and pedagogy derived from ecofeminism would put nature as a central concern. Ecofeminism would raise the natural environment to its rightful place as one of the major political concerns in composition studies. To gender, race, and class, we should now add nature, and in the process create a contextualized web of social, political, and natural concerns. (377)

McAndrew gains credibility in this article, as John Flynn does in his, by showing his indebtedness to women, especially ecofeminists. Rather than extensive use of paraphrase and summary, two methods often used by essayists to join other people's ideas to their own, McAndrew quotes extensively. From one perspective on authorship, McAndrew's rhetorical strategy often requires that he place himself in the role of editor who has arranged other people's ideas. I do not mean this as a criticism, since all male feminists are eventually in the role of editor and collaborator, but only as an acknowledgment of McAndrew's rhetorical strategy. For McAndrew's contributions are twofold: first, he brings together voices conversing about ecofeminism and, second, he argues for making nature, along with race, class, and gender, "one of the major political concerns in composition studies" (377).

Rather than aligning himself with a ready-made cause, one that has feminist concerns at its core, James Sosnoski in "A Mindless Man-Driven Theory Machine" re-sees an institutional problem—requirements for tenure and promotion—through a feminist lens. Sosnoski only *seems* to begin at some distance from the specific institutional reform he has in mind. "This is an essay," writes Sosnoski, "about the tie between the institutional construction of intellectuality and the social construction of sexuality" (33). Sosnoski then goes on to critique the principle of "falsificity," "that it is logically wrong (and therefore culpable and punishable) to mistake the incorrect for the correct" (35). For Sosnoski, and this is how his critique finds its institutional purpose, "falsification is a rationalization of academic competition, but, more significantly . . . it is a device for maintaining the patriarchal *status quo*" (35).

Thus, rather than committing himself to a ready-made cause which has feminism as its very foundation, Sosnoski's critique leads him to an insight into patriarchy that causes him to follow this mode of rhetorical inquiry further. He notes in passing well-known efforts of philologists, literary historians, and New Critics to give literary study the appearance of scientific objectivity, reliability, and even verifiability that has continued to haunt it. Sosnoski goes on to advance this notion by considering it in light of falsificity: "Since readings are accepted as 'true' at an earlier moment in time can at a later date be shown to be 'false,' the engine of this system [literary study] is falsification" (38–39).

When we consider the professional lives of those who have entered English studies, then, we are faced with an ongoing dilemma, the dilemma of careerism. In a career that involved intellectual competitiveness, "masculine qualities of exemplary male professors were imitated and became the traits of an idealized career profile" (40). And here is the feminist critique Sosnoski employs: "Modern literary study developed as a profession to the extent that the manner in which a particular man studied literature was widely imitated, to the extent that a man's way of 'doing' criticism or scholarship became a trait in the composite profile of the ideal professor of literature. Invariably, men were the models underlying the ideal profile of the scholar/critic at specific junctures in the development of literary studies" (40–41). This issue is compounded by the resulting need for critics to falsify their rival's conclusions, and also requires, to continue one's participation in the conversation, that scholars measure "the degree to which their own arguments are deemed falsifiable" (42). Sosnoski provides a label for this practice: "intellectual machismo."

These articles, then, by McAndrew and by Sosnoski, show two ways that men in the profession have successfully employed feminist principles to critique the profession as a whole. McAndrew's use of these tenets comes relatively risk free since he attaches his cause to another, one that already exists. Sosnoski's use is more rhetorical and less programmatic insofar as he critiques the profession's methods for accepting its members into the discipline and argues using a masculine rhetorical approach but from a feminist subject position. We might ask, who, after all, would argue against the notion of equality in our profession or in favor of the planet's destruction? As if already prepared for such uses of feminist principles, Flynn gives this caution: "One limitation of the feminization metaphor is that it suggests an essentialized and oversimplified conception of gender" (354).

THE PERSONAL DILEMMA: INTEGRATING PUBLIC AND PRIVATE

I have some things to admit before ending this chapter. It is obvious by now that I am a male, specifically a first-generation Italian American. I share some concerns of class with male scholars of color, who have written about the ways men have employed feminist principles in their lives (see Adu-Poku). And though it may not much influence a reading of this essay to know so at this point, I should say I am a former college football player who coaches the sport voluntarily at a middle school in eastern North Carolina, one for whom coaching, too, is teaching. When I handed my father, an Italian immigrant, a copy of my first book of poetry in 1977, he shook his head: "How is it that you went off to college a football player and came back a poet?" This statement should make clear my interest in what kind of role model a man should be to younger men. It should also explain why I want to argue that I am a different man at different times. If I cannot function directly and authoritatively as a coach, I cannot much influence these young men who play for me. If as a coach I am what Gerald Graff describes as a wimp, most parents (more fathers than mothers, I suspect) will not respect me as a coach.

I share these events because they are at the core of my dilemma and, perhaps, reflect the dilemma of other men as well: how older men, especially teachers, might model manhood for younger men. I say it is possible for us to learn from women how to bring younger men along as men but to do so with a recognition that we may be required by the occasions in which we interact with younger men to be different men at different times. We must keep in mind that younger men too have been socialized to do what their teachers say to do. My personal experiences force me to read Graff's "A Pedagogy of Counterauthority, or the Bully/Wimp Syndrome" with great interest. Yes, sometimes we *tell* students what we want them to know. As I coach football, I demonstrate for my players' benefits what I want them to do: "No," I might say, assuming what used to be an athletic posture, "*this* is what I mean." For Graff this effort to demand that things be done the way I say they must, this effort to control and thus dominate, is the bully portion of the equation. On the football field, I do not create situations where players can learn their own way of doing things or, with their teammates, construct knowledge about the game. There is very clearly the right way or the wrong way. This does not mean to me that anything goes; I have stood by and heard the head coach exclaim loudly that "we're going to give you guys skirts instead of uniforms for our next game." I forced myself to tell him, an ex-Marine drill sergeant, that I am uncomfortable with such slogans. What I felt as I told him reflects the dilemma a male feminist faces when he leaves campus: the values we hold in academe may not fit comfortably into the lives we live off campus. The drill sergeant/coach laughed and said, "You're kidding, right?" Respecting the hierarchy, I told him I wasn't kidding entirely; it was his team and he could say what he wanted. But I added my belief that if the players wore skirts the coaches should too. This is only superficially different in its theoretical context from the things Murphy says to his students in his classroom or Sosnoski says in his article on professional issues. If we don't consider how these matters of theory dangerously lead us into confrontations in the world off-campus, we have done little more, in the end, than pose. It takes manly courage to relinquish masculine privileges.

I am a teacher of young poets as well and a publishing poet trying to live with my father's concern over what would make a football player write poems, none of them about sports. I carry this construction with me into my classrooms, faculty meetings, and football practices. When I teach my young male students to write poetry, I make a space for their self-discovery. I try not to appropriate their writing. Sometimes I keep quiet while my students talk among themselves. This is the wimp in me (using Graff's distinction); I am that person sometimes too. Rarely do I employ the wimp role when I work with my young football players. What's more, sometimes I simply cannot be a wimp with my classes and still be an effective teacher. There are semesters, such as this one, when I have retirees from the armed forces in my classes, teaching as I do near Camp Lejeune, Fort Bragg, and Seymour Johnson Air Force Base. These men, nearly my age, challenge me repeatedly to deal with them directly, often forcefully. I am capable of meeting this challenge, but this is not the role I want to model for young men and students I encounter, including these men.

What do I want young men, especially those entering the profession, to learn from me? I want them to see that there is a range of ways of behaving between the wimp, on one side, and the bully, on the other. I would want them to see, as my experiences as an older male have shown me, how situations require them to behave in a particular way. Manhood, as it is constructed for us, is in large part response. We do not have to agree to constructions of manhood imposed on us from outside. But we had better be able to act out the roles we are given if circumstances require that we do. I would want the young men I coach at middle school football to see that I am compassionate—"the nurturing coach," as one parent describes me—but that I am also one who will make demands of them, require them to run through their pain *as I ran through mine* when I played. I want my students to see that I am willing to read their writing and hear their conversations in class with some sensitivity. But I also want them to see that I will respond to their challenges. I want them to see that I am more than a physical being, that I am spirit and intellect equally. But let's end with some notion of how this might apply in the classroom since I do not think men can wait for women to invite them in. We are not visiting their offices or homes; we are making a path for the young men who will follow us.

As the published literature discussed in this chapter shows, men need to critique openly in their classrooms the privileges they have been given through tradition. This may require that men give up some authority in the classroom, give students opportunities to reach conclusions about the materials being taught. Men, then, will need to think differently about teaching and therefore about how they respond to their students. When necessary—and men will know when they're challenged to do so—they must also take a position on a subject and hold it. Some men will not respect a "soft" man, one who gives in too easily when directly confronted. But I also believe we can make a classroom where such confrontations are unnecessary. I am not the authority on every issue and need not behave as though I am. While there can be no doubt about who's in charge on the football field, authority can be dispersed in the classroom. Sometimes I'm one type of man, at other times a different type of man entirely. The situation demands it of me.

But this leads to another interesting method for incorporating feminism in traditionally male issues. Conscientious men must at some point move their beliefs outside the classroom and into the public sphere. Interestingly, Sosnoski writes a thesis-driven essay but argues from a feminist subject position, employing a hybrid mode of argumentation. Men might model a kind of masculine, even macho, courage in the profession, as Sosnoski does, by tracking the history of specific professional issues and asking, in effect, "What if we had done this differently?" I believe Connors should have asked this question in "Teaching and Learning as a Man." In this way, men might demonstrate that they have read the history of the profession differently, seeking the central emphases and naming them as masculine, if they need to be so named. Men must not only recognize their indebtedness to women, but acknowledge that they have been trapped in the myth-making and social expectations of others who have preceded them into the field. Male teachers should talk to their students—men and women both—about the myths of manhood that have constructed them, the demands of a profession that has institutionalized masculine approaches to problem solving and ways of thinking about the profession as career.

Chapter 5

Guns, Language, and Beer

Hunting for a Working-Class Language in the Academy

Ann E. Green

CLASS AND THE ACADEMY: VIGNETTE #1

I'm team teaching feminist theory with a colleague from psychology. We have ten students, all white, eight women and two men. We're sitting outside discussing readings on environmental feminism. We've been arguing for about twenty minutes about vegetarianism and environmentalism. My colleague says, "And what about those guys with guns? Those guys who shoot everything up? Who are they?"

It takes me a moment to answer, "My Dad."

Students are surprised. "Your father hunts?"

"Yes, and I've hunted, too . . . sort of; I don't carry a gun and I've only been out in the early morning hunting turkey and we've never seen one."

What I don't say is that most men that I knew growing up hunted, that hunter safety was a required subject for sixth graders (and that I passed and got a florescent orange hunter safety card), that many of my high school classmates hunted (and many later enlisted in the army because jobs were scarce). I don't tell them about being ten years old and waking up early on December mornings, walking sleepily into the kitchen to discover that my father and his friends have already eaten eggs, pancakes, bacon, and ham cooked by my mother, and gone out to hunt at the first legal moment, the moment that the game commission determines is official sunrise. They woke at 3:30 a.m. and milked and fed seventy cows before leaving. They would return at noon for lunch with at least one deer carcass in the back of the pickup.

It's hard to write about social class in ways that don't recreate academic scripts about social class. It's also hard to make class visible in daily life, in daily encounters, even in the teaching moment that opens this chapter. To interrupt a conversation in feminist theory to talk about social class seems, on the surface, to be completely appropriate. To talk about the environmental movement as a classed movement, to consider who hunts and why, seems like a logical question to raise. So why didn't I do it? It seems to me that there are several complex reasons that talking about class and writing about class are difficult. Middle-class, white, assumptions of propriety and politeness dominate academic discourse and the assumptions about what is "polite" to say in an academic context. While assumptions about social class affect how we encounter one another, these assumptions are difficult to articulate. While I come from a Northern, white, rural, working-class background, grew up on a farm, have parents who didn't attend college, worked a number of "shit jobs" (custodian, bank teller, house cleaner, farm worker), these experiences are generally erased from my public persona, and this is not often a choice on my part. When I talk with colleagues about their summer homes or their children's private education, there is often an assumption that we share the same class background, and that background is one of privilege, upper middle class or higher—and, further, that if I don't have those material things, that I *aspire* to them. Like the assumption that because I am married and straight that I aspire to give birth to biological children, this assumption that I aspire to middle-class symbols of status is problematic. However, to interrupt a conversation about middle-class privilege with an assertion about a working-class past or a question about middle-class values is often considered "impolite" (and in some contexts, not "collegial"). And, sometimes, when teaching or writing, it's risky because the assertion can be misread or misinterpreted.

For example, when talking with a colleague's wife about her new baby, she went into a long digression about how fearful she is that our faculty tuition benefits at other institutions will be cut. I responded by saying, "Well, you have a lot of time and we can fight, the faculty can fight, to keep that benefit." She said, "But this really concerns me. Little

Johnny may not be able to go to college where he wants to, and you'll understand when you have children." I said, "If I have children, my children might not want to go to college." She seemed surprised, and said, "But-of-course-you-would-want-your-child-to-go-to-college." I said, "I don't know; maybe my kid would want to be a carpenter." But this was not the script. This was not the "polite" way I was supposed to respond, and the polite way would have been to affirm a middle-class person's "fear of falling." The resistance to discussing issues of class makes perfect sense when "[t]he university is, after all, the core institution of the professional middle class" (Ehrenreich 58). And because middle-class people are so trained not to "hear" the poor or the working class talk about their own self-interest, it's even more difficult to interrupt academic discourse or polite conversation by questioning someone's assumptions (Ehrenreich 139). In fact, this is one of the paradoxes of middle-class life: while middle-class people are supposed to have more choices (more money?) than working-class or poor people, middle-class ideas of success and failure effectively delimit any "real" choice that a member of the middle class has. While this is not new, this idea that capitalism works by presenting a variety of "choices" when there aren't really substantial ones to be made, what I want to think about here are the rhetorical choices that can get made to highlight class, and how these choices get misread because the script around class is so deeply embedded—given the history of the university, possibly more deeply embedded here than elsewhere.

In "Bi, Butch, and Bar Dyke" Michelle Gibson, Martha Marinara, and Deborah Meem explore the complexities of sexual identity and class in ways that highlight the "both/and" of identity rather than the "either/or." Marinara writes,

> I can talk or write about my working-class past, but I no longer live in it. I have no real identity there, and I have no real identity in the professional class; I have only the dream.
>
> The dream state makes one unable to belong to a particular social identity because the lack of authenticity, however problematic the concept, makes one's class, as well as one's sexual orientation, invisible. (74)

Language for class is almost invisible. Unless someone else talks about, for example, growing up in South Philly (a location that may provoke a particular read about "class" depending on the audience), class is assumed to be middle. And unless one speaks about the opportunities that one has had because one grew up working class, if class is acknowledged at all, it is as though that story of upward mobility is the one that matters. Mine is not a story about the "deprivation" of being a working-class child. Or, rather, while there were financial deprivations, there were also a number of opportunities and privileges of growing up working class—closeness to community and family, a sense of history, multiple religious commitments that were fluid rather than dogmatic, a knowledge that if something was broke, one could fix it, or learn to fix it, or do without it—that make me increasingly recognize the richness and complexity of this "poor," white, rural world.

I am trying to be attentive to the ways in which the narratives about class that I am using are white narratives. Dalton Conley describes learning about race as a process of learning a language, learning "a set of stories we tell ourselves to get through the world, to organize our reality" (25). In this case, the stories I tell about class are also stories about whiteness. White privilege enables me to pass more easily into white middle-class "norms," and this is part of the complexity of working with "class" as a category. Where, how, and when does it bump up against race, and what does it signify? In contrast to race, which is most often a category invoked by others for us based on physical characteristics, it may be that class, like ethnicity, is a rhetorical move that a writer can *choose* to invoke or make visible (Conley 37). This fluidity of rhetorical identity means that working-class ideas and ideals can be written about, but that they are often misread as being the story of upward mobility and success that capitalist, materialist culture perpetuates rather than the more complex and fluid identity that Gibson, Marinara, and Meem describe.

In my academic writing, I often present class as a "calling card" through stories and narratives. This strategy is effective because a story allows room for complexity that is richer and thicker than that conveyed by definitions. As Joanna Kadi describes it, "[C]lass identity comes from many places: education, values, culture, income, dwelling, lifestyle, manners, friends, ancestry, language, expectations, desires, sense of entitlement, religion, neighborhood, amount of privacy" (53). Because class is slippery and complex, narrative permits the shading and ambiguity necessary for developing a more complex way of thinking about class. And it is not for me about "passing" as middle class as much as it is about being neither one identity or another, being both/and rather than either/or, and where possible, making class visible, breaking silences around class. Except for drinking beer out of bottles (and drinking beer at all), there are few ways that class is written publicly on my body or through my words. And even that beer drinking identity is complicated. While I felt like I screwed up my first academic job interview dinner by asking the waiter for beer when the restaurant only served wine (clearly "out" as a working-class job candidate), the beer that I currently drink is not the red and white cans of Budweiser that I grew up sneaking sips from during summer kickball games. The beer that I drink now is most often from bottles and most often micro brewed. And when it's not, like last summer when I went to a week-long workshop for those who teach at Catholic institutions, where there was only Budweiser available, I am struck by how Budweiser, unlike a Proustian madeleine, does not invoke the sounds and sights of my childhood, but instead, well, just tastes like Budweiser.

Some of my work is what Linda Brodkey names a kind of "autoethnography," a kind of autobiographical writing that places the individual within/amongst a collective. It is writing as "a singular self" that "challenges received categories" (28). But I also use stories—either my own or others that I've heard—in the academic writing that I do, because, as Hephzibah Roskelly writes,

> Without any straightforward moral code to complete them, the stories told by the people in my father's family subtly taught values and ideals, strategies and subterfuges. Of all the things I have learned from being the child of a redneck farmer, the most useful and important to me has been this emphasis on the story as a tool for teaching. (295)

I learned through stories from my father while I listened to him as he talked with other men while they stacked hay bales or built fence together. When we worked together, my father would occasionally tell me stories about his experiences in school. My father did not do well in school. His stories were often about those moments. One story was about a day that all of the high school boys got out of school to help the volunteer firemen search for a depressed man who might have committed suicide. The boys walked through cornfields and pastures, through woods and across creeks, but no one found the body. It was finally discovered a few weeks later floating in a pond. He also told me about being unfairly accused of cheating on his math homework. His teacher wouldn't let him go to recess until he confessed. It took a week of missed recesses for him to confess to the thing that he didn't do. His story had a specific point—he vowed at that moment that he would never be bullied into confessing to something he didn't do again.

Dad's stories about school often resonated with my own experiences—school was a place where middle-class teachers exercised arbitrary power over working-class students. I was never a "good" student, but always the one who asked the questions. So often teachers write about teaching with the expectation that students should be quiet, thoughtful, polite, and aspire to middle-class status. My mother would have preferred for me to be one of these kinds of students because she received the bulk of flack for my rebellions, and she argued that without "good grades" I would never go to college on the scholarship money that I needed. My father, however, told me that it was better to be "well read." While he understood school as a necessary certifying agent for success (a college degree, he told me, would mean a million dollars more income over a lifetime than a high school degree), he was skeptical about the value of what was taught there. When I write about social class and teaching, I want to identify my subject position because I want to model a kind of skepticism about middle-class values and school that was useful for me as a model. Writing about class is one way to remain connected to the people and place I come from, but it is also a way of modeling a both/and, a way of aspiring to some aspects of middle-class life—a regular pay check, health insurance, and a certain amount of autonomy at work—while also validating those aspects of working-class identity—collectivity, connection, passion in speech, writing, and action, an ability to fix what's broken without buying something new—that I've found valuable as a person with working-class origins who chooses to continue to identify as working-class. Of course, even listing the qualities immediately creates questions about where and when (if ever) any of these ideals and ideas have existed. I am reminded by the dean who wanted to enforce rather rigid constraints on faculty office hours that middle-class professionals are increasingly supervised at work; working-class people can certainly buy rather than repair what's broken, particularly at the local Wal-Mart. However, creating play between these various aspects of identity, rhetorical play, can at least highlight the possibility of material choices that do not mirror those that fit neatly into categories emphasized in mainstream U.S. culture. Finding ethical ways to address class through stories is a part of the project.

Stories can disrupt the flow of academic discourse and build a connection with the reader. When I think about the connections that I would like to build with the reader, I recall the first time that I read Dorothy Allison in Janet Zandy's collection, *Calling Home: Working-Class Women's Writings.* When I read "Mama," I felt the shock of recognition, the sensation of seeing something that I hadn't read before in print. For the first time, I thought, it's okay to write about social class by telling stories about class. I had the same feeling when when I read bell hooks's *Teaching to Transgress* and found someone writing about social class in the classroom. The absence of hooks's and Allison's work and the work of others like them in graduate classrooms disappointed me, but it also energized me. It seemed to me that there should be a way to write with the passion and integrity of hooks and Allison in academic discourse—even within the boundaries of that most academic of forms, the dissertation, and that there existed methods to write for a wider audience.

CLASS AND THE ACADEMY: VIGNETTE #2

When I taught first-year writing as a graduate student in a large state university, a fellow TA who had grown up in New York City and went to an Ivy League undergraduate school told me that the "narratives" we let students write were potentially dangerous sites of bad writing. I should, he advised, tell students that they couldn't write about drunk driving, a dead grandmother, or deer hunting. Rural students, he said, they all want to write about getting that first deer. To save myself from clichés, he suggested that I should tell students they couldn't use those topics.

Instead, I let my students write about whatever they wanted. One young woman wrote a series of papers about her family's farm. Her final paper was a persuasive argument to her family about how her role in running the farm shouldn't be subordinate to her brother's because of her gender. I liked reading papers about hunting, and I was a decent audience for them because if I didn't know about a particular type of gun or hunting strategy, I could ask my father. I remember arguing in the TA training class about why students should be able to write about what they wanted to write, but at the time, I didn't think about how certain topics—deer hunting, drunk driving, farming—were particularly "classed."

As I've experimented with ways to write about social class, I've tried to reach a larger audience. I'm most happy with a short story about social class called "My Uncle's Guns." Fiction allowed me to pursue the kinds of rhetorical strategies that highlighted class and the problems of pedagogy for working-poor students. I wrote "My Uncle's Guns" as a first-person narrative, much like those that are often assigned in freshmen composition. The narrator, Maria, relates how she discovered two bodies by the roadside when she was out on a date with an old friend from high school. Both victims had been shot. Because it's been reprinted in *Teaching Developmental Writing*, at third year review my colleagues called it a story-that-works-as-pedagogy, and I rhetorically invoke class in ways that are similar to my academic writing. The story deals with language, class, and the way these factors are perceived by working-class and poor white people in a rural area. By writing "Guns," I found strategies for telling stories that I could then use in more traditional academic discourse. "Guns" functions as a kind of fictional ethnography, a story that represents a culture that is unfamiliar to most of its readers.

"Guns" was first published in *Writing on the Edge* in Fall/Winter 1997 and has since been reprinted in *Teaching Developmental Writing: Background Readings* as an account of a basic writer from the student's perspective. Until "Guns" was reprinted in *Teaching Developmental Writing*, I had never considered the main character, Maria, to be a "developmental" writer. But, because of her class background, because of her choice of writing topics, Maria could be classified as developmental. But then how does she represent a working-class point of view? While Maria writes in a sophisticated metadiscourse, she does not write what a middle-class teacher would expect in a first-year student's paper. Lynn Z. Bloom argues that the qualities we value in first-year writers are particularly American and middle class—"safety, order, cleanliness, efficiency" (655). Maria's prose is not orderly or objective, and her tone isn't neutral. She is angry and her words convey that anger. This short story is not written in "normative discourse in subject, point of view, or values implied" (Bloom 659). In "Guns," Maria moves back and forth between telling a story and commenting about how the story she's telling won't make her teacher happy.

> Are these the kinds of details that you mean when we talk in class about significant details? How am I supposed to know which details are important to you?
>
> I feel like I have to tell you all the details about deer hunting so you won't think we're simple or backward or country, getting all excited about looking at somebody's gun. Even though you assign us those Tim O'Brien stories with lists, you really don't think we'll write like that do you? And you would tell us we were too repetitive if we did. You're not from around here, and I can see you don't like us sometimes when we go outside on break from class and smoke and talk too loud about how we hate our jobs. You look at us and think that we don't know anything. You think that teaching us how to write can't help us cause we're not going to change our lives by reading some essays. But we all want to do well in this class. Can't you just tell us what you want us to write about? (37)

The question, "Can't you just tell us what to write about?" echoes what students regularly ask teachers about assignments, but what comes before this question is Maria's analysis of the gap between what professional writers can do and what she as a "student writer" can do. Her details, she feels, won't be significant because they aren't what her audience (her teacher) would find significant.

The story invokes class in other ways as well. Maria works as a bank teller. The other main characters in the story are an army sergeant, a custodian, and an electric company worker. No one earns more than fifteen dollars an hour. Some have health insurance, but it's not very comprehensive. They live from paycheck to paycheck. As bell hooks writes about life in a small town, "You always see someone you know. Interruptions, intrusions are part of daily life. Privacy is difficult to maintain" ("Close" 100). Maria is rarely alone, always participating in some sort of communal action. In fact, the only moment that she is isolated is when she's composing her essay, and only then does she acknowledge her fear.

GUNS, ANGER, AND SAFETY

Almost every short story I've written has had a reference to guns. For me guns are clear symbols of white, rural, working-class people. Before I got my PhD, my mother asked what I wanted as a graduation present. I wanted a rifle, not because I wanted to shoot, but because of what it represents. (My parents laughed and got me flowers.) There's a big difference for me between a shotgun and a revolver, between a concealed weapon and a deer rifle. I grew up with guns but not handguns. My father owns ten or so shotguns and rifles. He hunts deer with a particular 30.06. He goes out for turkey with a shotgun. My father often argues with his friends about gun laws. He's for handgun control, and he disagrees with the NRA's slippery slope argument about this issue. If those who advocate gun control had better rhetorical strategies and knew something about their working-class, anti-handgun legislation would be easier to pass.

Guns symbolize the lack of physical safety that working-class, working-poor people continually experience. While, as Bloom articulates, the middle-class values safety, security is not always possible for working-class, working poor people. Allison describes her mother's warning, "Push it down. Don't show it. Don't tell anyone what's really going on. We are not safe. There are people in the world who are, but they are not us" (143). When I started college, the news that I regularly got from home was often about someone who had died, often a young person, from either a drunk driving accident or a gunshot wound. Two years ago, a man I graduated from high school with shot his girlfriend and then himself at the Proctor and Gamble plant where they both worked.

He and I had been in first grade together, received first communion together, and graduated together. At our ten-year reunion, we drank a beer, and he seemed happy. But where I come from, Chris's story is not uncommon. He had a "good" job at P&G as a security guard and had a gun shop of his own on the side. He had access to guns, he was angry, and he was thirty years old with no real hope of "doing better." The double murder described in "Guns" was based on another actual murder and the stories I was later told.

Guns symbolize a way of life where people are fiercely independent and the despair that weighs on the underclass. My home community values guns because they're an available source of power. Hunting is an opportunity to exercise control, control that's not allowed in the "physically demanding, repetitive, or dangerous" and that "lack autonomy" jobs that working-class people have (Introduction, "Working-Class Women" 5). There are few opportunities for higher education and few jobs with a living wage and health insurance. In teaching students like Maria, I have to be aware that the violent story may need to be written, that she may need a way to describe the violence in her life. To deny a student the opportunity to tell her story does further violence. Whether or not a student writing in most academic institutions would choose to share a story of violence with her middle-class teacher is, however, another story.

Paradoxically, for the working class, guns represent a way to stay safe in a world that doesn't value its experiences. As Joanna Kadi articulates, "[S]tupid has become a cultural concept with a particular code and set of signifiers that describe working-class people as the middle and upper classes perceive and construct us" (48–49). Guns are a way of gaining power when you're powerless. If a man (or a woman) can hunt and shoot, he has a kind of survival skill that city dwellers don't have (see Dorothy Allison's "Gun Crazy" for more on this). In "My Uncle's Guns," rifles have the dual purpose of literally and figuratively being what can kill you and what can save you.

LANGUAGE

A professor who read an early draft of "Guns" told me she was concerned about my language, that I didn't write correctly, and I needed to "clean it up." She thought that I used too much passive voice, that too often my prose should employ better sentence structures. Her response shook me. "Guns" allowed me to recreate the voices of my childhood and the way those voices sounded. I explained to her that this was a deliberate choice. What I thought were valid ways of using language to portray a region and its social class, she attributed to "sloppiness" on my part and to a lack of efficiency with language. I had anticipated a conversation about plot, characters, and setting, and did not expect the focus of the conference to be on grammar. When I spoke about what I wanted the story to do, how I wanted the story to portray a world often omitted from most middle-class fiction, my teacher advised me to read John Dos Passos because what I wanted to do was "political" rather than "artistic."

One of my professor's particular complaints concerned passive voice.[1] The rural, white language that I'm most familiar with uses passive voice regularly to deflect agency. Rather than "Mrs. Brown denied my loan," a farmer might say, "My mortgage was denied." The applicant is likely to know the unsympathetic loan officer, and rather than blame her directly, the speaker masks agency. The use of passive voice doesn't mean that the language isn't filled with metaphor and simile ("It rained like a cow pissing on a flat rock."), but it does suggest that indirection is more valued than confrontation. Like the working-class people that Finn describes in *Literacy with an Attitude*, the working-class and poor people in "Guns" reply on implicit, context-driven language (89). Unlike Finn's description, Maria is able to speak back to authority through the metanarrative.

While my professor's remarks were well intentioned, they replicated what Bloom argues is one of the purposes of first-year writing as middle-class enterprise: "to patrol for clean language and a suitably respectful authorial stance" (664). However, as Valerie Miner writes, one goal for a working-class writer is to make her work accessible (80). I want language to reflect the people it is written for and about, and this means that word choices and sentence structures are inflected with a tone and voice that I'm trying to create. After this experience, I initially felt that: (1) I no longer passed as an academic writer; (2) the place that I come from wasn't worth writing about; (3) language betrayed me. At that moment, "Guns" became a double-voiced narrative. Prior to my professor's critique, the narrative had only a single voice, one with no metacommentary, no speaking back to the teacher. Now, the story had two layers—one that related the events and the plot, and one that challenged the assignment, the requirements for the course, and the teacher's middle-class subjectivity.

"Language is also a place of struggle" (hooks, "Choosing" 146). Language and guns are complex, powerful tools that can be used to protect or to harm. Language can convey meaning, but it can also betray you. It can work to represent class and explore class, but only in certain contexts. My writing has been criticized for class-based moments. For example, I tend to swear often, deliberately, sometimes behaving in ways that are not polite in middle-class circles. When obscenities have appeared in my academic writing, I get comments about "toning things down" or about if such language is "necessary." For me, it is. It reveals a subjectivity that doesn't conform to middle-class norms, that is passionately angry, and that doesn't fit neatly into a box labeled "academic discourse." In "Guns" this language appears in the following metavoiced commentary by Maria:

> I don't know if this is the kind of dialogue that you say "reveals character." We said "fuck" a lot more than I'm writing down now, but you probably don't want that in a paper. It's probably one of those things that a professional author can use, but that we can't yet. Like we have to get good at knowing the big words first, before we can write like we talk. (40)

I wanted Maria to express class loyalty and connection. As Dorothy Allison writes, language connects you to your family. "Language then, and tone, and cadence. Make me mad, and I'll curse you to the seventh generation in my mama's voice" (Allison 144). What do students lose in order to sound middle-class? What is lost in the veneer of polite conversation? In the constraints of the middle-class story? What happens to those of us whose stories don't fall neatly into the middle-class categories?

SHOTGUN STRATEGIES

Creative writers such as Allison, hooks, Jordan, and Kadi help position my writing ethically. By ethically I mean that I do not undertake these positions simply to promote one singular "I" in the world but to write *with* those people who are "subjects" in my research. As Jacqueline Jones Royster writes, " '[S]ubject' position really is everything" (29), consequently, the writing that I do must, account for the subjectivity that I bring to the work. Throughout my writing I employ alternative patterns to the traditional, linear, objective academic argument. In some cases, I adopt the essayist's voice to interrupt the academic narrative and to problematize the "data" presented; in other instances, such as "My Uncle's Guns," I use ethnographic fiction as a method of presenting "data" that disrupt the authoritative voice of an academic researcher. Since much of my writing is done from the perspective of a teacher-researcher, how I use student voices in the writing itself becomes important. Reflecting on my own voice prevents me from simply using student voices to prop up an argument without acknowledging my own subject position.

I have learned that since there can be no neutral or objective voice, the academic voice I use cannot pretend neutrality or objectivity. And this voice cannot simply be a few sentences at the beginning of a scholarly article that establish my whiteness, my gender, or my class of origin. While a "calling card" is generally presented first as a means of introduction, a subject's position must be woven throughout the article, book, or manuscript. This continuous process of packing and unpacking, of re-seeing and re-visioning, requires constant immersion in the writers and teachers and students who continuously teach me new ways of being/writing/thinking in the world.

In a recent class I taught called "Literacy as a Social Practice," we talked at length about race and class and the implications for literacy work. This class was exceptional in that they went farther into thinking about whiteness and race privilege than any other class that I've ever had. They made wonderful connections between the readings they did and the service learning that they performed and were creative in developing what they named "anti-racist literacy practices." We discussed essays from Lisa Delpit's book, *The Skin that We Speak* in order to develop ideas about systemic change that would address the causes of illiteracy, and it surprised me that one group, a group with three of the four self-identified working-class students in the class, said that the systemic change that they imaged was getting parents more involved in teaching their children. They argued that parents were responsible for instilling middle-class values and aspirations and reasoned that they were in college because of their parents. All of the students who made this argument were white. This moment made me angry and also incredibly sad. It was as though what we had read and talked about before had no value. And for these working-class students, I felt a great deal of pain that they couldn't imagine anything about their working-class pasts that they wanted to respect, to maintain a connection with.

We talked about it. Or, rather, I held forth about systemic change and injustice and questioned what it means to place responsibility for literacy on parents. It was uncharacteristic for me because I lectured, drawing from previous readings to ask questions. And I also came out, forcefully, with a working-class past and how that conflicted with my present identity as a university professor. In the lecture, I said that what is valuable in middle-class life are the money and the security and choices that come with it, but that working-class identities, the connections between community and home are, ultimately, more important to me. What I hope happened is that what I said got heard, and that what got said contrasted with the academy, with academics, as "tweed: white, middle class, and heterosexual" (Gibson et al. 86). I hope that those students, particularly those from working-class backgrounds, got a sense that they didn't have to erase their working-class identities to become middle-class, that fluid identities are possible. And I hope that, by incorporating part of a personal story into the academic theory, what students and I talked about might mean that both hearts and minds can be changed.

When hearts and minds change, social justice is possible. Most academic discourse addresses only the minds of those who read it, and I would like to write in such a way as to reach both the heart and the mind. Actress, playwrite, and teacher Anna Deavere Smith describes the problem with assuming that simply educating the mind will change the world in this way:

> I came back to that sixties expectation that education is the answer to racial strife and inequality. . . . [A]s a bonus, an important bonus, was the notion that, having gotten to know one another, we would make a better, more equalized society. . . . Education gives us more facts, more evidence, but it does not give us empathy. (160)

I think that there are ways to write about race, class, and gender that nudge the reader toward empathy, and that empathy is the beginning of change. To do this, I try and undo some of the conventions of academic discourse. While I don't achieve all of these goals all of the time, I hope that by using narratives and telling stories to disrupt the flow of a linear argument, by holding open the possibility of other readings, and by including self-conscious reflections of my subject position in relationship to my students, that the hearts and minds of readers can be changed.

CLASS AND THE ACADEMY: LAST STORY

At Christmastime I'm in Ashland, Oregon, with my in-laws. Ashland is the part of Oregon that Oregonians feel is most like California because it's settled with a variety of retired Berkeley professors. My in-laws, retired Berkeley professors, are scientists. The house is filled with their local friends for their annual Christmas party. Some people have just come back from building houses for Habitat for Humanities in Ecuador. Others are deconstructing the problems with *The Lord of the Rings* (it's been out for two days, they've seen it twice). Someone mentions that they had spent some time earlier living in a town next to the volunteer firehouse, and that it was painful to hear the siren going off all of the time. A woman with a glass of white wine asks why they didn't join the volunteers? Didn't they have a pickup? A gun rack? Didn't they want to chew tobacco? Everyone sympathizes with how the noise from the firehouse must have driven down real estate prices. I go to the fridge and get myself another beer. It's a local, Oregon beer, probably the locals drink Budweiser. My mother-in-law offers me a glass, but I'm happy drinking from the bottle. I don't tell them that my father is a volunteer fireman, and that his job is standing hip deep in pond water making sure that the hoses don't clog with ice as the water is pumped toward burning buildings. And I don't describe for the guests the snapshot of me as a toddler wearing a plaid jacket and a red scarf and grinning happily from my father's knee as he kneels, posing with me in front of four or five hanging deer carcasses, gutted and butchered after a day of hunting. I don't tell them stories, but I know that I'll probably write about what happened later.[2]

NOTES

1. White, rural passive voice contrasts with what June Jordan argues about the fundamentals of Black English. She finds that Black English uses active voice and present tense to convey its "person-centered" values, and she further finds that "there is no passive voice construction possible in Black English" ("Nobody" 129).

2. Thank you to the Saint Joseph's University Junior Faculty Writing Group (Tom Brennan, Melissa Goldthwaite, April Lindner, and Jo Alyson Parker) for their thoughtful comments and discussion of an earlier version of this chapter. Thank you also to Susan Naomi Bernstein, University of Cincinnati, and Amy Winans, Susquehanna University, for their feedback and the conversations on race, class, and gender, and to Richard Fusco, Saint Joseph's University, for his graceful and precise editorial suggestions.

Part II

Refiguring Culture, History, and Methodology

Chapter 6

Smarts

A Cautionary Tale

Valerie Lee

> Of course, one of the dangers of standing at an intersection—particularly at such a suddenly busy, three-way intersection—is the likelihood of being run over by oncoming traffic.
>
> —Ann DuCille, *Skin Trade*

As an African American scholar in the academy, I have been negotiating traffic at a busy intersection for the last twenty-five years. For me, race, gender, class, disability, sexuality, and a range of categories of social difference have not been faddish, fast-moving sports cars on an academic highway. Rather, they have been the permanent routes, however fluid and contested, that I have chosen to pursue. As if traveling the routes of social difference were not enough, I have followed an itinerary that has been further complicated by a joint appointment in English and Women's Studies, as well as courtesy appointments in the Departments of African American and African Studies, Comparative Studies, The Center for Law, Policy and Social Science, and the Center for Folklore Studies. This type of interdisciplinarity and intersectionality has demanded that I have a clear sense of methodologies and theoretical frameworks for my research. Confronting promotion and tenure committees with anything less than knowing what I am doing and how I am doing it would have left me as *roadkill* on academe's outer belt—never arriving close enough to its city of power to make any difference. So, I have been strategic about my analytical tools and the arguments that I have formulated that allow me to employ those tools.

In *Granny Midwives and Black Women Writers: Double-Dutched Readings*, I demonstrate what it means to pursue research at the nexus of race, gender, culture, and class, and create an accommodating methodology. I began my research with the question: Why do the novels of so many contemporary African American women writers contain portraits of black lay midwives and women healers who are simultaneously constructed as obstetricians, chemists, rootworkers, and psychotherapists? In pursuing this question, I realized that I would have to study the historical lives of the many Southern, rural black women who during their heyday, the 1920s and '30s, numbered more than forty-three thousand and who, although described in some government publications as "uncompetent nigra women," in their own communities, "stood as tall as God" (*Granny Midwives* 6, 24, 88). I had decided to tell the historical grannies' stories in tandem with the fictional representations of their stories. However, my first roadblock was that at the time that I was researching my book, no one had written about the lives of the black lay midwives. There was one book on one particular granny midwife,[1] but there were no collected histories of their lives. I could not believe that these women, who had delivered thousands of black and white babies, who birthed and healed a nation, had not commanded scholarly attention. How was I to do what I wanted to do with the literature when the history was not there? Scholars of color in the academy often must first fill vacuums before they can do their work.

Although I had not originally planned to do all the archival and ethnographic work, I had to do it. If there was "no there there," as Gertrude Stein would say, then I had to do the research that would validate the lives of the black lay midwives as a first step to understanding how their lives resonated with the literary characterizations of a long list of conjure women: Toni Morrison's Pilate (*Song of Solomon*) and Marie-Therese (*Tar Baby*); Gloria Naylor's Sapphira Wade and Mama Day (*Mama Day*); Toni Cade Bambara's Minnie Ramson (*The Salt Eaters*), Tina McElroy Ansa's *Baby of the Family*, selected Alice Walker's short stories, and many other authors and texts. I had to bring together the medical history, the cultural history, and the literary tradition in a way that my colleagues in the discipline of English would find credible and a way that I felt was culturally responsive to the material. My task was to talk about all of these *sistah conjurers* without sounding like a conjure woman myself. For although I knew that the original meanings of *conjure woman* were closely associated with *double-headed* and *double wisdom,*[2] and thus an empowering idiom for diasporic sisterly powers, I could not count on my colleagues to read *conjure* apart from its European inflected meanings of black witchcraft. Scholars of color in the academy are always suspect.

I wanted a methodology that would fit my subject matter. It had to be a methodology that was grounded in multiplicities, able to accommodate my project's interdisciplinarity. It also had to be a methodology that was at ease with a culturally grounded text. I wanted to follow in the footsteps of African American scholars who were using indigenous metaphors for writing African American experiences: Elsa Barkley Brown's "quilting" of history; Henry Louis Gates Jr.'s "speakerley texts"; Mae Henderson's "speaking in tongues" trope, bell hooks and Cornel West's "breaking bread" metaphor. I wanted my methodology to travel to what Karla Holloway calls a "cultural mooring place" (Holloway 522). One day, while sitting at the kitchen table with a laptop, a PC, and a printer, I noticed my daughters in the driveway jumping double-dutch. As I watched the turning of multiple ropes, listened to their chanting of folk rhymes, and saw them negotiate space between the two ropes in front of a company of neighbors waiting their turn, I knew that I was witnessing the performance of my methodology. Here was an art form that was closely associated with the experiences of young black girls. In *Granny Midwives*, I transform jumping double-dutch into a practice of reading dual cultural performances, the performances of the historical grannies and the performances of the literary texts. Just as jumping double-dutch requires the jumpers to listen to the chanting and sound of the ropes, then multiply locate themselves between ropes, I ask my readers to hear the orality of the two sets of texts and multiply locate themselves between my narrative ropes (*Granny Midwives* 3).

Jumping double-dutch is much harder than merely skipping rope. It requires a company, a community of jumpers. It is difficult to learn, for one must perform a set of verbally sung instructions while the two ropes are turning. Jumping in requires a number of false starts. Jumpers sway their bodies back and forth as they try to match the rhythm of the ropes. Building on double-dutch as a trope, I discuss the ropes of my analysis as an intertextual, interplay performed against a polyphonic range of black women's voices, providing the interdisciplinary freedom my work requires.

Not having found a methodology that complemented my role as an "indigenous ethnographer," I risked creating one. One of the benefits of having done so is watching how others who practice women of color feminisms have made use of the model. Imagine my surprise when someone sent me a tape of a womanist theologian who spoke at a large convention and introduced her work as "double-dutched ministry," citing the work that I had done. In addition to the methodological work the historical recovery work has attracted an audience. Medical groups such as LaMaze International and Midwives Alliance of North America (MANA) have not asked me to speak at their national and/or regional conventions. Although I never planned to build bridges between medicine and literature, there was work that needed to be done, a gap that needed to be filled.

Just as rewarding as academic and professional responses have been the responses from African American communities. Interdisciplinary work and methodologies that resonate with frameworks familiar to one's home community engage populations outside the academy. Perhaps it was the Varnette Honeywood picture of young people jumping double-dutch on the cover of *Granny Midwives* that caught the attention of the editors of the hip-hop magazine *Vibe.* In any event, in the special Notorious B.I.G. death keepsake issue there's a review of *Granny Midwives* as a text that does cultural work. The practice within my department is to place reviews on a bulletin board. Usually the reviews are from canonical, professionally approved journals. I had the pleasure of tacking on the wall the *Vibe* review, a review that placed *Granny Midwives* next to books with titles that usually do not grace the hollowed walls of academe: *Tough Love: Cultural Criticism and Familial Observations on the Life and Death of Tupac Shakur* and *Fuck You Too, the Extras+More Scrapbook.* Scholars of color in the academy often go where no one has gone before.

SMARTS

What or who gave me permission to go my own route? When I became full professor, I gave myself full permission. When I was leaving graduate school, a well-known professor of Victorian studies told me to "not waste my mind on African American literature, for it would blow over before I came up for tenure." Fortunately, I never took his advice and have always insisted on the importance of African American literature, especially African American women's studies. Nevertheless, it took a specific moment in time to make the type of university-wide public statement that I wanted to make about privilege, authority, entitlement, knowledge systems, "smarts." That occasion presented itself in a forum that the College of Humanities sponsors. Upon promotion to full professor, each person presents a lecture of his/her choosing. I selected this moment of my academic career to most fully reveal my thoughts. By critiquing academe at the very time that I entered its most hollowed halls, I was at best performing what African American poet Thylias Moss refers to in her latest collections of poems, *Last Chance for the Tarzan Holler*. "Last Chance for the Tarzan Holler" is whatever you grapple with the moment before entering some final passage, the moment before any life-changing event. It is a holler that "affirms and resists the very situation it heralds."[3] At worst, the moment of promotion to full professor is when one finally receives what Mari Evans calls in her poem, "Status Symbol," "the key to the white locked john." It was at this moment in my career, the passage from associate to full, that I decided to share my strategy for engagement with my white colleagues, who had all come to praise "her fullness." It was time to reveal that although I had played by all the rules, I never bought their definition of "smarts."

When one does work that engages a range of categories of difference, when one theorizes difference and diversity, the academy does not always see such an endeavor as smart. What happens when one finds oneself caught between two intellectual traditions, caught between communities that define "intellectual" in different ways? How does one negotiate separate communities when what one community calls "presence of mind," the other calls "stoned out of one's mind"? Many scholars, especially scholars of color who practice black feminist criticism, have dual allegiances. Their home communities expect them to "give back and reach back"; yet they work in structures where their success depends on how well they can distance themselves from that community. As such, black feminist scholars become Trojan horses[4] in the academy, doing what Chandra Mohanty would call oppositional work with institutional space.

Historically, African Americans often have shaped knowledge from different interpretive frameworks. Most academic units have written and shared notions of what excellence in teaching, research, and service means. Prior to the times when scholars of color presented their calling cards at the academy's door, faculty members were pretty smug about the meaning of such words and phrases as "canon," "rigor of thought," "cutting edge," "the educated mind." Contrastingly, a survey of African American folk stories and literature reveals a distinction between education and *edumacation*. The space between the two concepts is a contradictory space, as most complex spaces are. That is, even as most African American communities have praised literacy and education as the way to freedom and success, there has always been another discourse that says you have to watch out for white folks' education, derisively called *edumacation.* In Ebonics, the extra syllables indicate pomposity, extremity, as when Langston Hughes's character, Jesse B. Simple, calls worry, "worriation." Worry can stress you out; but worriation can kill you. *Edumacation* is academe's corruption of smartness. *Edumacation* is what folks at home think you are getting when they start asking, "Now how long have you been in school? What degree did you say are you working on *now*?" *Edumacation* calls into question many of academe's ironclad canons.

Take for example Jessica Care Moore's poetry. Why is it that at the Apollo, where one misspoken word or note can get one laughed off stage, so many of the new groups of hip hop poets are bringing down the house with poems about learning and scholars? How is it that Jessica Care Moore, the poet who has an unheard of winning record of five weeks in a row at the Apollo theatre's Amateur Night Slam Nation Competition, has touched audiences with poems not only about drugs, violence, poverty, or some other stereotypical subject matter, but also with poems about T. S. Eliot, the grand old man of modernism? Moore dedicates "There are no asylums for the real crazy women" to Vivienne, T. S. Eliot's wife. The poem begins by calling Eliot "an English tea drinking dog / Who quietly and without remorse / Stole his wife's spirit." At another point in the poem, Eliot is an "Anglo nerd knight of the canon kings" (Moore 38–39). What happens when as a professor of literature, you find yourself caught between one intellectual tradition that says T. S. Eliot is father of a noble tradition and the other that calls him "an English tea drinking dog," "Anglo nerd knight of the canon kings"? How does one read the multiple discourses at the nexus of race, gender, and culture? Is the academy the only audience to whom one has to answer? How can anyone learn to read something as contingent and contentious as race? In a piece entitled "Unleash the Queen," Marlon Riggs irreverently critiques the academy's attempt to certify him as race and sexuality resident expert: Can Miss Thing "comprehend discursive intertextual analysis, can she engage in postfeminist, neo-Marxist, postmodern deconstructionist critique? Does she understand the difference between text, subtext, and metatext? Does she know she's part of a subaltern universe? Can she, in a word, *really* read?" (*Black Popular Culture* 102). In the essay, Riggs speaks of academe as a place where he gives his most prize-winning performances. Like Moore's poetry, his words echo the distinction between education and *edumacation. Edumacation* is using a critical vocabulary to dazzle one's audience. Education is understanding that critical vocabulary well enough to choose simpler, common words.

SMARTS IN AFRICAN AMERICAN FOLKLORE

Smarts and Physical and Psychic Survival

As a parent of four teenagers, I have attended a number of middle and high school graduation ceremonies in recent years. One folk story that I have heard repeatedly at commencement services at predominately black schools is one that gives warnings of where *edumacation* can lead to. Even as the black speakers praise the students for their accomplishments, they caution them with such stories as the one about the boy, the scholar, and the minister. It's a flight story, as so many stories in African American folklore and literature are, and there are many variations of the story. A white minister, a young African American boy, and a white scholar board a small plane. The white scholar is Dr. So & So with an expertise in Such N' Such. His research is rigorous, groundbreaking, risk-taking. When the plane is having engine trouble, all three passengers must parachute to safety. There are two parachutes and three passengers. The scholar immediately grabs a parachute, exclaiming that the world cannot afford to lose his expertise. With one parachute left, the minister, exercising his Christian virtues, tells the young boy that he may have the remaining parachute. They argue back and forth because the young boy keeps insisting that they both can parachute to safety. When the minister asks him why he feels that way, the little boy replies: "You know Dr. So & So with all those degrees, who said the world couldn't live without his brains? Well, that wasn't a parachute he grabbed. That was my backpack."

A contemporary folk story that circulated to black literary listserv groups is another flight story. This time the plane is a large plane with all white passengers, except for an African American mother and her daughter. When the plane begins to have engine trouble, the white pilot throws off cargo to lessen the weight. Still the plane is too heavily loaded. The pilot must throw off people. Thinking to get rid of the African American mother and daughter first, the white pilot announces that he is going to throw off passengers in alphabetical order. He voices what sounds like a racially neutral policy, "When I call the alphabet of your identity, please step forward." He calls out, "A." The woman and her daughter remain seated. He calls out "B." Although obviously black, the woman and her daughter, still remain seated. Frustrated, the pilot calls, "C"—thinking certainly the mother and daughter will recognize themselves as colored. When the mother fails to move, the daughter says, "Ma, I thought we were African American, black, and colored." Clinging to her seat more tightly, the black mother tells the daughter, "Today, we are Negroes." Smarts is resourcefulness. It is what one uses to dodge bullets, lynching mobs, and public policy schemes that have racist effects.

Smarts and "Old Massa" Stories

Slavery generated a canon of stories that posited smarts as one upmanship on some beast (usually mules, foxes, rabbits, and buzzards) and one upmanship on "old massa." As such, smarts is relational. Staying ahead of massa constitutes smartness. One such story is about the slave, John, and his master. Massa wakes up one morning and tells John that he went to "nigger heaven," but he didn't have a good time because everyone was loud, the place was dirty, and a host of other stereotypical details. John quietly listens and then tells his master that he had a dream too. In John's dream, he goes to "white heaven." John reports that everything was neat and clean, the streets were pearly and white. But, as John explains, "dey wuzn't uh soul in de whole place."[5]

This type of traditional *outsmarting whitey story* is not unlike the contemporary stories that emphasize smarts as using common sense to settle matters that whites in authority find baffling. For 101-year-old and 103-year-old African American sisters Elizabeth and Sarah Delany in *Having Our Say*, Old Massa becomes Congress, a group of men easily outsmarted. Elizabeth writes of her ability to make judgments that white congressmen found difficult: "That Clarence Thomas mess, the Supreme Court nomination. He's lying. That girl, Anita Hill, is telling the truth. And Sadie says, 'How do you know?' Well, I'll tell you something, Honey, I know a rascal when I see one!

Sadie and I watched the whole thing on the TV, and when I saw all those silly old white men asking those stupid questions I almost got myself on a train and went down to Washington. I could have straightened out that whole Clarence Thomas mess in ten minutes, yes sir! I should have gotten myself on a train and gone on down there but Sadie wouldn't let me" (*Having Our Say* 285).

Smarts and Individual and Systemic Racism

> I'll tell you what takes real intelligence—dealing with people's ignorance. Crazy questions that white people ask.
>
> —Black woman from N.C., (*Streetsmart & Motherwise)*

Many folk stories and jokes argue that smarts is knowing how to deal with individual and systemic racism. The many DWB (Driving While

Black) stories admonish their listeners to smarten up. According to these stories, in a racialized world, African Americans need to know that when driving, they are as likely to get a ticket for DWB as for anything else. The DWB stories are numerous. Willie Gary, a well-known African American attorney tells one such story that combines literacy and racial profiling. He tells of driving South in the late '60s in a nice car when a white Southern cop pulls him over. Remembering that he did not have his driver's license on him, he feverishly pulls out the first card that he does have in his wallet. Upon seeing that it is his NAACP membership card, he fears that he is going to be lynched for sure. Not only is he driving an expensive car, but also he has just offered evidence of what he imagines the cop will consider a radical political group. The cop takes the card, looks intently at it, and says, "Boy, this is a funny looking license; you go on and don't come back." The cop could not read.[6]

Smarts in African American Literature

As with African American folklore, African American literature redefines "smarts." In Ralph Ellison's *Invisible Man,* the protagonist at an all-black school controlled by white trustees is supposed to show a trustee around campus. He takes the trustee to a place where the black school president did not want the trustee to go. It is a place where so-called poor, ignorant blacks reside. Although the trustee turns out to have the same sexual appetites as the poor ignorant black farmer he is taken to visit, the black college president is angry with the very scholarly student who mistakenly carries the trustee to the wrong side of town. The president is furious that the protagonist has revealed to the trustee this side of black life. Angry, the president rants, "[T]he dumbest black bastard in the cotton patch knows that the only way to please a white man is to tell him a lie! What kind of education are you getting around here?"(*Invisible Man* 107). The protagonist was making progress toward his degree, but he isn't smart enough to pick up on racial relations—so he is expelled.

Smarts is Resiliency. Characters such as Langston Hughes's Alberta K. Johnson and Jesse B. Simple are savvy folks who make it in life because they have managed to keep their wits despite forces that seek to demolish them. As Simple explains,

> I have been fired. Laid off, and last week given an indefinite vacation, also Jim Crowed, segregated, barred out, insulted, eliminated, called black, yellow, and red, locked in, locked out, locked up, also left holding the bag. I have been caught

> in the rain, caught in raids, caught short with my rent, and caught with another man's wife. (And if that's not enough): I have been underfed, underpaid, undernourished, and everything but undertaken. . . . I been abused, confused, misused, false-arrested, tried, sentenced, paroled, blackjacked, beat, third-degreed, and near about lynched. I was born with the measles! Since then I had the smallpox, chicken pox, whooping cough, appendicitis, athlete's foot, tonsillitis, arthritis, backache, mumps, and a strain—but I am still here. Daddy-o, I'm still here. (*The Best of Simple* 60–61)

Simple refuses to let obstacles stop him from moving forward in life. He walks urban streets dispensing wisdom, arguing for an alternative type of knowledge and accountability, much like the characters in Toni Cade Bambara's "The Lesson" do. Told through the voice of a young black girl in urban environment, the story is about a teacher who takes her class to FAO Schwartz, the very expensive toy store. She wants to teach her poor, urban students about economics and class privilege. Her lesson is both patronizing and even cruel, for she assumes that her students, Flyboy, Junebug, Q.T., Sugar, Fat Butt, and the rest have been too ignorant to conceptualize their position in society. The teacher, Miss Moore, gives each child $5.00 to spend and emphasizes that this is real money. The narrator complains that "Miss Moore asking us do we know what real money is, like we a bunch of retards. I mean real money, she say, like it's only poker chips or monopoly papers we lay on the grocer" (*Gorilla, My Love* 81–82). After a wild cab ride, where the kids start making all kinds of unmentionable sounds with their armpits, they finally arrive at the store. When they see the high prices, one student asks, "Can we steal?" (83). Dispirited by their own lack of resources, one student inquires, "Watcha bring us here for, Miss Moore?" (87). When Miss Moore asks the students what they learned, their response is, "White folks crazy" (88). Rather than have their difference judged as a deficit, the students make statements that validate their meager but sensible negotiation of goods and services.

In *Granny Midwives,* I discuss how African American women writers critique notions of objectivity and principles of empiricism by giving us portraits of men of science and learning whose paradigms and methodologies are culturally biased at best and inhumanely dangerous at worst. Scholars, whether black or white, become targets of critique and ridicule. Gloria Naylor's Reema Boy in *Mama Day* goes to college and returns home with erroneous and extravagant theories to explain everyday life. When he tells his hometown that he is doing *field*work, they mockingly point out that he "ain't never picked a boll of cotton or head of lettuce in his life" (*Mama Day* 7). They question his use of the term *field* and mockingly perform their roles as native informants by spitting tobacco into his tape recorder and other such antics. It is not the experience of college that the novel devalues. Rather, it is the arrogance that assumes that one's home communities that have survived slavery and its aftermath are ignorant. Nikki Giovanni's "Alabama Poem" demonstrates the clash. A college coed walks down a dusty road and meets an elderly black man and an elderly black woman. The old man shouts out to her, "Girl! My hands seen /more than all/them books they got /at Tuskegee," and the old woman tells her "My feet/ seen more than yo eyes / ever gonna read." The warning here is to make use of hands and feet that know cultural terrain as a site of struggle.

A number of African American novels speak about the damage that some white scholars routinely do when they analyze the world from what they see as a neutral standpoint. Adam Nehemiah, the white historian in Sherley Anne Williams's *Dessa Rose,* tries to write Dessa's story of rebellion from the perspective of someone who can only imagine the slave woman as "darky" and "wench." The history he writes competes with the history written on Dessa's body—a body where a whip has lashed a tale "writ among her privates." At the story's end, Adam, distraught over the fact that no one believes him when he identifies Dessa as an escaped slave, is an indictment of all would-be scholars who take it upon themselves to commodify and colonize the experience of others.

Even more disconcerting is the white educator called "schoolteacher" in Toni Morrison's *Beloved.* As a scholar, schoolteacher has kept a ledger of Sethe's human and animal characteristics. Instead of a redneck overseer, *Beloved* uses schoolteacher, a man of learning, to show how one is required to be complicit in one's own destruction, for Sethe was required to make the ink for schoolteacher's writings. Sethe also understands that scholars such as schoolteacher can "dirty you so bad you couldn't like yourself anymore. Dirty you so bad you forgot who you were and couldn't think it up" (251). Schoolteacher's and Adam Nehemiah's methodologies do not work in emancipatory ways for Sethe's and Dessa's lives. Each woman has to map out a different terrain for her life. And therein lies a cautionary tale. In *Yo' Mama's DisFunktional!: Fighting the Culture Wars in Urban American,* Robin D. G. Kelley argues that scholars and policymakers play the dirty dozens with black people's lives. By blaming black women and black family structures instead of indicting institutional racism, Kelley argues that scholars have done more to talk about black people's mamas than anyone else (Kelley 1–13).

In sum, I created a methodology that resonates with the lives of many African Americans because I wanted to close the distance between how race, gender, and culture are discussed in the academy and how African American lives are lived outside the academy. To do so I had to recognize that there are experts in both camps. Scholars of color who cut off their home communities lose a valuable resource. Alice Walker's poem, "For My Sister Molly Who in The Fifties" describes how her older sister was transformed by college, learning new words and new concepts, but whose transformation failed to do anything for her family and home community other than make them feel like country bumpkins. The poem does not fault Molly because her education took her to many different places; it faults her because she did not know how to travel to those places and still travel home again. The poem is a good companion piece to Walker's story, "Everyday Use," which makes a case for going one step farther than merely using cultural artifacts, such as quilts, to adorn one's college room. In the story one daughter, Dee, wants her grandmother's quilt because quilts are good grassroots symbols of a poverty-stricken backwoods past from which she has distanced herself; however, that past is in vogue. The other daughter, Maggie, who did not go to college, wants the quilt because as Dee tells us, Maggie is "backward enough to make them everyday use" (33).

Today, in many black churches, even as the congregations praise the accomplishments of their graduate students, they take great joy in pointing out that the PhD stands for "pray heaven delivers." It's quite common for graduates to give a testimony where they claim that although some have graduated *cum laude, magna cum laude, summa cum laude,* they are thankful simply to have graduated "praise the lawdy." Laughter usually follow these declarations, not to belittle the achievement, but to affirm that the graduates have not let their education become *edumacation,* and to signify that they are planning to do something transformative with their "smarts"—like put it to everyday use.

NOTES

1. Katherine Clark tells Onnie Lee Logan's story in *Motherwit: An Alabama Midwife's Story* (New York: E.P. Dutton, 1989).
2. See *Granny Midwives,* "Who are Sistah Conjurers?" 12–14.
3. The book jacket to *Last Chance for the Tarzan Holler* says that the holler of the title (and of the title poem) is born when the sentient being—man, woman, or child—grapples with mortality at the last moment: at the moment before baptism or, for Susan Smith's sons strapped in their car seats, just before the lake waters close over them. It's a last burst of vivacity, a holler that affirms and resists the very demise that it heralds."

4. See Layli Phillips and Barbara McCaskill's discussion of black women in academic settings in "Who's Schooling Who? Black Women and the Bringing of the Everyday into Academe, or Why We Started *The Womanist, Signs* (Summer, 1995): 1008–10.

5. In Black Writers of America, eds. Richard Barksdale and Kenneth Kinnamon, call this folktale, "Swapping Dreams." See pp. 230–31.

6. I heard Willie Gary tell this story at a banquet in Columbus, Ohio, in the mid 1990s.

Chapter 7

Naming and Proclaiming the Self

Black Feminist Literary History Making

Joycelyn Moody

> I have been . . . thinking about ways in which books get not only reread but also rewritten—both in one's own language (with the ambivalence of the writer and the back-and-forth between editor and writer), and in translation. The liberties translators take that enhance; the ones taken that diminish. And for me, the alarm. There is always the threat of not being taken seriously, of having the work reduced to social anthropology, of having the politics of one's own language, the politics of another language bury, rather than expose, the reader's own politics.
>
> —Toni Morrison, "Home," 1997

To prepare for an upcoming research excursion, I read *Under Its Generous Dome: The Collections and Programs of the American Antiquarian Society* and *A Quarter Century of Visiting Fellowships at the American Antiquarian Society, 1972–97,* publications the AAS has sent to all of next year's designated scholars. I will be in residence there in April 2003, so this spring I want to take advantage of my proximity in central New York. During my fellowship month I will read through the AAS's extensive collection of early American newspapers and broadsides, specifically to locate news accounts, graphic images, all that's there on black women enslaved in antebellum America—research for a book that will explore how some such women managed to get their lives into print in spite of their illiteracy.

Reading *Under Its Generous Dome,* I am surprised to find extremely few references to Africans, African Americans, slavery, even the Civil War. First, I check the index and table of contents: no obvious signs there. Then I skim every page, looking for the barest allusions to my topic. I get very pessimistic—and begin to wonder why my proposal was accepted. What does it mean that the collection, which prides itself so unabashedly on having archived just about every imaginable "profound and mundane" document, save "a first edition of Audubon's *Birds of America*" (Neely), either in fact has very few items representing early *African* American culture, or in 1992 does not consider those particular holdings noteworthy in a book boasting the Society's resources?

Then I read *A Quarter Century of Visiting Fellowships at the American Antiquarian Society, 1972–97,* looking again, or still, for materials on enslaved women of the antebellum era. This time, even less. I had spotted a photograph of the 1992 AAS staff in *Under Its Generous Dome.* In the second book, there're photos, too: one, a snapshot of shelves at the American Antiquarian Society, teeming with texts researched there. I recognize a book prominent in the display: Nell I. Painter's biography *Sojourner Truth, A Life, A Symbol.* Painter has extolled the resources at Worcester, but I wonder that none of the materials she must have consulted are anywhere highlighted in these two Society publications. So now I want to know how Painter intuited that she could research Truth there *and find her.*

Next I listen again to a brief interview with the Society's current president, Ellen Dunlap. She is talking to Barbara Neely, host of *Commonwealth Journal,* WUMB's weekly arts radio show. Dunlap identifies herself as a Texan and "sounds white." She does not mention slavery; the closest detail is her note that the Society's thousands of collectibles extend to "the end of Reconstruction." Again, I'm confused: how can archives of early Americana not contain the stuff of slavery, the greatest catastrophe in the nation's history between the Revolution and Reconstruction? Why a "Reconstruction" anyway, but for slavery?[1]

The process of reconstructing nineteenth-century African American women's literary history begets many challenges. To be sure, the specific difficulties pervading my research exacerbate the academic's usual anxieties about scholarly work and worth. After all, as Hattie Gossett chastises, "Who told [me] anybody wants to hear from [me]? [I] aint nothing but a black woman!" Nonetheless, I go on finding ways to conduct this research because early black women's performativity thrills me and because it strives still to fight injustice directed against U.S. black women. As long as folks equate being black and female with being unintelligent and incapable, there is a critical need for my work.

Fulfilling my scholarly goals requires unconventional scholarly approaches. Fortunately, I learned to infer what I needed to do an early age, in all-black schools in Mobile, Alabama, despite Wallace Regimes I and II. These days I pursue posts such as the Kate B. and Hall J. Peterson Fellowship that will take me back to the American Antiquarian Society. I read across disciplines, using the Internet to access databases of resources in American history, law, religion, rhetoric and composition, linguistics, and education as well as in women studies and American ethnic studies. I use e-mail for consultation and networking. I attend conferences to meet other scholars working on related topics and to nurture established professional connections. I review manuscripts for a range of scholarly journals and presses to participate in decisive conversations and to keep abreast of current movements. Because in K-12 ten proud black women taught me to pay attention to "the poets in the kitchen,"[2] perhaps my most vital work is listening to women, mainly women of color. For, like Barbara Christian, I grew up around women who "continuously speculated about the nature of life through pithy language that unmasked the power relations in their world" (281). So, I place weekly long-distance calls to my mother, to my only sister almost as often; my lover is a Latina; and at the University of Washington I belong to a multidisciplinary feminist writing group comprised of four other women of color and two Jewish women. Significantly, however, none of these colleagues is black. Moreover, only one other is not a social scientist. Although my work thrives with their help, my experience with them can ironically underscore the singularity I often feel as a black lesbian feminist academic. I counterbalance an absence of blackness among the women who bolster my research in two ways: I "write myself into being" in autobiographical essays such as this one, and I try to "convert a racist house into a race-specific yet nonracist home" (Morrison 5) through scholarly collaborations with other black feminists.

As a child-volunteer for the public library in my redlined neighborhood, I hungered 'round grown-women librarians who fed me a bountiful diet of books: we insisted that a text be "interesting," and in the 1960s and '70s, nothing beguiled us like blackness. I relished most the movable feast of James Baldwin's *Autobiographical Notes*, from which I learned to value my own voice and reason, and to exalt those voices and minds the librarians valued—their own, other black people's. Given this particular background, then, it is clear as a goblet why I teach black women's texts, black folks' autobiography, and black feminist epistemology.

To these roots I further attribute my current book project: "Silent Language," the title taken from a cryptic admonition of the narrator of *The Story of Mattie J. Jackson* (1866). Near the autobiography's end, Jackson bitterly tallies the cost of institutionalized illiteracy: "I could read a little, but was not allowed to learn in slavery. I was obliged to pay twenty-five cents for every letter written for me" (28). Then, curtly, Jackson "advise[s] all, young, middle, aged or old, in a free country to learn to read and write. . . . Manage your own secrets, and divulge them by the silent language of your own pen" (29).

By the time I first read these words, I'd already read the 1863 *Memoir of Old Elizabeth*, another former slavewoman's story. Though illiterate, Elizabeth skillfully subverts her amanuensis's naïve Christian abolitionist agenda with a more dynamic eyewitness account of racism, religion, sexism, and slavery. When I later encountered similar rhetorical subversion in other bondswomen's dictated narratives, their interlocution disclosed a veritable *pattern* of interplay of (pre)literacy, power, and dominance that struck me as incomparably compelling. Thus, "Silent Language" examines intersections of race, rhetoric, linguistics, and emotional risk in a wide variety of discursive forms that disseminated enslaved women's self-representation. Yet my Southern "home-training" has endowed my literary scholarship with an arrant irony: I propose to expose the academic fallacies that privilege literacy and manuscripts over orality and spoken texts precisely by amplifying the definition of *autobiography* to include first-person life histories as reconstructed in diverse antebellum print media—among them, abolitionist broadsides, legal documents, slave advertisements, regional and race serials, plantation diaries.

Broadly put, I study early African American women's acquisition of literacy; their attitudes toward English language proficiency; their pursuit of formal academic education, and conversely, their rejection of formal academic education; the publication of their lives in slavery; their subversion of institutionalized illiteracy; the extent to which their "resistant orality"[3] includes subversive testimony dictated to amanuenses about their experiences in bondage, and thus, their circumscription of amanuenses and publishers both cavalier and compassionate.

I also study the parallels between nineteenth- and twentieth-century black women's acquisition of literacy and formal education, often in the face of odds all but insurmountable.[4] Moreover, I study the history of African American ambivalence about the relative value of formal academic education, or "book sense," mistrust rooted in veneration of orality, in apprehension about pernicious applications of script and texts,[5] and in disgust for the Eurocentric equation of intelligence with erudition. Indeed, Geneva Smitherman's dictionary *Black Talk* offers no definition of "education," but defines "educated fool" as a "person with a formal, 'book' education, but no common sense, no motherwit" (104)—the latter term denoted as "intuition; wisdom not taught in school or found in books" (163).[6] No wonder Hattie Gossett grieves: "Theres a national literacy crisis and a major portion of [black women writers'] audience not only cant read but seems to think readin is a waste of time" (175).[7] Ambivalence about women's education forms Susan K. Harris's subject in "Responding to the Text(s)," which surveys "the contradictory impulses, or themes, motivating [nineteenth-century African- and Anglo-American] women who desired to participate in their culture's system of intellectual authority. On the one hand, they sensed its power, both socially and spiritually—they suspected that if they could attain it, they would be transformed into 'what I am not.' On the other hand, they understood—and often agreed—that education for a woman was legitimate only if it helped her help others" (264).

I want to examine the eloquent ambivalence that impassioned black feminists such as Anna Julia Cooper and Frances W. Harper expressed when pursuing education for all women[8]—and to trace more contemporary sisters' attitudes about blacks' proficiency in English. Where my own work focuses on the production of early black literature, recent scholarship by Elizabeth McHenry undertakes the similar project of identifying an antebellum black readership: her goal is "to decenter formal education as the primary institutional force behind the reading of literature" (478).[9] McHenry warns that celebrations of African oral and vernacular cultural elements have turned us from the history of (Northern) black literacy, so she asks scholars "to look in new directions at the various reading cultures that existed within antebellum black communities and at the impact black readers had on the development of both an American and an African-American literary tradition" (477). Finally, I study the intersection of blackness and what James L. Machor calls "reading as a sociological activity and the material conditions affecting the availability of reading material. . . . the relation between readers and books as commodities and artifacts" (x). I want to ascertain the verity of such claims as that made by Max Rodríguez, publisher of *QBR: The Black Book Review*: "For blacks, books speak to a lifestyle. It's more than just reading; it's also what reading represents, education. . . . We want to build our libraries of books we cherish" (qtd. in Arnold 2/3). So, in progress, "Silent Language" yokes together various aspects of African Americans' relationships to texts and textuality.

INSTITUTIONAL CHALLENGES

Various institutional challenges impede the completion of my scholarly work. First, there are few archival sources available because of a patriarchal pejoration of U.S. black women's lives. Moreover, black women themselves have historically had little opportunity to preserve their legacies in conventional forms. Hence, perhaps, the difficulty of locating them among archives as profuse as the American Antiquarian Society. However, black women's lives *can* be recovered in word, song, art, and artifact. The untraditional forms they (might) assume call for an expansion of scholarly referents for "text" and "document," to encompass the range of enslaved women's gifts. Because our interpretative tools have been exclusionary, contemporary scholars must, as Jacqueline Jones Royster has advised, "learn to count experience variously" (ix). Then, in part because of the demographics of the U.S. professoriate, there are relatively few scholars engaged in work like mine; thus, there are few colleagues with whom I am able to share resources. On the whole, I experience this scarcity as institutional disregard for my area of specialization. Moreover, it is increasingly true that African Americanist scholars are not also African Americans. And if Gerald Early is right, the future of black studies could well be less black than its present, for "more than half of all bachelor's degrees in ethnic studies are now awarded to whites" (Early 1/7). This shift means that I now interact with colleagues who share my work but not necessarily my impetus for doing it and so not the same type of commitment to doing it. I do not mean "to discourage white graduate students from exploring black literature" (McKay 363), and I am not arguing for different-but-greater hegemony in the academy so much as for a recognition—and a reckoning—of the impact of racism and elitism on what is studied and who permitted to study it and with what access. What does it take to become professionally "connected" enough to be informed about where to find diverse pertinent resources, to gain access to them? Students of color now compete with white African Americanists who may be better mentored (frequently, by black faculty like me[10]) and thus better affiliated. In short, highly profiled academic stars aside, rank-and-file *black* African Americanists cannot escape racism inside the academy any more than they can outside its ivory walls; consequently, we are burdened by the effects of oppression there, too—as evident in cases of black professors denied tenure when not altogether prematurely derailed from the tenure track. Institutional oppression may further manifest as black women's professional insecurity, internalized racism, and intra-racial conflicts with one another.

UNIVERSITY IMPEDIMENTS

At the university level, a variety of impediments also obstruct black feminist literary history making. At my own West Coast state university, unrelenting economic crises keep depleted funds once available to support released time from teaching duties, to say nothing of travel to distant archives. Adequate funding for faculty research is hardly a regional problem, however. Then there are the turf wars. Arguing for the administrative elevation of black studies from university program to department, Nell Painter, former chair of the Princeton Black Studies Program, observed, "Departments don't have to be intellectual ghettos, especially not departments that depend on communicating with other disciplines" (qtd. in Boynton 7/7). I concur, ironically, situated as I am in *English*, a discipline notorious for exclusivity. Before the salvation of my interdisciplinary feminist writing group, I consistently felt isolated within an "intellectual ghetto." Perhaps this was so because there are *no* other professors in our department of more than sixty voting faculty who engage African American literature to the extent that I do, and perhaps so for other reasons—poor collegiality, professional estrangement, subspecialization factionality, teacherly demoralization, or less generously, racism, classism, antifeminism, homophobia. I have felt alone because I am not aware of all the folks in my large department, nor obviously the larger university, who teach or research African American texts.

DISCIPLINARY OBSTRUCTIONS

One particular disciplinary challenge doggedly shackles black feminist scholarship while sustaining a debate about disciplinarity that has seeped over into women studies[11]: "Is it [i.e., black studies] a form of feel-good nationalism for the black community or a dispassionate academic field? And what are the parameters of [its] scholarship" (Boynton 1/7). Ironically, this challenge fetters my productivity even though I have three degrees in English, and work in a "Research One" English department. Unquestionably, I am situated in "a dispassionate academic field." And yet, many persons in my department as well as across the academy, to say nothing of the nation at large, consider what I do mere "feel-good nationalism." Defending such an attitude consumes vital resources clearly better applied to my research. Moreover, that attitude protracts my worry about the anomalousness of my scholarship: my own private brain drain.

Princeton professors confronted related issues when they strove to upgrade black studies there to departmental status; proponents argued that maintaining program status "suggests that the field of study and the people being studied are not of central importance to the university's intellectual and social missions" (Boynton 5/7). The conflicts at Princeton parallel those in African American studies at my home institution. With three full-time faculty positions, it is subsumed under American ethnic studies (AES), a department as fraught as at most other Research One universities, if not more so. Undergraduates can major or minor in AES but not exclusively in African American studies, and the university does not yet offer postbaccalaureate degrees in either area. The English department has made no express hires in African American literature since it hired me in 1991, even then as now I specialize more in nineteenth-century American than in African American. Back then I joined three other African American department faculty, all peripheral to literature studies: two specializing in creative writing, and the third tenured in AES and adjunct in English. For a few years a fourth black assistant professor served in English, but has since moved on. I recall *one* graduate student in English (an African American woman) who has concentrated on African American literature in my ten years. Certainly, others study it, yet they do not select black faculty to chair their doctoral committees. Notably, though, those few do seem invariably to want an (any?) African American professor to serve on a committee led by a nonblack professor with less expertise. As Nellie McKay bluntly asserts, "It is not unwarranted pique or territorial jealousy when black scholars condemn incompetents' claims to authority in African American literature" (365). While my colleagues are not incompetent, in such cases, they exhibit grave disrespect toward African American literature, and more injuriously, they risk disserving students.

Sardonically questioning whether English departments are "Ready to Disband the [Phillis] Wheatley Court," McKay further shows that "the scarcity of African American PhDs in our discipline is one manifestation of the white academy's earlier reluctance to recognize the significance of developments in black literature" (363). My participation in a panel revisiting *Uncle Tom's Cabin* on the 150th anniversary of its publication suggests that such reluctance is yet *au courant.* That is, the reception of my contribution confirmed for me that some nonblack academics continue to believe that black African Americanists draw not on painstaking research but on cultural proximity for our scholarly output. As if descendants of slaves "just know" ("jes' grew"?) data of the antebellum era intrinsically or intuitively! Rather, I spent a good deal of time preparing a selected bibliography of nineteenth-century African American women's literary responses to *Uncle Tom's Cabin,* to distribute to my audience. They received it eagerly. And yet I had the distinct feeling that, in some cases, the enthusiasm was rather awe that I had

had to research the bibliographic entries and, in other cases, that there in fact exists a body of literature to be thusly mined. That when some said they were impressed, they meant they had been oblivious, and moreover, had assumed that "illiteracy" under the slaveocracy meant that Langston and Zora were the first blacks who wrote, or at least who wrote anything that was "any good."

Besides such instances of the "talking horse syndrome" that betrays most academics' importunate lack of knowledge about the sheer breadth of nineteenth-century African American literature, there is the gender imbalance. That is, when a black person *is* thought capable of writing in English in 19th-century America, that *man* is considered as rare as a talking horse. So, despite recent years' happy failure of Barbara Christian's prophecy that black women's creative literature would "in no way [be] supported by the academic world" (288), it remains true that critically more attention is paid to texts produced by nineteenth-century black men than by early black women. One example of this imbalance is Raymond Hedin's 1993 essay "Probable Readers, Possible Stories," which examines early black narrative for "felt restrictions on voice and physical presence" as well as nineteenth-century black writers' "relationship between the seemingly desirable end of being listened to and recognized by whites and the danger of being contained, controlled, or diminished by them as the price of attention" (180, 181). Hedin's article has rich implications for my scholarly project, but he too easily conflates black *male* writer into "black writer." Moreover, his complete gender analysis summarily appears as a single brief endnote (205n10). In particular, his assessment of the detrimental intrusion of amanuensis Thomas Gray into *The Confessions of Nat Turner* parallels my own frustration with the Reverend H. A. Mattison's prurience in the 1861 *Louisa Picquet, The Octoroon.* For though Mattison apparently functions as Picquet's advocate, in her 1861 dictated slave narrative as in Turner's 1831, the "central battle enacted within the text is a battle of voices" (Hedin 183). Yet Hedin's representative inattention to gender construction in an article on black and white masculinity aggravates my thinking about miscegenated femininity, notwithstanding the stunning parallel between what Gray depicts as Turner's black male savagery and what Mattison depicts as Picquet's white female beauty.

MY OWN STUFF

An ongoing critical hurdle I have to jump in the academy is loneliness. The multiethnic, interdisciplinary feminist writing group I joined in Fall 2000 notwithstanding, I often continue to feel isolated in my research. Back in Mobile, I was surrounded by blacks who cared about what I care about, who taught me to care for black matters. Now I must forge a community of my own if I am to have one, an exigency for me that requires immeasurable time and energy, resources many of my colleagues can expend on work. A good portion of time for my scholarship is preserved by an e-mail service called Zephyr. I have rarely had the luxury of a research assistant, so I have been particularly grateful that the graduate library at my school offers this on-line research service. Specifically, it posts me each month lists of the most recent publications on topics I have specified: slave narratives, African American literature, nineteenth-century American literature, women's literature, women's education, and women's literacy. It has revolutionized my research in that through the dozens of citations it generates exclusively for me, I become familiar with sources I would usually not encounter.

Often the most stimulating items are empirical studies from the social sciences. Ironically, however, they underscore the limitations of academic training in a single discipline: inevitably, I waste time by reading articles that ultimately do not bear on my work, or that I lack the skill to interpret or apply in meaningful ways. For example, I recently read *what appears to me* to be an astounding study on adult literacy instruction, an area obviously pertinent to "Silent Language." However, I have a great deal to learn in order to assess the actual merit of this article and to make any application of it and others like it consequential, precise, authoritative, or even merely valid to my scholarship. While junior colleagues may represent the "emergence of scholars who," in Noliwe Rooks's words, "have been trained in its [i.e., an interdisciplinary department's] methods," I do not. Instead, as associate director of black studies at Princeton, Rooks might say that I am still a "lit person who just wants to do 'other stuff' " (qtd. in Boynton 6/7). So, another impediment to successful completion of my research is a struggle with interdisciplinary methods. After humbly filling the endowed chair of a highly interdisciplinary women studies program in 2001–2002, I feel more conviction than ever about holding students of every academic department accountable to the rigors of interdisciplinary work. Rooks rightly notes that there are comprehensive, established methods that not only should be respected but that *do* govern all meritorious interdisciplinary research. I want to cultivate this methodology for myself; I want it for my students.

Moreover, I have found that much of the research that excites me as I complete "Silent Language" emerges at disciplinary intersections. Two exemplary texts vital to my thinking about antebellum literacy and dictated narratives, for example, are Melton McLaurin's *Celia, A Slave* and Nell I. Painter's "Representing Truth." For their respective historiographical studies, the two U.S. social historians draw on documents and tools of an impressive variety of disciplines. To reconstruct events surrounding "State of Missouri Versus Celia, A Slave" (October 1855) and the life of the enslaved woman on trial for the murder of her "owner," McLaurin researched documents detailing relevant concomitant legal cases; antebellum histories and state census reports of Virginia, Kansas, and Missouri and of the Missouri Compromise; pertinent local and regional newspapers; slave narratives; and contemporary feminist theories of women's bondage, rape, and murder. Similarly, to reconstruct the epistemologies that Sojourner Truth rejected and embraced, Painter also studied and incorporated relevant state histories; genealogies; slave narratives and their conventions, and she drew as well on court cases in which Truth was enmeshed; diverse antebellum religious and theological histories; antebellum educational records; women's life, literary, and cultural histories; feminist reading practices; relevant regional newspapers; suffragist histories; histories of photography; antebellum art; literature and studies of literary texts mediated by white women amanuenses. The interdisciplinary scholarship of these two projects alone both daunt and inspire me.

Without graduate students pursuing projects related to mine, I rely on my writing group and like-minded colleagues for support, encouragement, collegiality, and collaboration. Graduate students in my department who decide to incorporate "race studies" into their course work seem to find it easier to "do race" with my nonblack colleagues, most of whom have far less experience with African American literature than I do and many of whom seem not to ask students to reflect politically, ethically, self-critically on the stakes of their choice of concentration. In "Getting (The) Man Off (Our) Eyeball," Jeannine DeLombard somberly considers the role identity politics should play in white African Americanists' literary critical studies. How professionally compulsory, or moral, is it, she questions, for whites to foreground (their own) whiteness in their scholarship? In the end, DeLombard determines that white intellectuals make their "best contribution" to African American studies when they do not make much of their racial positioning (346). I disagree with her. While in an ideal nation, perhaps, the white scholar can now devote "his or her full critical energies to provide us with access to a previously neglected or misunderstood aspect of African-American culture and letters" (DeLombard 346), I am not ready to say that "we" have had sufficient discussion of the function of whiteness in the field of African American studies. I want still more critical articles like Anne E. Goldman's " 'I Made the Ink,' " published more than ten years before DeLombard's review. Goldman, a self-identified white feminist literary scholar, demands that whites "recognize in what ways we have stifled the speaking subject who is not white, and in what manner we continue to do so" (314). She unmistakably references white intellectuals in particular as those who "have stifled the speaking subject who is not white." To articulate the responsibility white academics have to (nonwhite) laborers "who underwrite the identity of the dominant group" (328), Goldman elucidates both black women's responses to whites' efforts to claim and consume their labors and whites' proclivity for refusing "to acknowledge [their] indebtedness to the real subject" (325). Am I willing to work with a nonblack student who will demand less, who would consciously understate her subject position with respect to black literature? Royster's proud words in *Traces of a Stream* resonate within me, too: "I have learned to accept that I cannot escape the connections to my own sense of identity as an African American woman or my intense desire to understand my own intellectual ancestry" (x), for I have come to know ways that my race, culture, gender, and sexuality identities matter in/to the scholarship I undertake. As I work with my department's (nonblack) graduate students in peripheral capacities, I am also aware that their social locations bear significantly on their own knowledge and training. I know that blackness and femaleness drive my work; by contrast, I need to know what motivates my students.'

In spite of the multiple difficulties I face in validating enslaved women's lives as they themselves narrated them, I cherish the excavation of narratives by nineteenth-century black women as yet unknown or unacknowledged. For all my esteem of indispensable studies such as Royster's *Traces of a Stream* that attend to what our foremothers wrote and published, I want to unearth and extol literary production by black women whom the "white folks didn't never help . . . to read and write no time" (Sylvia Cannon, qtd. in Hine and Thompson 73). That extant production exists in abundance, yet it must be uncovered. For all my foreboding, my initial visit to the American Antiquarian Society turned out to be an extraordinary and beneficial adventure even though the two publications I'd read about its holdings had not deemed black matters worth indexing. Sadly, I imagine that, without the promise of next spring's access to the archives, I might well have renounced my search there for enslaved women's voices, erroneously assuming that we do not exist there. But black women *are* there, as we are everywhere, as I mean to show, against all odds.

NOTES

I am grateful to Jacqueline Jones Royster and Lorraine Martínez for invaluable advice on drafts of this chapter. I am also grateful to the women studies program at Hamilton College, under whose auspices this chapter was written.

1. I first visited the AAS on May 14–15, 2002, and want to acknowledge my extraordinarily productive experience there, for which I am deeply indebted to the Society's expert and solicitous staff.

2. See Marshall.

3. I borrow this phrase from Harryette Mullen, "Runaway Tongue."

4. For two excellent analyses among the growing number of scholarly explorations of African American women and U.S. higher education, see Elizabeth Higginbotham and Johnson-Bailey.

5. See Goldman.

6. Perhaps Smitherman's and other dictionaries of African American English/vernacular such as Major's *From Juba to Jive* and Westbrook's *The Hip Hoptionary* paradoxically represent black scholarly efforts to bridge the gap between black reverence for literacy, on the one hand, and black suspicion of literacy, on the other.

7. While Oprah Winfrey's Book Club did not target blacks exclusively, it is safe to hazard that African Americans were among those who purchased "the hundreds of thousands of extra copies—sometimes more than a million—" that Winfrey warned publishers of club selections to print (Blewster 4/6). More recently, in Spring 2002, executive editor Janet Hill has founded Harlem Moon, a publishing imprint that will differ from others, for in Hill's words, "There's an extraordinary, healthy black readership market who are hungry for [black] writing, and the climate is great for quality trade paperback" (Arnold 1/3). Ironically, Hill also observes, "You can't overlook the importance of *word of mouth* in selling books, and that's very important among blacks" (2/3; my emphasis). For an analysis of Morrison's audiobook edition of *Song of Solomon*—her "talking book"—as Oprah Book Club selection, see Young.

8. Harris writes: "Cooper's Christian and racial arguments function as do [Catharine] Beecher's Christian and domestic ones: both deflect attention from the fact that women who had been educated like men would be likely . . . to move out of the private sphere of the approved feminine and into the male social and political realm" (275). And: "Yet like Anna Julia Cooper's and Catharine Beecher's essays, Harper's novel [*Iola Leroy*] places [black women's] aspirations within . . . a frame that lays claim to the equality of Christians, on the one hand, and to the equality of womanhood on the other" (277). See her essay for more of her analysis.

9. I am indebted to Joanne Chaison of the American Antiquarian Society for introducing me to McHenry's work.

10. Cf. McKay.

11. During the working conference on "The Ph.D. in Women Studies: Implications and Articulations," held at Emory University on Oct. 12–14, 2001, for example, questions about disciplinarity versus interdisciplinarity (versus multidisciplinarity) were persistently voiced.

Chapter 8

Speaking With and To Me

Discursive Positioning and the Unstable Categories of Race, Class, and Gender

Jami L. Carlacio

> I want to beg you as much as I can—to be patient toward all that is unsolved in your heart and to try to love the questions themselves. Do not seek now answers which cannot be given you because you would not be able to live them. The point is to live everything. Live the questions now. Perhaps you will someday without noticing it, live along gradually into the answer.
>
> —Rainer Maria Rilke, *Letters to a Young Poet,* 2001

INTRODUCTION: LIVING INTO THE QUESTION

The recent emergence of studies centering on the literacy and activism of antebellum African American women signifies a turn in rhetorical scholarship that warrants further analysis. African American feminist rhetoricians, including Gertrude Mossell, Shirley Wilson Logan, Carla Peterson, and Jacqueline Jones Royster, among others, have brought to light a tradition of women whose rhetorical practices have heretofore been largely overlooked until the latter part of the twentieth century.[1]

Their critical investigations have revealed the existence of a significant, multivoiced tradition of African American women's rhetoric; more important, they have brought to light the inherently racist, patriarchal assumptions undergirding the received canon of rhetorical history. Their work, and that of others,[2] has helped scholars in the field of rhetoric to locate and to recognize a tradition of these women's rhetorical practices in the nineteenth century. I have located my work here as well, and this chapter represents my attempt to question the assumptions that have shaped it. Specifically, my inquiry centers on how I identify with and how I theorize about the overlapping categories of race, gender, and culture and their impact on the Northern antebellum African American rhetorical tradition.

For the past several years, I have studied and written about the rhetorical practices of the first woman in this tradition who authorized herself to speak to the mixed audiences of free African Americans living in Boston during the early years of the 1830s, Maria W. Stewart. I have worked to make visible the raced and gendered rhetorical style that defines Stewart's oral and written performances, for she broke down the barriers that had previously determined the extent to which free African Americans could participate in the civic life of Northern antebellum culture. That is, she demanded her and other (Anglo- and African American) women's right to speak and preach publicly, and urged her community to "sue for their [African Americans'] rights" in general. These barriers were subsequently broken down further by the many who followed her, including Sara Remond, Frances Ellen Watkins Harper, Ida B. Wells, and Anna Julia Cooper, whose work has, at least within the last quarter-century, received continued (and necessary) scholarly attention by those interested in African American history, some of whom are raced white and gendered male.[3] Tantamount to my interest in Stewart's rhetorical practices are the challenges she faced as a woman who sought to unify her race in an effort to erase the distinction that justified the exclusion of African Americans from the designation of "citizen" generally and to break through the gender bias that precluded women from speaking (and preaching) in public specifically. As a black woman, moreover, Stewart challenged the Northern antebellum middle-class conception of "true (white) womanhood" whose attributes included piety, purity, domesticity, and submissiveness (see Welter).

In the following subsections, I show how Stewart deconstructed not only the categories of race and class but also the specific traits of "true womanhood" by examining her rhetorical performance in "Address Delivered to the Afric-American Female Intelligence Society of America" ("Female") and in "Mrs. Stewart's Farewell Address Delivered to Her Friends in the City of Boston" ("Farewell"). Concomitantly, I investigate my motives to accomplish this rhetorical work as a woman who is not racially a part of this group and reflect on how I have rewritten myself onto the pages of rhetorical history alongside Stewart, who has shown me a way to do this. In the end, I hope my work may stimulate further critical discussion of rhetorical scholars' appropriation of these categories—and why we do so—for textual studies.

WRITING YOU, WRITING ME: PATHWAYS OF INSCRIPTION

From the first moment I began to investigate Stewart's life and rhetoric, I have asked myself, "Why do I identify with Stewart?" On the surface, our lives couldn't be more different. She died eighty-five years before I was born and lived in what is one of the most contentious periods of America's racial history. I grew up taking my civic (and civil) rights for granted, whereas Stewart would never see these rights come to fruition. I have been accorded the privileges of a higher education and have been accepted into the ranks of the professoriate; Stewart, however, gained her literacy solely through Sabbath school instruction and independent Bible study. Following her public speaking career in Boston (1832–1833), she moved first to New York and then on to Baltimore before finally settling in Washington, D.C. Encountering mostly obstacles in her attempts to earn a living by teaching, and suffering political and racial prejudice along the way, Stewart died in relative obscurity. She was, however, finally recognized for her life efforts two months after she died, both in a moving eulogy written by the editors of *The People's Advocate* and in letters contributed by Alexander Crummell and William Lloyd Garrison, all of which were published in the February 28, 1880, edition. The editors write, for example, that "[f]ew, very few know of the remarkable career of this woman whose life has just drawn to a close. For half a century she was engaged in the work of elevating her race by lectures, teaching and various missionary and benevolent labours" (1).

The differences that separate Stewart from me are indeed significant, yet they fail to disconnect us completely. We are both outlaws: she repudiated social norms by speaking out in public to promiscuous (mixed) audiences—that is, to women and men who wanted no advice from a young, poor, widowed woman with no authority to speak except for those terms on which she authorized herself. In effect, she wrote herself into our rhetorical and historical consciousness by asserting the right to share public space with those for whom dominant culture had sanctioned that right: Anglo-American men. And just as Stewart inscribed herself on the pages of a history crowded with such company, I consider myself an outlaw, for I not only participate in writing Stewart into her rightful place, but I also presume to identify with her, to speak with her, and to take the risk of crossing a bridge that is still under construction. I enter this conversation hesitantly, acknowledging the historical and racial distance that separates not only Stewart but also my contemporaries from me, some of whom may consider me unauthorized to perform this rhetorical work.

And yet, it is Stewart who began to bridge this distance for me, since in her purposeful deconstruction of the categories of class, race, and gender, she invented her own "calling card" through which she (re)introduced herself to an audience of her contemporaries. In other words, Stewart rejected the grounds on which she should have identified as the culturally constructed black woman and reinvented herself by changing the very nature of the card (and the categories implicit in it) itself. Her work, in effect, created an opening whereby I might follow her lead in my attempt to understand why I have used the "calling cards" inscribed with these categories, and, more importantly, why I feel the need to do so. With Stewart's invitation, I reinvent myself (my *ethos*) by removing what I have imagined are fetters constituted by race, culture, and ethnic difference, thus enabling myself to speak with and to her as well as share in (re)telling a centuries-old story by complicating its cast of characters and their roles.

Both in her "Address Delivered to the Afric-American Female Intelligence Society of America" and in "Mrs. Stewart's Farewell Address Delivered to Her Friends in the City of Boston" Stewart attempts to justify her and other women's right to speak in public by drawing on biblical women prophets and medieval mystics and letter writers whose lives and work were proof of woman's power to prophesy as sanctioned by God. In the former speech, for example, Stewart exposes "true" womanhood as a racist and classist metaphor designed to exclude all but middle-class white women. In her effort to dismantle the symbolic structure of "true" womanhood, Stewart addresses her audience by using a double-voiced rhetoric that reaches out to "woman," regardless of her color or class status:

> O woman, woman! Your example is powerful, your influence great; it extends over your husbands and your children, and throughout the circle of your acquaintance. Then let me exhort you to cultivate among yourselves a spirit of Christian love and unity, having charity for one another, without which all our goodness is as sounding brass, and a tinkling cymbal. (55)

In this passage, Stewart reminds her audience that they are powerful, they have influence, and they are good (Christians). Such attributes are associated with white, middle-class women; by reframing the discourse, however, Stewart extends the meaning of "true womanhood" to include, in this case, African American women. She has taken the terms of the dominant culture and metaphorically turned them into terms that describe all women, regardless of race or class. Stewart has thus ostensibly destabilized the category of "woman" so that any woman might conceivably hold power and influence not only within her family but also within her community. This indeterminacy makes it susceptible to changes in signification, affecting how all women understand their social and cultural roles. This instability creates the opportunity for a new space not only for African American women such as Stewart but also for Anglo-American women like me to occupy, for we may use this to reinvent ourselves.

This marked effort to help women (all women, ostensibly) reenvision themselves as something other than what Northern white culture has constructed for them is also evident in Stewart's "Farewell Address." In her final public speech, she rebuffs criticisms from those in her community who have treated her with contempt by creating an ethical stance not unlike that of the New Testament's St. Paul. Because she knows all too well that her gender, notwithstanding her race, will conflict with the dominant view that women—black and white, working and middle-class—are expected to exert their "influence" solely within the private domain, she attempts to mitigate this opposition by insinuating herself as a "martyr" and by describing her purpose as "rousing [her community] to exertion." She implies that her "wretched and degraded" brethren need a strong advocate who will deliver them out of the bondage of slavery just as Moses delivered his people out of Egypt. Stewart is both teacher and leader, maintaining these roles by speaking to her auditors as a preacher whose role is to energize her community in faith.

Stewart claims for herself the *authority* to use Scripture as her means of expression, to become its agent speaking through her. Yet, she also appropriates the dominant discourse, creating a new form of authority. Doubtless, Stewart realizes her tenuous position in claiming both agency and voice, but she sees no other recourse. Because she has discovered a lack of leadership in the African American community, Stewart feels moved to step in and lead them. This she accomplishes by invoking a metaphoric kinship with St. Paul, whose conversion brought him to "the people in the fullness of the gospel of grace" ("Farewell" 66; Romans 15:29). Clearly, she believes herself to be the messenger of the Word, a builder of faith, a leader of communities. Stewart finally confesses to her auditors in her "Farewell Address" that "I will speak for thee [God] as long as I live" (67). In an effort not unlike Paul's, she addresses her community in order to strengthen or encourage their faith, continuing her missionary work when she moved from Boston to New York and finally to Washington, D.C. In fact, she indicates that she believes her mission to be the same as Paul's—to spread or encourage faith in a Christian God that would ultimately deliver African Americans from the bondage of oppression. In both a literal and a figurative sense, Stewart re-*places* Paul, speaking "humbly" for God and blending her voice with the most famous of Christian martyrs as she assumes her place at the textual pulpit.

Because she locates her *ethos* in the strongly rooted patriarchal tradition of the Bible, whose voices infuse her rhetoric, Stewart must reframe their words in her own style. Aligning herself with medieval women mystics who "had about them an inconceivable something, approaching to divinity," Stewart muses that "[p]erhaps that idea was only the effect of the sagacity common to the sex, and the advantages which their natural address gave them over rough and simple warriors" ("Farewell" 68). Deciding she might possess her own "natural sagacity," as well as an eloquent voice that will reach out to her community in advantageous ways, Stewart appropriates the voices of men and makes them her own. Relying on her own experience and knowledge, she rhetorically fuses her voice with those of dominant males, inviting us to consider the power of destabilizing the "normalized" categories of identification, such as her race and gender. Resisting these thus enables a perspectival shift.

With this shift comes the power to transform ourselves, from who we have been or how we have been constructed to be to how we want to be and how we envision ourselves. And while feminist rhetorical historians have demonstrated how different voices, different inscriptions, and different tellings reshape history's *ethos* and ultimately our own, such work has not come without its challenges.

METHODOLOGICAL AND ONTOLOGICAL CHALLENGES: CONSTRAINTS AND POSSIBILITIES

One of the key questions provoking my inquiry into Stewart's rhetorical practices concerns the race and class of scholars performing cultural and critical work similar to mine. While I cannot be certain how many of the rhetorical scholars currently investigating the work of those women I mention above are African American, I make the educated guess that a majority of them are (several of whose works are included in this volume). The coterie of rhetorical historians shaping the majority of scholarship in this arena motivates me to ask why it is that critical inquiries focusing on race, gender, class, ethnicity, and so on, are frequently carried out by those who occupy the same categories. Critical theorists have taken up this question of who can speak for/to/with whom, Linda Alcoff being among the most well known of these in the last decade. In her 1991 essay, "The Problem of Speaking for Others," she makes the argument that while speaking *for* someone ("othering" someone) is problematic, speaking *to* or *with* someone can produce the kinds of open dialogue that potentially liberate the oppressed (23). I wish to explore this aspect of her argument because it is germane to the questions I am asking. In her discussion of Gyatri Spivak's "Can the Subaltern Speak," Alcoff tells readers that she agrees with the latter's preference for "speaking to" others,

> in which the intellectual neither abnegates his or her discursive role nor presumes an authenticity of the oppressed but still allows for the possibility that the oppressed will produce a "countersentence" [in Spivak's words] that can then suggest a new historical narrative. (23)

Alcoff takes Spivak's argument an important step further, suggesting that "we [those of us in privileged discursive positions] should strive to create whenever possible the conditions for dialog and the practice of speaking *with* and *to* rather than speaking *for* others" (23; emphasis added). Alcoff's insight has helped me to envision how I might occupy more comfortably that space where I *authorize* myself to speak with and to Stewart. At the same time, I realize that unlike Spivak's voiceless subaltern, Stewart has demonstrated her ability to articulate a "countersentence" by speaking on behalf of women and of people of color, both to audiences of her contemporaries and to those of mine. The question that remains for me, then, is this: If Stewart can ably produce her own "countersentence," why have I assumed that I might take her words farther?

As I read Stewart's texts, I am hailed along with her nineteenth-century audience into a larger milieu where I not only recognize the extent to which we share a history but where I also inscribe myself more creatively into a history that has heretofore excluded our voices, our words, our actions. Despite the social, moral, and cultural proscriptions that would deny her the "right" to engage in any form of civic activity, Stewart authorized herself to speak to and with all women as well as to and with African American men. In doing so, she inscribed herself both as a woman and as a scriptural authority, thus allowing me to reinscribe myself beyond my race and class status, which would otherwise limit the possibility of my speaking with and listening to her.

Stewart's rhetorical work has in a material sense created a bridge for me that goes both backward and forward. That is, I am able to turn back more than a century and a half and recognize my relatively recent rhetorical antecedents and at the same time move forward to reveal a more productive direction for others like me who are not sure of our way. Besides Stewart, other women of color, including Phillis Wheatley and Sojourner Truth, have forged pathways of identification with women in diverse locations whose experiences potentially transcend race and ethnicity; the women they reached back then did not necessarily occupy the same social, cultural, and political status, just as women today do not. And yet, today many of us remain silent, wondering if it is we who are being addressed, spoken to, or invited to join in what ought to be perceived in many ways as a common struggle for our rightful place in a history that has elided our intellectual work and our rhetorical practices.

The importance of reciprocal bridge building across the color line was addressed by keynote speaker Shirley Wilson Logan at the 2002 Rhetoric Society of America conference. Traditionally, Logan reminded us, women of color have had to build a communication bridge that brings women of all races together because few Anglo- (white) American women have taken such an initiative. With Logan, I advocate identity building across the color line as well as across the lines of class and culture. Some of this two- or multi-way connection involves recognizing some of the commonalties that women share, particularly in relation to our place (or lack of it) in rhetoric's long history; at the same time, we must realize and acknowledge the important material differences that shape our lives. I urge all women, therefore, to risk crossing the lines that would otherwise circumscribe our ability to form collectivities and to acknowledge the value in and need for reciprocity. In short, we need to connect.

Such risk taking will not be easy and, thus, we should approach our work cautiously. By this I mean that I, for example, must realize my implication and complicity in a racist and classist structure where I enjoy the cultural power accorded me at least insofar as I am white and work as a university instructor. And yet, even as I recognize my relatively favored status when I compare it to that of women of color, I must be able to bracket difference to some degree in order to realize my affinity with Stewart so that the lines of communication across the discursive and material borders of race and class remain fluid.

Despite my insecurities about the space I occupy, I stake my claim as a rhetor(ical) historian who wants to excavate the practices of women whose voices, practices, and names have been elided or occluded from our collective history. This work should not be left to women of color only. It's up to all rhetoricians and historians, regardless of race or gender, to recognize a richer, more inclusive history. This is not simply about adding some women or people of color to history, for we all share in a twenty-five-century-old tradition; we have always been there, but we have not been accorded the attention that is due us. We must continue to challenge this, to "remap" history, in Cheryl Glenn's terms, to challenge the very definitions that have narrated a history to us that is ours as much as it was our Greco-Roman and African ancestors.'

One of the most significant methodological challenges I have faced concerns recognizing my own position as a white, middle-class woman in the elite circle of the academy. My research was motivated initially by my desire to understand a generally female-centered antebellum rhetorical tradition previously effaced by dominant accounts of the history of rhetorical theories; I moved beyond this, however, to locate the emergence of a distinct African American tradition that, as I explain above, has been uncovered and retold by a select few and this, only since the 1980s.[4] As I work through this challenge and through my attempt to discover my own motivations for such work, I look for guidance from Gayatri Spivak and Saidiya Hartman, who locate their work in postcolonial and feminist critical theories.

For my work to be accorded any value, I must be accountable for it; Spivak and Hartman offer some insight into how I might achieve this. In *Outside in the Teaching Machine*, for example, Spivak alerts us to the potential problem involved in translation. She argues that "one of the ways to get around the confines of one's 'identity' as one produces expository prose is to work at someone else's title, as one works with a language that belongs to many others. This, after all, is one of the seductions of translating" (179). Farther on, she articulates this idea more specifically by explaining that the translator "must solicit the text to show the limits of its language, because that rhetorical aspect will point at the silence of the absolute fraying of language that the text wards off, in its special manner" (183). In describing "the politics of translation" in this way, Spivak maintains the necessity of caution in taking up the words, the language, of the other. While she is describing the process of translating into English the texts of third world (women) writers, I find her directives to be applicable to the work I am doing in regard to Stewart: in the way that I write her and the way in which she interpellates me when I read/hear her rhetoric. Such an act has, for someone in my position, a potential for violence: by imposing my historically, culturally, and internally racialized reading onto Stewart's text, I run the risk of misinterpreting her rhetoric at her expense and to my putative gain.

In a similar move cautioning against what might be formulated as "unethical" translation (however accidental this may be), Hartman, in *Scenes of Subjectivity: Terror, Slavery, and Self-Making in Nineteenth-Century America*, echoes Spivak that, in Hartman's gloss, "there is no access to the subaltern consciousness outside dominant representations or elite documents" (10). In other words, whenever a dominant discourse is used to account for the discourse (or the materiality) of its opposite, it necessarily precludes the one it purports to elucidate. In this way, my reading of Stewart's rhetoric potentially effaces her words—the intentionality behind them and the conditions that made her rhetorical practices necessary to begin with. While Spivak and Hartman raise a necessary warning flag for me as I engage in this project, they do not discourage me from continuing to invest more time into it (about four years at the time of this writing). As a model for deconstructing the categories of race, class, and gender in an effort to expose their vulnerability to reconstruction, Stewart makes room for others like me who wish to engage in this critical work without appropriating "cards" that are meant to "authenticate" our work. As I introduce Stewart's voice into a different dimension of rhetorical history, I do the same with my own, for as I write her, I am necessarily changed (rewritten) in the process.

Both Spivak's and Hartman's work suggest the inherent damage done to the agency and the subjectivity of "the other" when dominant voices attempt to narrate and therefore authorize and define what constitutes the material conditions of the former. When scholars take these rhetorical risks, we potentially subdue the dominant voices and amplify our own. Nevertheless, the possibility that such silencing acts will occur should not dissuade us from attempting to re-vision rhetorical history; it should, however, serve as a reminder to be accountable to those with and to whom we speak.

One productive strategy that might help us to achieve this accountability is to consider the place of emotion—passionate engagement—in our scholarly work. Royster addresses this specifically in "A View From a Bridge," the concluding chapter in *Traces of a Stream.* In the process of negotiating her "place" as a researcher in relation to her subjects, Royster acknowledges the need to consider the extent of her identification with the women in her study. While Royster admits she "share[s] in kind, though perhaps not in degree, some of their material realities," she realizes she can occupy neither their time nor their space

(271). As I have tried to make clear, my historical location as well as my social and racial position necessarily distance me from Stewart but these differences do not mitigate the affinity I feel for a woman I consider to be both a rhetorical exemplar and a personal role model.

As I continue to focus on Stewart, I acknowledge Royster's forthright directive that as an "outsider in the community [I] study," I must "carefully articulate what [my] viewpoints actually are" rather than allow my assumptions and my approach to my work go unexplored (277). Just as this advice is clear, so too is her invitation to do this work with the right motivation. For me, this includes my identification with Stewart as a woman, as someone in rhetorical history with something to say and a provocative way to say it. In short, my intent has been to maintain an ethical regard for as well as an affective attitude toward my work on Stewart, for these are the values that guide me to do productive work in a community of my peers.

But my ethics and my feelings toward my subject reach beyond just Stewart herself. As we engage with any subject, we try, ostensibly, to maintain the integrity of history by making epistemically valid claims based on evidence we discover and by making educated assumptions about what we do not (and cannot) know, always keeping in mind the limits of context and the ethical concerns of the community of which they are a part. Scholarly responsibility also demonstrates for me the importance of acknowledging what Hartman calls "the interventionist role of the interpreter, [and] the equally interested labor of historical revision" (11). What I have learned as I have pursued my work is that any intervention in rhetorical history (or elsewhere) is interested, but it should not hinder my desire to engage in a dialogue about it with a community of my peers. I must continually assess my position, take risks, and remain open to critique and revision; in a word, I must listen rhetorically and share in what I hope will continue to be a productive scholarly exchange about histories that are always under construction.

CONCLUSION: CHARTING NEW TERRITORY, OR REMAPPING THE OLD?

I began this journey without a clearly defined conceptual map to guide my way, one that would undoubtedly have aided me in reading against the grain of a history informed by racist patriarchy; I have since realized, however, that there is no single "perfect" methodology within which to work. Part of the challenge in this undertaking is remaining aware of what motivates me and of my material position—my singular and finite perspective as a woman who occupies a number of categories on shifting temporal and spatial axes. As I "enter into the text" of "the other," I must allow it to speak to me, to wash over me, and to take me to another place as yet uncharted, refusing to quell its voice with my own assumptions. During the composition of this chapter, I have struggled to answer the key questions that motivate this chapter: Why am I invested in narrating (and in speaking with) Maria Stewart? What do I hope to gain from it? What potential costs will accrue when I "tell it the way I see it"? At the same time, what, if any, are the potential gains for the communities (women, African Americans) to/with whom I purport to speak? I feel the need to connect and I derive pleasure when I do.

When we engage in inter-, multi-, and cross-disciplinary work by discursively presenting our "calling cards," whose imprints bear the categories of race, class, gender, and so on, we must ask ourselves whether this is an act of symbolic representation used to authenticate our work, or whether it makes a positive contribution to clarifying the material conditions that made this textual, symbolic production possible. I have been playing both Stewart's and my cards—using hers to inform and complement my work and using mine to complement hers. In the process, I have been transformed from an Anglo-American rhetorical historian uncomfortable in what I consider to be unfamiliar terrain to one who recognizes the important work that must be continued on it. Stewart can never experience the gratification of knowing the extent of her contribution to rhetorical history or how her words have done their share in changing the way we perceive our role in it today, and I cannot wait passively for a vindication of mine. This is a conversation I feel compelled to enter, and I welcome the opportunity to engage in a productive conversation about who is authorized to narrate rhetorical history about and with whom.

NOTES

1. Gerda Lerner's *Black Women in White America: A Documentary History*, published in 1972, is one notable exception.

2. See, for example, Andrews; Brown; Condit and Lucaites; Henderson; Higginbotham; Lauter; Lintin; Stepto; and Sterling.

3. Logan, Royster, and Simpkins (see this volume) have done substantial work on these rhetors. Others include Jacqueline Bacon and Glen McClish; Karlyn Kohrs Campbell; Celeste Condit and John Lucaites; Philip Foner; Gerda Lerner; and Peter Ripley.

4. See Carlacio; Logan, *With Pen and Voice* and *"We Are Coming"*; Richardson; and Royster for specifically rhetorical treatments.

Chapter 9

Questioning Our Methodological Metaphors

Barbara E. L'Eplattenier

Of all the artifacts I saw in the Vassar archives, the calling cards enchanted me the most. Stiffened pieces of paper three-fourths of an inch by two inches, they were embossed or printed with the names of the women I was researching. When I held them in my hands, they seemed to embody tradition and refinement, elegance and grace, a gentler, slower way of life—a symbol of the middle-class lifestyle during the Progressive Era. Small, disposable, and static, they were a transient, fleeting way to show that you had come to call and left quietly. I adored them.

As a historian, though, calling cards do not represent what I do. I don't simply come to call and leave quietly. Instead, I come with a radical agenda: to "shape the future by telling over more precise stories of the past" (Kerber 310). I am a historian because I want to make a difference, the same way, I suspect, many of the contributors in this collection feel. Our interdisciplinary, cross-disciplinary, and multidisciplinary historical work is our contribution to social justice and change. When I research and construct a history, I do so out of desire to make the world a better place through historical representation.

My point here is not to criticize, but to remind us that metaphors are powerful tools—especially metaphors used to conceptualize the methods by which we carry out our work. They carry implications, possibilities, and limitations for the way in which we conduct historical research; our biases, known and unknown, are reflected within them.

In this chapter, I want to examine the implications and limitations of the prevailing metaphor of historical methodology in rhetoric and composition—that of the map as a guide. One source of this metaphor is Cheryl Glenn's 1995 *Rhetorical Review* article, "Remapping Rhetorical Territory." She begins the essay by saying:

> Until recently, we could pull out a neatly folded history of rhetoric out of our glove compartment, unfold it, and navigate our course through the web of lines that connected the principal centers of rhetoric. . . . Now we are turning to a new map, or rather, to new, often partially completed maps that reflect and coordinate our current institutional, intellectual, political, and personal values. (287)

These new maps are "created" by viewing the terrain from different angles, using different lenses to see what emerges in the landscape, a strategy that has been extremely fruitful for our field. My own work on female writing program administrators working at Vassar during the turn of the century developed as a result of overlaying multiple maps to see what appeared (L'Eplattenier). The results were impressive: previously blank landscapes suddenly became populated with people. Satisfied with what I found, I didn't question my methodology much; it was fairly transparent.

But Rose Schneiderman changed all that for me.

During the Progressive Era (1890–1920), Rose Schneiderman, along with her colleagues Clara Lemlich and Pauline Newman, worked to organize unions in sweatshops, eliminate human rights violations within the workplace, and help women obtain political power in the form of the vote. All three were Yiddish-speaking, Jewish immigrants from Russia who went to work in New York sweatshops in their teens to help support their families, and all had been exposed to socialist and Marxist ideas early in their lives. The stark material conditions and inhumane treatment of workers, combined with the women's socialist leanings and a desire to improve life for working women, turned them into lifelong union organizers and advocates for the laboring class. From their writings, it is easy to see what motivated them. According to Pauline Newman,

> Most of these so-called factories were located in old wooden walkups with rickety stairs, splintered and sagging floors. The few windows were never washed and their broken panes were mended with cardboard. . . . In the winter a stove stood in

> the middle of the floor, a concession to the need for heat, but its warmth rarely reached the workers seated near the windows. During the summer months the constant burning of gas jets added their unwelcome heat and smell to an atmosphere already intolerably humid and oppressive. . . . There was no drinking water available. . . . Dirt, smells, and vermin were as much a part of the surroundings as were the machines and the workers. (quoted in Orleck 32)

The financial rewards were no better. Schneiderman describes her first job at age sixteen as a capmaker:[1]

> So I got a place in the factory of Hein & Fox. The hours were from 8 am to 6 pm and we made all sorts of linings—or, rather, we stitched in the linings—golf caps, yachting caps, etc. It was piece work, and we received from 3 1/2 cents to 10 cents a dozen, according to the different grades. By working hard we could make an average of about $5 a week. We would have made more but had to provide our own machines [and thread purchased from the employer], which cost us $45, we paying [*sic*] for them on the installment plan. We paid $5 down and $1 a month after that. . . . We were helpless; no one girl dare stand up anything alone. Matters kept getting worse. The bosses kept making reductions in our pay, half a cent a dozen at a time. It did not sound important, but at the end of the week we found a difference. ("Story")

Shortly after taking this job, Schneiderman began organizing and leading walkouts and strikes.

The women were further galvanized by the tragic Triangle Shirtwaist Factory Fire of 1911; all three lost friends in the fire.[2] Clara Lemlich was forced to search the rows of bodies for a relative. A newspaper reporter "described her as convulsed with tears and hysterical laughter when she finished her gruesome task without finding a cousin who she feared was among the dead" (Orleck 66). For the rest of their lives, Orleck writes,

> the 1911 Triangle Shirtwaist Factory Fire was their recurring nightmare. It filled them with an urgency that precluded considerations of ideological purity. . . . Memories of the charred victims haunted them throughout their careers,

> reminding them that women workers could not wait for change. They adopted . . . the common sense of the working woman in their approach toward social change: whatever route was the quickest, whichever path seemed most promising, they would take. (5)

I'm fascinated by these women, the work they did, and their impact on the contemporary working world; rights such as the eight-hour day, minimum wage, overtime, pensions, health benefits, job security, and a safe working environment are the direct result of their work (Dash). A significant portion of their work—indeed, one could argue, all of their work—required a keen sense of audience and significant rhetorical ability. As organizers, Newman, Lemlich, and Schneiderman were effective at their jobs, partially because of their youth and appearance, but mostly because of their eloquence. Their rhetoric was fiery and militant, unapologetic, committed to fair working practices for both men *and* women, and unyielding in its demands that the working class unite and empower itself. Their rhetoric, especially when addressed to a working class audience, is unflinching.[3]

Despite the uniqueness, eloquence, and availability of their rhetoric in the form of speeches, newspaper accounts, and archival artifacts, rhetoric and composition scholars—indeed most historical scholars—have paid minimal attention to women such as Schneiderman, Lemlich, and Newman. The historical work in rhetoric and composition done on the postbellum and Progressive Era periods has focused mainly on the rhetorical activities of people who ascribed to the literary practices of the middle class and, who, in one way or another, wished to rise to the middle class or were already positioned there. Most of our histories are based on maps that "reflect and coordinate our current institutional, intellectual, political, and personal values": curriculum, pedagogy, student writings, literary practices, and/or uplifting social work through rhetorical activity (Glenn 287; Fitzgerald; Connors; Schultz; Berlin; Clark and Halloran; Crowley; Johnson; Mattingly; Adams; Mastrangelo).

The Progressive Era, however, was much more than education, literary practices, or the uplifting social work of middle-class women with money and leisure time. Other powerful and influential social movements were occurring—movements in which rhetoric and rhetorical ability played a significant component. Labor and business owners fought long bloody battles about the rights of workers in the country; modern investigative journalism began as a result of muckraking reporting by people such as Nellie Bly, Ida Tarbell, and Upton Sinclair; the Eugenics movement was (unfortunately) gaining credibility and popularity; and the West was being "civilized" at the expense of the Native American and Mexican peoples who resided there. But these movements, despite their long-reaching consequences, don't readily appear on the historical map we've constructed; they are still excluded from our "alternative" rhetorical canon.[4]

Jacqueline Jones Royster eloquently points out in "When the First Voice You Hear is not your Own," that " 'subject' position really is everything. . . . Subjectivity as a defining value," she writes, "pays attention dynamically to context, ways of knowing, language abilities, and experiences" (29). Our own subjectivity needs to be more specifically acknowledged within our metaphors so that we have a space in which to talk about how we developed our research agenda and interests. (For example, my own interest in these women developed precisely because they were so different from myself.) Maps don't simply appear; they are constructed by cartographers, who choose what to emphasize and highlight; who set criteria for determining what is significant enough to deserve recognition and what is not. The way that we describe our methodology should allow a greater space for descriptions of how we choose our subjects: What pushes us to them? How do we choose that which we find significant? How do we begin to represent our participants? (our research subjects? the objects of our interest?—exactly how do we describe the dead people in whom we find our job security and prestige?). Where in our methodological metaphor is there space for an explanation of my fascination with Newman, Lemlich, and Schneiderman? Where in the metaphor can I incorporate my admiration for their work in the face of blatant sexism, racism, homophobia, and general disinterest from people around them? My respect for them and what they have done? My recognition of their limitations, flaws, and failures? Their positions in my life as role models? How all of this affects the stories I tell about them? How this might limit the stories I see about them? How do we incorporate our own twenty-first-century subject position into our metaphor and our research? Similarly, how do we acknowledge or note our own inherent limitations in the stories we are able to see within the archives? Acknowledging our own subjectivity might allow us to see additional stories available to us or at least acknowledge that there are stories we do not have the schemata to tell in a respectful manner. By answering these questions and others like them, our methodological metaphors can help "construct paradigms that permit us to engage in better practices in cross-boundary discourse, whether we are teaching, researching, writing, or talking with Others, whoever those Others happen to be" (Royster 37–38).

In addition to not granting the researcher a position, the map metaphor suggests a concept of history in which a "complete" historical moment, event, movement, and/or person is gazed down upon, much like Gulliver looking down at the Lilliputians. I have two difficulties with this concept. First of all, viewing the map from straight down or even at angles implies that we hover above the story, our own views never impacting the picture we see. This cannot be farther from the truth. While I agree with Berlin that no history is apolitical, the map metaphor allows us to briefly acknowledge our agenda/subjectivity (see, we're viewing it from a different angle!) and then move on. Subjectivity is *implied* by the notion of viewing the map from different angles, but this moves the researcher/historian outside of the data. It doesn't recognize that the historian selects what is significant, determines which boxes to look at in the archives, or goes to the archives intent on locating information that supports a preestablished conclusion. It doesn't acknowledge that we work within the information found in the archival documents, constructing the tale as we come across additional information, revising and altering as we uncover more and more that helps us put previously unimportant information into context, shaping a story we assume exists. The historian, as shaper of the story being told, exists only in the periphery of the map metaphor. Additionally, the map metaphor implies that we have a complete map—a complete picture to discuss, present, and interpret.

Let's be honest. History is a messy business. We don't have a map—we have various and sundry fragments we piece together. We are comparable to the scholars piecing together the Dead Sea Scrolls: a bit here, a fragment there, suddenly a gloriously large section, a couple more little fragments and suddenly we have a sense of what *might* have been, what it could all possibly mean. We are cobbling together a story, a tale, a suggestion of what probably happened. My colleague, Laura Smoller, a professor in the University of Arkansas—Little Rock history department, always reminds me that "history is like doing a connect the dot puzzle of a zebra . . . except you don't have all the dots and you're not sure it's a zebra." Our metaphors need to reflect the fact that we are telling the best story that we know how to tell—*at that particular moment in time with the information we have available to us.* It should reflect how much of the writing of a history is a fabrication, a factional tale spun out of old papers, memoirs, newspaper accounts, interviews, census data, and other factional histories. Perhaps a more accurate description might be that of an incomplete mosaic, with the historian discovering a few tiles, moving them around, discovering a few more, shifting the existing tiles until the new ones fit in, and continuing until there appears to be a recognizable picture. Newly discovered tiles might change that picture entirely.

In addition to highlighting our own role as researcher, the way we talk about "doing research" needs to allow for ways to represent the tensions and intersections of the multiple forces that constrain and impact (whether positively or negatively) the lives of those whom we study. Schneiderman, Newman, and Lemlich's lives were filled with overwhelming levels and amounts of complexities, all of which appear in different combinations and with different amounts at various points in their lives. She and her friends fought sexism (from both males and females), classism, homophobia, attacks on their devotion to their work, and a general lack of belief in their abilities despite clear evidence to the contrary.

For example, sexism came from both their allies and their enemies. Within the Women's Trade Union League, an organization dedicated to the empowerment of working-class women, the middle/upper-class allies and the working-class women differed strongly on what the League's work should be. Working-class women wanted (and needed) practical, day to day advise on organizing, leading, and sustaining strikes that would allow them a better quality of life. The middle-class women often advocated for educational activities designed to introduce the workers to culture through trips to art museums, or teas, or dances, or reading discussion groups.[5] Many strikers resented the classist and patriarchal overtones of their relationships with the wealthy suffragists who worked with them. Pauline Newman wrote to Rose Schneiderman during a fund raising trip: "My work is horrible! The keeping sweet all the time and pleading for aid from the 'dear ladies' and the ministers is simply sickening" (Dash 45–46). Similar sentiments appeared in Rose Schneiderman's "Reply to Senators on the Delicacy and Charm of Women":

> We hear our anti-suffragettes saying, "Why, when you get the vote it will hinder you from doing welfare work, doing uplift work." Who are they going to uplift? Is it you and I they want to uplift? I think if they would lift themselves off our shoulders, they would be doing a better bit of useful work. I think you know by now that if the workers got what they earn, there would be no need for uplift work and welfare work or anything of that kind.

At the same time, the working-class women recognized their need for upper-class women's prestige and money. Only when the "Mink

Brigade" appeared on the picket lines and the public became aware that "respectable women" were being beaten and thrown in jail did the police violence against the strikers, which was truly brutal, dissipate somewhat.

A similar situation existed within the American Federation of Labor, at that time the most powerful union in the nation. Samual Gompers, head of the AFL, was openly scornful of women's efforts to organize and this attitude appeared also within the lower ranks. When the leader of the WTUL met with Gompers at the 1915 AFL convention, she reported back that

> [h]e stated . . . that the Exce. Council of the American Federation of Labor recognized the need of organizing women, but they did not think that women were qualified to organize women, that, in the first place, women were very difficult to organize, if they could be organized at all; that secondly, women organizers were rarely worth anything, that they had a way of making serious mistakes—and used some other language which, frankly, I don't want to repeat. (Tax 102)

This attitude infuriated Schneiderman, Lemlich, and Newman, all of whom recruited thousands of women into unions, and deeply impacted their ability to do effective organizing. But it was not just the AFL that held this attitude; the International Ladies Garment Worker's Union also reflected sexist attitudes. At one point, the ILGWU sent Newman to Cleveland to provide support to striking workers. She quit when she learned that the male organizer sent after her was being paid a higher wage than she was (Orleck 69). Yet the women also recognized that they could not continue without the money, connections, name recognition, or backing (however grudgingly given) of these various groups.

Throughout their lives, Schneiderman, Lemlich, and Newman walked a tightrope of alliances, with each connection both helping and hindering them. Their world and their ability to be politically effective was built around a tenuous web of networks between wealthy allies who supported either suffrage and/or the labor movement, union officials, Christians, "native-born" Americans, politicians, various immigrant groups, as well as others (Payne). As Orleck puts it:

> From the time they left the shop floor until the end of their careers, they operated within a tense nexus of union men, progressive middle- and upper-class women, and the working women they sought to organize. These alliances shifted continuously, requiring the four women to perform a draining and politically hazardous balancing act. (55)

Many of their rhetorical strategies and their political actions can be understood only in response to these tensions.

What metaphors can guide us through these complexities? These forces/tensions rose up at different points with different impact; different intersections of these forces created different points of tension. A colleague suggested that these forces are similar to tectonic plates, shifting and moving underneath to change the contours of the map, but I am dissatisfied with this image. First, it suggests that these are unseen forces at work, when in reality, all three women were keenly aware of these forces and their impact. Secondly, it does not acknowledge that these forces existed as both *de facto* and *de jure* prejudices that rose up at various points in time, in various degrees, dependent on the political changes the women were attempting to implement. Our metaphors need to give us a way to include and consider the external pressures which occur both systematically and intermittently and push/pull on the people we study.

Additionally, our metaphors should be able to take into consideration the cultural and historical factors that had impact upon the people with whom we work. As Jews, Schneiderman, Lemlich, and Newman grew up with a very different feminine ideal than the one that existed in Progressive Era America. In contrast to the sheltered middle-class housewife ideal dominant in the United States, Eastern European Jewish religious tradition glorified strong, economically sophisticated wives and mothers; Jewish women—especially poor Jewish women—were believed to be "innately suited to competition in the economic sphere" (Orleck 19). Because the community valued life-long religious study for men, many Jewish women economically supported their families, either as business owners or as workers. This created women for whom economic stability and justice was a crucial factor in their ability to create a home life. Additionally, many Jewish immigrants found validity in the speeches of Zionists, Yiddishist, and Socialist speakers who advocated revolution and equality. Jewish immigrants brought these teachings to American when they immigrated. Without considering this specific cultural heritage, Schneiderman and her colleagues become more than anomalies—they become freaks who not only defied the WASP social expectations of their era, but to some extent, the cultural expectations of our own era. Without an understanding of the impact of religion and culture, these three become women who don't fit into the social norm of a woman—whether in terms of race, age, ethnicity, culture, or ideology. Our metaphors need to take into account how culture shapes whom we are studying—especially when that culture is outside the white middle-class norm.

The final issue I want to raise here is the representation of chronology and/or changes that occur over time. Maps are static, top-down views of a specific topography at a specific point in time; indeed, their need to be continuously redrawn attests to the fact that they actually represent something non-static. But we study rhetoric—the ability of people to create change. Schneiderman—known early in life as "Red Rose" because of her fiery speeches and ties to socialism—was so successful with her rhetoric that she became an unofficial advisor to FDR and Eleanor Roosevelt on labor issues. As a result of her friendship with them and Francis Perkins, she was named to the Labor Advisory Board of the National Recovery Administration during FDR's term as president. Although clearly a useful and powerful position from which to effect change, her success weakened her effectiveness with the rank and file and she became increasingly conservative as she grew older. Suddenly, she was "Pink Rose." Her desire for respectability drove her throughout her latter years and contributed to her conservatism. The co-author of her autobiography, *All for One*, refused to have anything to do with the book after its publication. She accused Schneiderman of "a mania for respectability which suffocated the story and robbed it of all drama or controversy" (Endelman 271). Schneiderman's ability to be rhetorically successful dramatically changed who she could be rhetorically successful with; she moved from persuading sweatshop workers to unionize to creating national labor regulations.

Clara Lemlich, on the other hand, married a working-class man, had four children, and continued to organize for the rest of her life. This time, though, she organized working-class wives and mothers, recognizing both their roles within the economic cycle and how such women could make an impact on capitalist society. She organized rent strikes and boycotts of grocers and kosher butchers; she advocated for more low-cost housing and municipal unemployment benefits. She was, in the words of one of her neighbors, "a spark plug" who could get the women of the neighborhood excited and committed (Orleck 229). The woman simply never stopped organizing. At age eight-two, less than a year after entering the Jewish Home for the Aged, she'd shamed the management into supporting the United Farm Workers grape boycott—mostly by constantly reminding them of the work of Jews in the labor movement. She then convinced the nurses and orderlies at the home to unionize. During the later years of her life, though, Lemlich's effectiveness occurred only at a local level; if Schneiderman lost her ability to influence the rank and file, Lemlich lost her ability to influence the national leaders of the union. She was forced to beg the union for her pension; they refused to give her one because she hadn't worked fifteen consecutive years. Finally, David Dubinsky, long-time friend and president of the ILGUW, arranged a "lifetime" pension, more out of pity, embarrassment, and regret than out of the union's willingness to support a lifelong member and supporter.[6]

I contrast the career paths of Schneiderman and Lemlich because I think it important we recognize what is lost as well as what is gained when we examine rhetorical strategies. Using a metaphor of maps suggests that historians examine a single moment in time—a snapshot—when, in reality, nothing could be farther from the truth. The methodology we choose to work with must be flexible enough to recognize and allow a space for the shifts that occur as a result of rhetorical work. As historians, we must always recognize that the context of which the people we study can shift dramatically in a moment or subtly over the course of time. Our methodology needs to accommodate changes, gains and losses, as well as the passage of time.

This chapter has been difficult to write because I am keenly aware of my own inability to develop a metaphor that adequately addresses these issues. I have thought of multiple ones, all of which lack some critical aspect. At this point, I'm not convinced that one metaphor can address all of these issues; I do know, however, that how we *conceptualize* the development of histories impacts the histories we actually create. I also don't want to imply that we should develop our methodologies only around the issues that these women's stories raise; they are the vehicle for which to discuss what I see as the limitations of the map metaphor. For now, I draw inspiration from Linda Kerber's words in *Towards an Intellectual History of Women.* Historians, she argues, need to create holistic histories that present more representative versions of the past. Kerber writes, "[T]he new [historical] narrative will be disconcerting: its author will have to have the ability to render multiple perspectives simultaneously" (98). It is my belief that rhetoric and composition scholars are uniquely suited to do such a thing. But first, our metaphors need to be flexible, changeable, and responsive to our subjects so that they help us work systematically through our archival records and present stories with multiple perspectives.

NOTES

1. Schneiderman had spent three years working as a runner in New York department stores. Her pay was $2.75 a week. She left when she realized another woman who had worked there for fourteen years was only making $7.00 per week (*All for One* 36, 43).

2. On March 26, 1911, The *New York Times* reported:

> 141 Men and Girls Die in Waist Factory Fire;
> Trapped High Up in Washington Place Building;
> Street Strewn with Bodies; Piles of Dead Inside
>
> Three stories of a ten-floor building at the corner of Greene Street and Washington Place were burned yesterday, and while the fire was going on 141 young men and women at least 125 of them mere girls were burned to death or killed by jumping to the pavement below. . . .
>
> At 4:40 o'clock, nearly five hours after the employes [*sic*] in the rest of the building had gone home, the fire broke out. The one little fire escape in the interior was resorted to by any of the doomed victims. Some of them escaped by running down the stairs, but in a moment or two this avenue was cut off by flame. The girls rushed to the windows and looked down at Greene Street, 100 feet below them. Then one poor, little creature jumped. There was a plate glass protection over part of the sidewalk, but she crashed through it, wrecking it and breaking her body into a thousand pieces. . . .
>
> They jumped, the [*sic*] crashed through broken glass, they crushed themselves to death on the sidewalk. Of those who stayed behind it is better to say nothing except what a veteran policeman said as he gazed at a headless and charred trunk on the Greene Street sidewalk hours after the worst cases had been taken out:
>
> "I saw the Slocum disaster, but it was nothing to this."
>
> "Is it a man or a woman?" asked the reporter.
>
> "It's human, that's all you can tell," answered the policeman.

The Triangle owners were found not guilty during the trial and never made restitution to the workers and their families. For the complete report and other primary sources related to the Triangle fire, please see http://*www.ilr.cornell.edu/trianglefire/texts/*. To read a description of the working conditions in the Triangle Factory, read Pauline Newman's letter to Michael and Hugh Owens in May of 1951 at the same website.

3. See, for example, Schneiderman's speech at a fundraiser/memorial for the victims of the Triangle fire held by heiress Anne Morgan, daughter of financier and capitalist J. P. Morgan. This speech, given to an audience of the wealthy, middle class, and working poor, refuses to let the culpability of the citizens of New York go unnoticed. Schneiderman lays the blame for these deaths—and others—at the feet of capitalists and advocates militancy for the working class. It was an immensely popular speech. Newman wrote Schneiderman, "You really gave them hell, [and I] am glad of it. . . . I wonder how Miss Morgan felt after you got through" (Orleck 66).

4. I was pleased to see that *Available Means,* edited by Joy Ritchie and Kate Ronald included work by Sarah Winnemucca (a Paiute Indian) and Emma

Goldman, well-known anarchist, but disappointed that the working class was represented mostly by middle-class white reformers. Another important text for examining union/labor rhetoric at the turn of the century is Susan Kates's *Activist Rhetorics and American Higher Education 1885–1937*, which presents the rhetorical training done by the Brookwood Labor College. Brookwood was founded by Fannia Cohn, a close friend of Schneiderman, Lemlich, and Newman's, who gave up a family fortune to work with and for the workers. She spent her entire career in the International Ladies' Garment Workers' Union's Educational Department, organizing educational programs for union organizers, rank and file, and leaders. To fund Brookwood, Cohn violated her union/organizing principles and begged her family for the money, something she swore she would never do. Kates's discussion notes neither Schneiderman or Cohn's role in founding Brookwood.

5. An excellent example of the attitude the allies held toward the working-class women is found in a letter from Laura Elliot to Leonora O'Reilly:

> You can not push me out, and you can not make me afraid of any working girl sister, or render me *self conscious* before them. I refuse to be afraid to tell them that I can teach them music, that I can take them to the Metropolitan Museum and *teach* them and help them.
>
> Dear Sister, get on the Cosmic Band Wagon and be a Monist, and hear the Human Counterpuntal Symphony, where every *point* is sustained by every other *point*, then you will see that it takes all kinds of men to make and run a world. . . .
>
> You, like all Jews, seem to be so oppressed with oppression. I have never heard you *say* that you believed relief was coming. And yet I thought this was the meaning of Socialism—the coming of power to the working classes. (Tax 112)

I suspect that striking workers found the Counterpuntal Symphony did little to put food in their stomachs or clothing on their backs.

6. The pension suddenly stopped in 1959. When Lemlich inquired, she was told there had been no lifetime pension, but rather, a special sum to be paid out quarterly and that sum had been exhausted. In 1960, after much protest, she received *another* special sum of $2,000; she never received another penny from the union she helped shape into a major political force.

Chapter 10

Pretenders on the Throne

Gender, Race, and Authority in the Composition Classroom

Amanda Espinosa-Aguilar

INTRODUCTION

During the last two decades, a growing number of scholars in rhetoric and composition have focused their research on examining the influence of race, gender, and culture on English studies and teaching. Several others (e.g., Bruffee 1984; Murray 1969; Elbow 1973), have addressed such issues by promoting collaborative learning and shared classroom authority as methods for opening new space to allow for diverse voices. These approaches, generally referred to as critical pedagogies or liberatory pedagogies (Freire 1970; hooks 1994; Shor 1996), have contributed to a paradigm shift in educational practices from teacher-centered pedagogies to student-centered ones. For the most part, the impact of this shift on students has been positive in enabling traditionally disenfranchised students (working class, minority, GBLT, etc.) to navigate academia more easily. At the core of these practices is the assumption that authority in classrooms should be shared, a strategy that has typically helped students to feel empowered, to have a clearer sense of their own agency, and to operate confidently as learners. Missing still from our research, however, is attention to the impact of these strategies on the teachers who use them, and especially when the sharing of authority fails.

After five years of applying critical pedagogy in my own teaching, I have not experienced the success generally proclaimed by others. Instead, I have come to understand from a very personal perspective an important point made by Don Dippo and Steven Gelb (1991) in criticizing proponents of shared authority. They observed that those who promoted sharing classroom authority (e.g., Bruffee, Murray, Elbow) are white males who, given typical classroom dynamics, are the least likely to have their authority questioned in the first place. Academics (typically white, male, and older) whose authority is established because they already embody normed expectations about authority have fewer factors to balance and ultimately less difficulty democratizing their classrooms. This observation raises the question of what happens when the professor is not a white male? My experiences as a female faculty of color offer a different perspective. In my view, success with liberatory pedagogies is linked to the extent to which a professor is perceived to hold authority. In my case, despite my holding the position of professor, as a woman of color, authority is not automatically granted for me, and using an approach that often requires me to relinquish what little authority I command can be a problem.

Many studies (e.g., Bauer 1990; Ellsworth 1989) have shown that women already come into the classroom facing students who disrespect them more than men. For example, Joan Gallos (1995) summarizes the experiences of numerous female faculty when she notes that male students are prone to "calling [female faculty] derogatory names, throwing objects at them during lectures, informing them that they hated being 'stuck by the schedule' in a section taught by a woman, [or] commenting publicly in inappropriate ways about the woman's appearance and more" (66). Challenges to authority are exacerbated when the woman is also a member of a historically underrepresented group. This essay, then, explores some of the problems that can occur when the person who is using liberatory pedagogy is a woman of color, and it serves as a cautionary tale especially for faculty who have not yet been tenured.

A QUESTION OF AUTHORITY

In my first tenure-track job I practiced liberatory pedagogy by including many student-centered activities in my lessons. The more I brought activities into the classroom that required active student involvement, the more the students challenged my methods. For example, one strategy that I used was having a range of voices represented among the readings that I chose in order to extend the frames of reference for the voices that my students might choose in their own essays. When I assigned both James Baldwin's "A Talk to Teachers" and Malcolm X's "My First Conk" in the same class, I received a number of evaluations noting that the readings were boring, not relevant, a waste of time, of questionable value, lacked connection to the course goals, or "not what I was used to." In other words, the students resisted seeing anything "appropriate" about these materials and responded with vitriolic evaluations. They did not want to be "liberated," and they questioned me, therefore, as a person who would do such "different" things. They questioned my knowledge, preparation, credibility, and my authority to teach them. At the end of my second year, the evaluations were so low that I was informed that my future at the school was in question.

At first, I believed this backlash was due to the demographics of the students. Most of my career I have taught eighteen- to twenty-four-year-old, white, middle-class students. They were entrenched in mainstream ideology, and when I highlighted hegemonic thinking practices to them and encouraged them to critique viewpoints and values, their course evaluations suggested that they took their own discomfort with these ideas out on me. On further reflection, however, I began to see other dimensions of this situation. After more than a decade of teaching against such resistance, I have come to realize that it wasn't just the topics and the pedagogy that resulted in the poor reviews. I realize now that I had trouble because I literally did not embody the authority they expected in their teacher, and I also did not wield the authority they had come to expect from their teachers.

Generally, by the time students come to college, they have observed years of punishment for not playing by the teacher's rules, for not assimilating to the classroom culture, and for failing to understand each instructor's whims. They know, for example, that a question such as, "Is that how we turn in our homework?" is a veiled command, chastising the student for not following directions. To most students, these are the ways that instructors wield their authority. Students are savvy; they know to wait for the other shoe to drop when a teacher claims she will share authority or implement student suggestions into the curriculum.

Despite shifts in some schools toward more liberatory pedagogies, many students are still likely to have been indoctrinated with the concept of following directives, such that when they enter a college class and are told there are no correct answers, they may be inclined to conclude that the instructor who claims this must have, must be, a problem. They think, "She must have missed the lesson where she was supposed to learn that the students are told what to do by the teacher, explicitly and plainly." Besides that, often the instructors in their other classes, the majority of whom are often older than she and male, are likely not to purport that there are multiple answers. With this contrast, then, students can easily conclude that their female instructor of color lacks the credentials and training to teach the class, and she isn't to be trusted. Her authority to teach the class must be called into question.

Over the years, many of my students have fallen into these categories. They have come to my classroom with their expectations of what authority looks like and how it works, have rejected me and my attempts to use student-centered critical pedagogies and to share authority. These students, in their neat rows and Scantron worldview, didn't want to be given any power over the class curriculum and rejected the responsibility that comes with holding power. They thought it was my job to explicitly tell them how to write papers, to tell them what the assigned texts meant, and to make all of the connections for them. If I didn't do it, I wasn't doing my job. They didn't think that they should have to think seriously about or actively engage with classroom materials on their own. As Louise Rosenblatt (1995) asserts, students have been "given to understand that there are proper ways to react, there are certain things to look for" and that their "remarks on the work must satisfy the teacher's already crystallized ideas about it" (60). By telling my students that varied interpretations were valued, I didn't perform as they expected. I had to contend, therefore, with reestablishing my authority and needing to defend myself against normed expectations.

Beyond facing student expectations about proper teacherly behavior, as Myra and David Sadker (1994) have documented, a professor's ability to share authority in the classroom is undermined even further when the person doing the sharing is a woman. Their research indicates that male students ask for and receive more attention, praise, feedback, and speaking opportunities in a class than their female classmates do. Students have experienced years of reinforcement that "normal" females don't participate, don't lead, and don't speak authoritatively in classrooms. And, it isn't just the males who question female authority. Young women can also strongly resist female faculty who don't reflect the status quo and who challenge their passivity. Sally Reis (2002) suggests that "[b]eing perceived as pushy, aggressive, or even ambitious is troubling to many talented females who often consciously or unconsciously refrain from speaking too much for many reasons. Fear of sounding too aggressive or too smart, stereotypical views about who should speak more often, manners which have been instilled by parents, and other issues related to negative perceptions from the opposite sex cause smart women to become confused about their roles" (25).

In my own discipline (composition studies), the essentialist image that female teachers should be mothering, nice, friendly, affirming, noncritical, giving, caring, silent, nonintimidating, empathetic, and submissive is still a predominant one. With the acceptance and deploying of this image by many in the field, we have made it harder for those women who don't want to be their students' friends or surrogate mothers—who don't encourage submissiveness, whose goal is to create critical thinkers of their students—to do (and retain) their jobs. It is no wonder that female faculty sometimes find themselves, as Frances Maher (1999) argues, in preassigned roles: "Her role tends to be theorized as that of the relatively passive, nurturing, enabling female 'other' of the 'active' masculinized child" (45). I have a problem with this and all of the other metaphors that equate effective female teaching with acting like someone's loving and nurturing mother. The reification of this stereotype of acceptable female roles in the classroom makes it harder for women, especially the younger junior faculty who resist them, to be accepted in their own classrooms. When they don't play the motherly part their students may expect them to play, the authority of these instructors is subject to unwarrented challenge, and especially so when these teachers use liberatory pedagogies that require students to critique and broaden their own frames of reference, and demonstrate independent thought.

The questioning of authority is even more pronounced for female faculty of color who, regardless of discipline, are often challenged or tested publicly in class, especially by young white men. Such public accusations frequently occur when female faculty of color embrace critical pedagogies or feminist pedagogies and ask students to interrogate inequalities in race, gender, and culture in class readings, assignments, and discussions. Some students feel threatened by what are often perceived to be hot topics. They often resist through the use of dismissive language that directly questions, not the text or the issues, but the instructor's credibility and authority. The students' conflict and unease can often come at a high price for the instructor. At evaluation time, students frequently criticize these instructors for being biased (e.g., for going against their normed expectations), for having an axe to grind (e.g., for insisting that students critique values and assumptions), for promoting an agenda (e.g., for using classroom materials written by marginalized people), for propagandizing and not being open to other points of view (e.g., for not keeping sacred the perspectives of the dominant culture), etc.

Eduardo Bonilla-Sliva (2003) has argued that "contemporary racial inequality is reproduced through 'new racism' practices that are subtle, institutional, and apparently nonracial" (3). He refers to this as color-blind racism. Instead of using out and out racial slurs or discriminatory practices, whites now reproduce the prevailing, white supremacist order by engaging in "racism-lite" (3), expressions of resentment and reverse racism hidden behind semantic shields that allow them to save face. One way students engage in color-blind racism is using disclaimers to preface their remarks. Rochelle Smith (1999) writes about challenges to her authority in her essay, "Walking on Eggshells: The Experience of a Black Woman Professor." In the essay, Smith recalls a student evaluation that stated, "I'm not a racist, but I believe that I would have gotten a better grade if my skin color was different" (69). This is a clear example of what Bonilla-Silva calls a discursive buffer. He claims that phrases such as "Some of my best friends are . . ." and "I'm not a racist but . . ." are used by whites to explain away any overt racism in their remarks or actions. Hence, Bonilla-Silva claims that "color-blind racism is racism without racists" (29).

Moreover, challenges to the authority of female faculty of color become clearer when contextualized within the growing scholarship on "color-blind" racism. Smith describes an experience with a white male student who could not accept her as his authority. She writes:

> His complaints, comments, accusations, and demands suggested to me that negotiating power and authority was not an option to which he would submit. . . . In an ideal world, I would have been respected from the beginning, my authority never would have been questioned, and the student would have remained an active participant in the class. Racism, however, is like a diseased patient who has not accepted treatment. (72)

Whites will use frames and semantic moves to criticize people of color in a passive-aggressive way. In the Smith ancecdote, color-blind racism occurs when the students challenge her authority based on "presumed cultural practices as fixed features and uses that as the rationale for justifying racial iequality" (Bonilla-Silva 39). Smith writes, "To be color-blind is an impossibility because the concept is predicated on the idea that one is color-blind within a system of rules, but the majority rules. We are not all the same; therefore, we should not ignore our differences but emphasize their value" (72).

THE IMPOSTOR SYNDROME

Recent studies by McCombs (1989), Heilman (1992), and Fontaine and Greenlee (1993) reveal that faculty of color are often questioned not only by their students but also by their colleagues (sometimes implicitly, sometimes explicitly) for their credibility or ability to lead a class. Stories abound about female faculty of color who are constantly asked to justify their hiring (Oh, you're just an affirmative action hire) or to prove their credentials (Do you have a doctorate? When did you graduate? How long have you been teaching? How many classes have you taught? Have you ever taught this class before? Have you ever taught [fill in the blank] population before? Are you old enough to teach this class? How can you teach writing when you have an accent, come from a nonwhite culture?). In her review of the literature on racial minority women in token situations, Yolanda Flores Niemann (2003) notes, "Women of color faculty report feeling increased pressure to outperform others, outshine and outthink their colleagues, feelings of isolation, pressures to assimilate, lack of mentors, difficulty communicating with majority group members, gender discrimination, being left out of the 'old boy' network, role complexity and doubts from their majority group counterparts regarding their competency" ("Psychology" 108). These types of pressures contribute to a phenomenon psychologists call the Imposter Syndrome or IP.

In the first major study of IP, Pauline R. Clance and Suzanne A. Imes explain that people who perform roles that are atypical for their age, sex, race, etc. are likely candidates for IP because their "uniqueness" contributes to feelings of standing out, of not fitting in, of being other. Julie King and Eileen Cooley, summarizing Clance's 1985 study, find that "as children, impostors believe their talents are atypical for their family, race, or gender" (305). Those who experience IP

> feel that they have fooled everybody and that they are not as competent or intelligent as others think they are. Success is attributed to luck, compensatory hard work, or "superficial" external factors such as physical attractiveness or likeability. Some of them are incredibly hard workers; they are always overprepared. However, they cannot accept that they have intellectual gifts and ability. They experience a constant fear that their imposturous existence will be found out, that they will not be able to live up to others' expectations and catastrophe will follow. (Kets de Vries 676)

Research has found that those who experience IP often exhibit low self-esteem, generalized anxiety, depression, frustration, and/or a lack of self-confidence.

Many of these studies have looked specifically at the incidence of IP among women of color. Joan Harvey notes, "High achievers who are female and black represent a 'double minority.' If they are successful in a career, they may have violated social stereotypes for both their sex and their race. That immediately gives them two reasons to have trouble adjusting their self-images to their success" (184). Clearly, academics of color, especially women, are set up by the stereotypes and negative expectations that surround them to internalize a view of themselves as impostors. Yolanda Flores Niemann (1999) also notes that faculty of color are susceptible to

> stereotype threat, which is defined as being vulnerable to internalizing the negative stereotypes about one's own group in a given situation, even when one does not endorse these stereotypes. A prevalent stereotype about Latinas/os and African Americans is lack of competence in academic domains, making faculty from these groups particularly vulnerable to the self-undermining effects of stereotype threat. . . . Obstacles faced by faculty of color involve interactive forces of two types of undermining—that done by others, and the self-undermining of competence. ("Making" 111)

Instructors who feel that they stand out, rather than fit in, are often less satisfied with their jobs because of the isolation they feel from being the only person of color, or worse, from being a double solo: the only female and the only faculty of color in the department.

EFFECTS AND CAUSES

With a combination of student resistance and the possibility of IP, the question still remains, however: Why do some faculty of color experience resistance when sharing their authority? In my view, there are several reasons that are supported, not only by my own experiences, but also the anecdotal experiences of others and research that has been emerging. One reason has already been suggested: some first- or second-year students believe that the proper task of authority is to convey absolutes to the student learner. It stands to reason, therefore, that an authority figure who fails or more importantly, purposefully chooses not to convey absolutes about her area of expertise, cannot possibly be seen as an authority. The dualistic student resists interrogation of topics that have no right solution, and prefers (and provides higher evaluations to) teachers who supply justifiable, preferably quantifiable, answers. As Kenneth Bruffee notes: "We derive our authority as teachers from being certified representatives of the communities of knowledgeable peers that students aspire to join, and that we, as members of our chosen disciplines and also members of the community of the liberally educated public at large, invite and encourage them to join" (658). By not living up to this idealized, reified image of a professor, the liberatory pedagogue often undermines her authority.

Another reason that faculty of color experience resistance is that Anglo students often resist and resent readings and activities written by or about people of color who challenge hegemonic thinking. Valerie Lee notes that "some students are comfortable, indeed, with sexist, racist, and classist thinking, and when [we] ask them to read and write about difference, these students vehemently resist considering the value of critical alternatives" (22). Some Anglo students particularly resist reading ethnic literature that contains examples of white discrimination. These students aren't moved to action because they have difficulty accepting the experiences and the anger that often accompanies the injustices being described. Lee also observes that a frequent response these resisting students have to ethnic literature is a feeling of resentment that some "ethnic writers do not seem to accommodate Anglo readers as much as they could" (28). For example, ethnic authors don't always translate the words and phrases they use from their first languages. When writers of color allude to "insider information" regarding myths, legends, history, or religious symbols, they are often considered poor writers or even un-American by some students.

A third reason that students challenge liberatory teachers is that they reject what some of them perceive to be these teachers' utopian call for students to challenge complacency and question "the way things are." Challenges come when students aren't invested in the possibilities for growth and change that a liberatory class invites. Students who lack experience with injustice naively adopt the attitude "if it hasn't happened to me it must not exist." This attitude is exacerbated when the resistant student perceives the utopian call as too much work outside of class, and therefore, unfair. When students are asked or even required to question the values they see as the foundations of their held beliefs, they perceive the instructor as threatening and possibly even disingenuous.

A fourth reason for so much resistance to liberatory pedagogies is that the students may not believe that our contestatory classrooms are truly safe environments for the expression of their views. Louise

Rosenblatt (1995) writes, "Tolerance of other points of view is extremely important for the teacher" (124). This is vitally important when discussing race, gender, and culture since many student reactions will be based on their maturity, experience, economics, politics, etc. Many faculty establish tolerance policies early, in conjunction with the class. A result can be that some of our students feel left out of the conversation before it even starts, or they respond defensively when discussing texts dealing with explicit forms of institutionalized oppression. Students may feel as though they can't express their true thoughts, or that, if they do, they will be labeled racist, or worse yet, offend the teacher and hurt their class grade.

A final reason for some students' resistance is that they sometimes like or even need an authoritative instructor because they don't want the added responsibility of co-creating the class' curriculum. Maybe we are most effective sharing authority only when the students buy into the concept of authority without authoritarianism. Otherwise, we wind up with classes that bell hooks describes in *Teaching to Transgress* as "full of 'resisting' students who did not want to learn new pedagogical processes, who did not want to be in a classroom that differed in any way from the norm" (9). And the norm often is equated with a white, non-accented, native-born American.

There, of course, exist many other reasons why students reject liberatory pedagogies. To be noted is that rejection for whatever reason is not a reflection (or prediction) of ability, intelligence, or promise. Students across ability levels, across class, gender, race, and ethnicity are all subject to be vulnerable to a need to resist these types of pedagogies. Such resistance is often tied to both conscious and unconscious expectations. Teachers, then, don't just face students. They also face the students' expectations about what it means to teach and learn and who they think can be authorized to do the job.

ASCENDING THE THRONE, ASSUMING AUTHORITY

What can be done to ascend the throne of classroom authority? First, one can reject the Impostor Syndrome. We aren't impostors. We would never have made it this far if we were. Second, despite the seemingly pessimistic tone of this essay, I still believe in using student-centered pedagogy, but with some caution. Faculty in tenuous positions (i.e., untenured, part-time, person of color) should be ready to defend their use of these methods. They must be ready to deal with the inevitable challenges to their methods in the spirit of transforming the academy itself. While faculty of color may desire to enact a critical pedagogy, it may not be a simple or straightforward choice to do so without some job security. In most school situations, the pressure for students to conform is very great. Students are typically pressured by fellow students and sometimes by their other instructors not to ask too many questions, and to avoid actively engaging in the learning process. Instructors and students alike are rewarded (via their grades, tenure, publication, evaluations, etc.) for maintaining the status quo system of learning. Until there are systemic changes in academia that reward participatory learning, use of these pedagogies will continue to result in students challenging faculty, and especially female faculty of color.

While the desire to use liberatory pedagogies may be held by faculty of color such as myself, a reality is that enacting this desire may be a risky business with regard to student evaluation and peer evaluation, especially when the professor does not have the security of tenure. Ultimately, faculty of color must accept that what works for Anglo colleagues and male professors simply may not really work for them. Because faculty of color embody difference and, overwhelmingly, their white colleagues embody the idealized norm, it is fairly inevitable that they will be compared against that norm. Faculty of color go against naturalized constructs of what faculty who are endowed with authority look and act like from the minute they walk through the door. We just aren't likely to become naturalized authority figures as professors until there are many more of us, and not just more hired, but more retained and tenured throughout academe.

In the meantime, my choice is to continue using the pedagogical approaches that I deem best for accomplishing the teaching/learning goals that I embrace in my classroom: assigning readings by people of color that disturb my students because doing it challenges the status quo; asking students to critique the frames of reference for their values and assumptions; requiring students to demonstrate independent thought by not reguritating my beliefs back at me. Using these methods enables me to watch the personal and intellectual growth that my students achieve when I refuse to act as the only authority in my classes. My commitment, though, as I have tried to do in this chapter, is to be clear in my analysis of this situation, to be articulate in explaining what I do and why, and to be assertive about making it crystal clear that I am not a pretender in this academic arena. I am a well-prepared professional.

Chapter 11

Veiled Wor(l)ds

The Postcolonial Feminist and the Question of Where

Akhila Ramnarayan

A 1989 interview of Gayatri Spivak in *The Postcolonial Critic*, conducted by Lola Chatterjee, Rashmi Bhatnagar, and Rajeswari Sunder Rajan in New Delhi, India, foregrounded indigenous and diasporic identity politics, the hot topic in postcolonial studies during the 1990s. The interview took place when Spivak was a visiting professor at the Jawaharlal Nehru University, New Delhi. Its main focus was what the interviewers read as Spivak's constitution of herself as "the post-colonial diasporic" and of indigenous scholars—such as themselves—as "native intellectuals." Spivak countered this characterization, dubbing both native and diasporic Indians as "postcolonial intellectuals." She said that her admittedly privileged stance as a postcolonial scholar operating out of the Western academy is one "into which I have been written. I am not privileging it, but I do want to use it."[1]

And use it she has. Alongside Edward Said and Homi Bhabha, Spivak has been regarded as the chief spokesperson for postcolonial studies. Her hallmark essay, "Can the Subaltern Speak"—a case study of widow immolation in India—became the foundation of a theory that was to influence perceptions of the colonial encounter and the colonized subject in both first and third world universities.[2] Her work in the areas of cultural studies, literary criticism/pedagogy, and postcolonial feminism has been often emulated and/or attacked, but seldom ignored.

As a PhD student in postcolonial studies, I struggle in more ways than one to both resist and adopt the tone, the voice, of established South Asian postcolonial and postcolonial feminist scholars. I am personally invested in the postcolonial conversation in terms of my own scholarly identity and the processes by which it has formed. I started thinking about the binding identity associations of "home" and "abroad," "native" and "diasporic," "third world" and "first world" in connection with gender, race, and postcolonial scholarship as an undergraduate and MA student studying English literature in Chennai, India. Doing college-level work in a discipline that almost exclusively privileged the British literary canon entailed questioning the relevance of what I was studying to the Indian and Tamil cultural context. In the late eighties and early nineties, moreover, many scholars were reassessing the role and fate of English departments in the postcolonial Indian university, a debate that influenced the way I thought about my own studies.[3] I was excited to find when I went to Chennai in Winter 2003 that English departments all over India have made radical changes to the ways in which they teach English studies.

This chapter is intended to clarify and vex my position as a South Asian woman writer in English literary studies writing a dissertation in the United States on the twentieth-century Tamil novel. Despite this somewhat exclusively demarcated subject position, I believe the representational concerns I raise are pertinent not only to my situation but also to scholars interested in what I like to call the politics of the fringe, investigating representations of the racialized, classed, sexualized, gendered other in mainstream and alternative discourse while trying to intervene in both. I try to pay attention in the essay to the ideological battles facing such scholars, asking specifically in my case, what it connotes to be the female native informant in the Indian and U.S. academies. I hope this chapter will speak to those in the humanities who are forced time and again to defend and legitimize their scholarly endeavors to both the conservative and liberal factions in their fields of study. Focusing on identity debates in postcolonial scholarship, I reflect on my role as a teacher, writing center consultant and administrator, researcher, student, and feminist of color in the Indian and U.S. academies, grappling with Western and indigenous patriarchies at home and abroad.

The debates that revolve around postcolonial identity invoke the "postcolonial intellectual" and the "third world feminist," debates in which both Gayatri Spivak and Rajeswari Sunder Rajan, one of Spivak's interviewers, continue to participate. I see Sunder Rajan's work as offering a counterperspective complementary to Spivak's pioneering efforts in postcolonial theory, criticism, and feminism. For me, the former represents a postcolonial sensibility that stems, not from a diasporic consciousness, but from the experiences of the indigenous subject. By defining the scope of postcolonial identity debates, I draw attention to the complex relationship between postcolonial and postcolonial feminist theory, criticism, and pedagogy. I look also at how intervention might be undertaken by the feminist scholar in postcolonial contexts of global capitalistic enterprise and mediatization.

Both Spivak and her interviewers (Sunder Rajan included) are positioned as voices for the subaltern. Their positions relative to each other bring me to the central questions surrounding this chapter. How does the postcolonial feminist construct and compose herself as an embodied sociocultural actor and writer? In particular, the South Asian woman scholar (herself) writing the third world woman away from "home" is constructed to undertake certain kinds of representation for the postcolonial subject. To examine these writers' subject positions vis-à-vis the worlds they represent, I look at how they identify both the postcolonial condition and their own scholarly investments in their writings. The chapter outlines the indigenous and immigrant contexts that inform South Asian women's scholarly identities. Using this lens, I problematize the ethical debates about the postcolonial intellectual in the U.S. (Western) academy.

Two South Asian theorists, Aijaz Ahmad and Arif Dirlik, are prominent in debates about the postcolonial intellectual. Ahmad's 1992 publication, *In Theory: Classes, Nations and Literatures*, interrogates postcolonial scholarly practice, questioning, among other things, Fredric Jameson's category of Third World Literatures, and Edward Said's notions of traveling theory and exile.[4] Writing from a staunchly Marxist position, Ahmad argues that scholars such as Said and Homi Bhabha, and writers such as Salman Rushdie, privilege the immigrant position for various erstwhile unexamined reasons. This position leads to a research focus on themes and topics welcomed in the Western academy, allowing immigrant scholars to participate in discourse authorized and sanctioned by the metropolitan university while maintaining their apparently oppositional status.

Self-interest aside, Ahmad notes that third world academics are often *required* in the Western academy to undertake the burden of representation: "The retribution visited on the head of an Asian, an African intellectual who is of any consequence and writes in English is that he or she is immediately elevated to the lonely splendour of a representative—

of a race, a continent, a civilization, even the Third World" (98). These scholars are further exoticized because of their exilic status, though they might have voluntarily moved to the first world for their own professional self-advancement. "[T]he upper class Indian who chooses to live in the metropolitan country is then called the diasporic Indian,' and 'exile' itself becomes a condition of the soul, unrelated to facts of material life. Exile, immigration and professional preference become, synonymous and mutually indistinguishable."[5] The implication here is of collusion between the postcolonial critic and the metropolitan academy to preserve the former's status and privileged position. Similarly, in his 1994 essay titled "The Postcolonial Aura: Third World Criticism in the Age of Global Capitalism," Arif Dirlik points specifically to the number of Indian immigrant intellectuals teaching in U.S. universities, seeing the preeminence of postcolonial scholarship as complicit with and contingent upon the forces of global capital. The arrival of the immigrant scholar in the first world, Dirlik posits, signals the advent of a fashionable postcoloniality and studies surrounding it.[6]

What both Ahmad and Dirlik imply here and elsewhere is that the immigrant scholar and the first world academy "other" the third world by neglecting the material conditions of the (still) colonized subject at "home," by misrepresenting or ignoring ongoing processes of decolonization and neocolonialism in which they are implicated, and by retreating into the text through postmodernist and poststructuralist abstractions. By this argument, such scholarship is not really interventionist though it claims to be. Spivak's "not-quite-not citizen, an economic migrant with a toehold in postcoloniality" in *Outside in the Teaching Machine*,[7] begins to take on a somewhat less glamorous cast.

In fact, it might be said that postcolonial studies maintains a somewhat predictable focus on the same, well- rehearsed themes—colonialism, nationalism, hybridity, syncreticism, exile, diaspora, place, gender, subalternity, sexuality, and class—signaling its cooptation into the Western academy. The academy is a "niche market" for the import of Indian postcolonial theories and intellectuals from the East. A terminology of colonial contact continues to pervade postcolonial discourse about texts written in colonial and ex-colonial contexts alike.

LIFTING THE POSTCOLONIAL VEIL

Today's scholar of gender, class, sexuality, and race writes in a climate of multiculturalism, transnationality, and globalization, encountering new/revised geographies as well as disciplinary boundaries in the search for theoretical paradigms. Postcolonial and transnational feminists seek to go beyond race and class elisions that have occurred in feminist history. The identity of Indian woman scholar bears investigation in terms of the various transcultural patriarchies she must face. How is she produced?

Speaking to Deepika Bahri and Mary Vasudeva, Spivak reflects, "When I talk about my life I try to see it as representative of various kinds of historical lines, political lines, class lines and so on. . . . It is not necessarily useful as feminists to decide that talking about lives is not intellectually okay."[8] If subject position is pre- or overdetermined, how one presents oneself and one's location to others in metropolitan and indigenous contexts, both within the academy and without, may be the key to feminist intervention. And if, as Spivak has argued throughout her career, our subject positions are revealed through life and word language, we need to think about our scholarly activities, both written and oral in this regard.

In Spivak's case, the feminist-postcolonial critic is produced in the literary realm (canonical and non-) and in the realm of Western critical thought, in India abroad. In "Can the Subaltern Speak," Spivak uses a combination of Foucault, Marx, and Deleuze to theorize the position of the Third World woman/worker. *In Other Worlds* offers her early attempts at feminist readings of Dante, twentieth-century Bengali writer Mahasweta Devi's short story "Breast Giver," and to foreground the marginal feminist autobiography that occurs during such critique. Even at this stage in her career, Spivak is conscious in her analysis of Devi's work about the use of "elite methodologies and subaltern material."[9] She writes with more than a trace of irony in 2001: "I was never allowed to translate any Derrida again, whereas the call to translate Devi becomes more and more urgent."[10]

In 1999's *A Critique of Postcolonial Reason*, Spivak writes, "Increasingly, there is the self-marginalizing or self-consolidating migrant or postcolonial masquerading as a "native informant" (6). This, by now, is the charge against which every postcolonial scholar must struggle, and a debate that Spivak must herself acknowledge. She notes in *The Postcolonial Critic*, "I am viewed by the Marxists as too codic, by feminists as too male-identified, by indigenous theorists as too committed to western theory. I am uneasily pleased about this" (68). Perhaps such uneasy pleasures are a privilege only a select few can afford.

In Sunder Rajan's work, the concern for representation leads to a dynamics of intervention rather than poststructuralist paralysis. She resists easy classification in the trajectory of her career, self-consolidating or otherwise, as a critic of the diaspora. Unlike Spivak, whose student and teaching career were largely shaped by her experiences in the U.S.

academy, Sunder Rajan lived and taught for a number of years in New Delhi, before taking teaching and research positions abroad.

Sunder Rajan interrogates the category of "intellectuals in India" and resists unilateral classification as a radical interlocutor."[11] She claims that identity based on location should not be seen as a guarantor of (socialist or radical) politics, a stance that complicates Ahmad's view. These characterizations, she argues, betray an indifference to the reality of indigenous scholars. Located in the Indian academy, and later the United States and the UK, Sunder Rajan has published extensively on many subjects including English literary studies in the Indian university, feminist literary criticism, women's movements, and the law, and edited anthologies that have included contributions from scholars both in India and abroad.[12] While her selective usage of "Western" theory might constitute a problem for its detractors, her perspective on the third world intellectual seems generally more palatable to both indigenous and immigrant camps.

Writing that postcolonial intellectuals, whatever their location, are constituted much the same in terms of class and socioeconomic privilege, Sunder Rajan notes specific differences in the Indian context related to the reception and discussion of published materials in the public sphere, differences that facilitate a relationship with grassroots activism. These factors connect the published text and its scholar more tangibly to different types of sociopolitical interventions.

In her work, Sunder Rajan repeatedly focuses on female oppression in its present-day guise. In her 1993 book *Real and Imagined Women: Gender, Culture and Postcolonialism,* she shows a strong commitment to indigenous feminist agendas,[13] offering useful and easily accessible perspectives on Indian feminist issues and alternative paradigms for feminist literary criticism. Treating the practice of *sati,* she interrogates Spivak's and Lata Mani's conceptualizations of the phenomenon.[14] "The preoccupation with the sati [victim] as a colonial female subject" (55), also, in their case, a preoccupation with the textual, leads these two critics to focus on and get frustrated with the *sati*'s (woman's) absence. Sunder Rajan argues that this then becomes a space for the postcolonial critic's self-aggrandization, where her own scholarly voice substitutes for the *sati*'s.

Sunder Rajan's case study of the immolation of Roop Kanwar, a village woman in Rajasthan, in 1987, is written along alternative lines. Through Kanwar, she studies the female body in pain, drawing on the methods of Spivak and Elaine Scarry but cautioning us of their limited applicability.[15] Whether treating Kanwar's *sati,* the Shahbano case (a controversial alimony dispute involving a divorced Muslim woman in 1986), representations of the character Draupadi from the Indian epic

Mahabharata in the postcolonial context, Sunder Rajan carefully establishes contemporary relevance through historical data, media reports, court records, current legislations, and recent literary texts and films dealing with the topic.

In more recent years, Sunder Rajan's work has retained its focus on indigenous issues. Her essay on the intense political debate surrounding a Uniform Civil Code (UCC) in replacement of personal (religion-based) law in India concerns different Indian women's groups' negotiations of the state and the religious groups.[16] In it, Sunder Rajan fears that the UCC will result in a uniform Hindu law, rather than in secularization, and the further marginalization of women. In advocating women's issues, Sunder Rajan is careful not to elide caste and religion-based differences between communities of women.

In the same essay, however, Sunder Rajan also advocates women's solidarities, seeing as empowering in the Indian context "the identity and function of women as workers or producers" (74). Seeing the workplace as a site for shared interests in an India where more and more women, sanctioned/recognized both by the state and their own communities, work outside the home, Sunder Rajan calls for "work-related activisms" which might lead to "women's participation in the political process" (74). In this regard, her 2003 publication *The Scandal of the State: Women, Law and Citizenship in Postcolonial India*[17] might be read alongside that of sociology/globalization studies scholars such as Saskia Sassen, who, on a wider scale, sees the capital market itself as "a space where women can earn visibility as individuals and as collective actors, and come out of the invisibility of aggregate membership in the nation-state."[18]

Today in India, Hindu nationalist discourse announces the failure of secular nationalist project, instigates religious revivalism and essentializes gender roles, a cause for concern among many Indian scholars and activists. Indian postcolonial feminists such as Zakia Pathak, Sunder Rajan, Anupama Rao, and Nivedita Menon move away from literary-discursive realms to examine women subjects in relation to socioeconomic and political institutions such as the state and religious communities, in an Indian legal and political system recognizing personal (religious) laws.[19] They employ poststructuralist analyses with varying degrees of success.

GLOBAL LOCALITIES

My own research preoccupations in literary studies—postcolonial theory and criticism, postcolonial feminism, globalization, and subaltern studies—have arisen from reading the work of both Spivak and Sunder Rajan. While I am more sympathetic to Sunder Rajan's work, I cannot ignore the scholarly debt I owe Spivak and "Can the Subaltern Speak." Spivak's work has since oriented me toward more "difficult" and against-the-grain readings of texts with the woman question at the fore. From Sunder Rajan, I have learned more lessons about the treatment of gender, most crucially, to demand greater contextualization of the local, regional, and the national, and more nuanced arguments about the postcolonial subject and her constitution.

Writing, reading, teaching, and thinking in the present epoch of global capital, I have learned not to ignore the socioeconomic, political and cultural eventualities that accompany its spread. While aware of the global designs[20] of capitalistic enterprise, I am invested in context-specific ideological and cultural critique. That is, the global must be conceptualized in its distinctive relationships with the national and the local, as "distinct spatialities embedded in the territory of the national yet retaining their own specificity."[21] Such an approach would help counter what Arjun Appadurai describes as a type of "double apartheid" in the U.S. academy, where "globalization [is] an object around which to conduct its [the academy's] special internal quarrels about such issues as representation, recognition and the 'end' of history."[22] Appadurai sees this position as a narrow vision at odds with "vernacular discourses" of the global. Further, he argues that the "poor and their advocates" are alienated from such national and international discourses of globalization relating to the very issues that affect them.

In ex-colonies such as India, the backlash to colonial impositions has been a profound antisecularism, and the deliberate invocation of traditional and religious rhetorics to counter the hegemonies of the West. Postcolonial scholars in India have taken on this issue in the face of a rising Hindu fundamentalism, both among the populace and in governance. Janet R. Jakobsen and Ann Pellegrini note, "[S]ecularism is itself born in and enacted through the violence of modernity, particularly the violence of colonialism and the violence of the imposition of the secular over the traditional."[23] It is crucial to investigate colluding Western and indigenous patriarchies in differing local contexts, as Sunder Rajan advocates.

Reading postcoloniality and gender together in literary texts is a scholarly habit I have developed from exemplars in the field such as Spivak, Sunder Rajan, Leela Gandhi, and Ania Loomba. Because I am a Tamil, Indian, upper-caste woman reader, the two lenses become inseparable for me. Emily Apter asks: "When the problem of a globalizing mass culture and public culture is approached from the perspective of translatability, new and important questions of cultural commodification and, thus, ideology, arise. How do some works gain international visibility, while others do not?"[24] Following Apter, I am acutely aware that I contribute through my own acts of translation, metaphorical and otherwise, to the selective visibility of indigenous texts. Recognizing my own identity, I am deeply troubled by the compromises I have to make by focusing on indigenous writing and articulating my feminist project in relation to such writing in the United States.

Given the worldwide encroachments of global capital and pancultural religious revivalism, I am reminded of the risk of reducing feminist intervention to textual/literary effects, when both patriarchal oppressions and resistances occur at multiple levels, including those involving the physical and material realities of postcolonial subjects. My own work will, I hope, articulate a postcolonial and feminist literary model based on a specific local context. I seek to locate (the discrepancies in) Western and Indian metropolitan assumptions/standards that might nuance or problematize this model. If, as feminists we engage in rigorous critique of language, we have the potential for change, however circumscribed.

EPILOGUE

Chennai, India, 1999. When I was home, I occasionally went about the city in my grandparents' blue and purple auto-rickshaw, a motorized miniature cab on three wheels that is a familiar sight on Indian roads. Driving anywhere in Chennai took a while as the streets were usually heavily congested with all kinds of traffic, including pedestrians, bicyclists, moped and motorcycle riders, cars, bullock carts, and the occasional stray dog, goat, pig, or cow (guaranteed to stop traffic altogether). The purple auto was one of the relatively few privately owned such vehicles in the city, and so was recognized by neighbors, passers-by, local shop owners, and street vendors, who would greet it with waves, yells, and things to take home (ordered earlier by my grandmother).

I spent a lot of my time on the road talking and joking with Murugan, the genial auto-rickshaw driver in his early twenties, who had been in my grandparents' employ for at least five or six years. Murugan and I exchanged news about India and America, and on the states of our respective families. He updated me on regional and national politics with many a shake of the head, and pointed out all the new restaurants and pool halls that had mushroomed in my absence. He gave me a scrupulous account of my entire family's goings-on, and in turn demanded news of my new home, my studies, and my work. Having watched me grow out of a none-too-becoming adolescence, Murugan was vastly amused at the thought that I was now an English teacher, and that I had to cook, clean, and pay bills for myself. Once he quit chuckling, he asked a question that stumped me.

"Akhila, there is one thing that is very famous in America. I saw it in a Tamil film. What is it?" I tried a variety of monuments and places of interest as possible answers—the Statue of Liberty, the World Trade Center (this was before September 11), Mount Rushmore, Disneyland, the Grand Canyon, even McDonald's, the Rock'n Roll Hall of Fame, Yankee Stadium, and Barbie—only to be met every time with strenuous head shakes. Murugan himself, try as he might, could not remember what it was. It did not help that he wasn't sure whether the thing he meant was an object or a place or a character or a building. And pronouns in Tamil were no help.

The minute I got into the auto the next day, Murugan said jubilantly, "I found out the answer to the question I asked you myself." His eyes were mischievous. "What is it? Tell me," I demanded. "Hollywood," he said. At this point, I had to own shamefacedly to Murugan that I had never been to Hollywood, that the U.S. city I lived in was smaller than Chennai, and most appalling of all, that I hadn't kept up with the Indian film scene so I didn't know even from the movie's name what he meant by the most famous thing in America (I seldom watched popular Indian musicals even when I lived at home). Initially disappointed, Murugan was magnanimous enough to give me the healthy dose of popular culture that I hadn't received up to that point. He proceeded to fill me in on all the new movie releases in Chennai, with detailed plot descriptions and the titles of all the hit songs on various soundtracks. And so the good part of an hour was spent.

This encounter has stayed with me for many different reasons, some obviously pleasant and others not so. While at home, I had to negotiate hierarchies of class, caste, and gender in complex social interactions such as the one above, the kinds of interpersonal dynamic that I normally do not experience in the United States. Seated in the back of the auto, with Murugan in the driver's seat, I had to wrestle with an inherent asymmetry of power in our relationship. My family owned the auto and employed Murugan, and in that sense, I was, at least temporarily, an arm of authority, though neither of us dwelt on the fact. As a young, upper-caste brahmin woman riding alone with a young (lower-caste) male, I had to be sure, both for his sake and mine, that certain proprieties of language and conversation were not breached. Conventional roles aside, Murugan, as a Tamil speaker with a little

English, depended on me for information about America, information that I failed to provide. Instead, Murugan subverted processes of cultural transmission by himself providing the answer to his own question.

The incident also forced me to think about what counts as popular cultural currency and capital, the Hollywoodization, as it were, of Indian cinema and its audiences. It reminded me that often, the popular media everywhere are complicit in the very institutional discourses I want to critique. This, I tell myself now, is an awareness I need to maintain. The postcolonial feminist scholar cannot afford to exist in a rarified literary/theoretico/textual realm. For, as I speak of elisions, subversions, hegemonies, and marginalizations, I write Murugan himself, an adult human being who lives and laughs and thinks and works, out of my story.

NOTES

1. See *The Post-Colonial Critic: Interviews, Strategies, Dialogues,* ed. Sarah Harasym (New York: Routledge, 1990).

2. Gayatri Chakravorty Spivak, "Can the Subaltern Speak: Speculations on Widow Sacrifice," *Wedge* 7, no. 8 (Winter/Spring 1985): 120–30.

3. See Gauri Viswanathan's *Masks of Conquest: Literary Study and British Rule in India* (New York: Columbia University Press, 1989) and *The Lie of the Land: English Literary Studies in India,* ed. Rajeswari Sunder Rajan (Delhi: Oxford University Press, 1992).

4. Aijaz Ahmad, *In Theory: Classes, Nations, Literatures* (New York: Verso, 1992). See especially chapter 3, "Jameson's Rhetoric of Otherness and the 'National Allegory' " (95–122) and chapter 5, "*Orientalism* and After: Ambivalence and Metropolitan Location in the Work of Edward Said" (159–220).

5. Ahmad 86.

6. Later published in Arif Dirlik's book of the same name: *The Postcolonial Aura: Third World Criticism in the Age of Global Capitalism* (Boulder: Westview Press, 1997), 52–83.

7. Spivak, *Outside in the Teaching Machine* (New York: Routledge, 1993), 270.

8. Deepika Bahri and Mary Vasudeva, "Transnationality and Multiculturalist Ideology: Interview with Gayatri Chakravorty Spivak," in *Between the Lines: South Asians and Postcoloniality,* ed. Deepika Bahri and Mary Vasudeva (Philadelphia: Temple University Press, 1996), 64–92, 65.

9. *In Other Worlds: Essays in Cultural Politics* (London: Methuen, 1987), 245. Spivak was later to translate and anthologize Devi's short stories in a collection now in widespread use among U.S. universities. See Mahasweta Devi's *Imaginary Maps,* trans. Gayatri Chakravarty Spivak (London: Routledge, 1995).

10. Spivak, "Questioned on Translation: Adrift," *Public Culture* 13, no. 1 (2000): 13–22, 15.

11. Sunder Rajan, "The Third World Academic in Other Places: The Postcolonial Intellectual Revisited," *Critical Inquiry* 33, no. 3 (Spring 1997): 596–616, 599.

12. See endnotes 3 and 14. Also see You-me Park and Rajeswari Sunder Rajan, eds., *The Postcolonial Jane Austen* (New York: Routledge, 2000).

13. Sunder Rajan, *Real and Imagined Women: Gender, Culture, and Postcolonialism* (New York: Routledge, 1993).

14. See chapter 2, "Representing Sati: Continuities and Discontinuities" (40–63).

15. See chapter 2, "The Subject of Sati: Pain and Death in the Contemporary Discourse on Sati" (15–39).

16. Sunder Rajan, "Women Between Community and State: Some Implications of the Uniform Civil Code Debates in India," *Social Text* 18, no. 4 (2000): 55–82.

17. See Sunder Rajan, *Scandal of the State: Women, Law, and Citizenship in Postcolonial India* (Durham: Duke University Press, 2003).

18. Saskia Sassen, "Toward a Feminist Analytics of the Global Economy," *Global Legal Studies Journal* 4, no. 7 (1996): 7–40, 18.

19. For an introduction to the problematics of gender in the Indian context, see Rajeswari Sunder Rajan, ed., *Signposts: Gender Issues in Post-Independence India* (New Brunswick, NJ: Rutgers University Press, 2001).

20. I take the term from Walter Mignolo. See *Local Histories/Global Designs: Coloniality, Subaltern Knowledges, and Border Thinking* (Princeton: Princeton University Press, 2000). Also see L. Elena Delgado and Rolando J. Romero, "Local Histories and Global Designs: An Interview with Walter Mignolo," *Discourse* 22, no. 3 (Fall 2000): 7–33.

21. Saskia Sassen, "Spatialities and Temporalities of the Global: Elements of a Theorization," *Public Culture* 12, no. 1 (2000): 215–32, 228.

22. Arjun Appadurai, "Grassroots Globalization and the Research Imagination," *Public Culture* 12, no. 1 (2000): 1–19, 1.

23. Jakobsen and Pellegrini, "World Secularisms at the Millenium: Introduction," *Social Text* 64 18, no. 3 (Fall 2000): 1–27, 18.

24. Emily Apter, "On Translation in a Global Market," *Public Culture* 13, no. 1 (2001): 1–12, 2.

Chapter 12

The Paradigm of Margaret Cavendish

Reading Women's Alternative Rhetorics in a Global Context

Hui Wu

I have encountered many problems in reading the rhetorical works of Margaret Cavendish and Chinese post-Mao literary women: methodological difficulties in evaluating their works using available feminist theoretical frameworks. The problems grew out of two theoretical assumptions about rhetoric, though probably they both stem from the hierarchical patriarchy that feminism claims to subvert. First, rhetoric as a discipline seems to require that scholars prove the credibility of the women they promote, so there has been much focus on historical women whose rhetorical pieces and bases of arguments meet the criteria of rhetorical tradition and academic feminism as well, for example, the U.S. feminists in Karlyn Campbell's collection *Man Cannot Speak for Her*, in the rhetorical women in Cheryl Glenn's *Rhetoric Retold*, and in the second edition of Patricia Bizzell and Bruce Herzburg's *The Rhetorical Tradition*. Second, studies of women's rhetoric have recently been directed mainly by a set of analytical dichotomies developed in gender studies: gender versus sex, equality versus difference, and public versus private (Bock). The core concepts in feminist theory stand in opposition to the earlier gender dichotomies—male versus female, culture versus nature, rational versus caring—which are now recognized to have distinct roots in Euro-American traditions (Hall and Ames 83–84). Yet, insofar as the feminist binaries have also developed in the Euro-American intellectual context, they, too, have grown out of Western historical and cultural influences, as exemplified by the very pattern of using binaries. Combined with a new twist, some feminists now ask whether gender predisposes women and men toward different virtues (Raphals 223). The masculine/feminine distinction is used to reconstruct another dichotomy between "the maleness of philosophy" and "the idea of a female ethic" (Hall and Ames 83). For more than two decades, both sets of dichotomies have been used as dominant, essential concepts in feminist studies of texts and rhetoric (see also Condit and Arthos). Looked at closely, underpinning the oppositions in feminist theoretical frameworks—gender/sex, public/private, reasoning/caring, and equality/difference—is the similar conviction inherent in the patriarchal tradition: rhetorical women worth historical documentation must meet the traditional criteria; the only difference is that they must also meet the standards of today's mainstream feminism.

While feminist efforts have indeed created a new trail for research on rhetorical women, enlivening scholarship by criticizing the patriarchal nature of rhetoric for limiting women to the private realm, the emphasis on the same traditional characteristics—an agonistic, logical approach—carries prejudices and exclusions, as Carol Mattingly observes, ("Telling Evidence" 101). Scholars have been hesitant to include Margaret Cavendish's notes on eloquence and her collection of imaginary speeches in anthologies of historical women's rhetorical writing. The hesitation may stem from the conclusion that her thoughts and writings are less conventional (Stark) and thus hard to interpret (Sutherland) according to the traditional analytical categories. More probably, however, the reluctance grows out of the assumption that Margaret Cavendish can hardly be considered a feminist from the perspective of today's academic feminism. She is often read as not questioning or confronting the dominant patriarchal doctrine of female virtues. The contradiction between her practice of rhetoric and her criticism of Aspasia makes it difficult to position her in the new rhetorical history reconstructed by feminist critics. Although she could not help but envy Aspasia's "attractive power" of speech in its being equal to that of statesmen, her negative remarks on Aspasia as a "whore" and thus "a great Blemish" to Pericles (Fitzmaurice 42–43) could be read as representing Cavendish's contemporary mores in the sense that these values buttressed patriarchal traditions and excluded women from public function. On the one hand, Cavendish herself defied the traditional definition of women (although not without many apologies) by trying her hand at writing a collection of eloquence for imaginary public occasions, *Orations of Divers Accommodated to Divers Places.* On the other hand, however, the exchanges of opinions on female virtues between her imaginary female speakers did not show Cavendish's commitment to either side. Some scholars concluded that Cavendish was a practitioner of rhetoric whose work did not develop into a coherent theory (Sutherland). From today's academic feminist viewpoint, Cavendish even joined with males to maintain patriarchy (Sutherland). Interestingly, this conclusion parallels the feminist evaluation of some temperance women in nineteenth-century America, for instance, Frances Willard, whose discourse was problematically associated with rhetoric reinforcing existing patriarchal values (Mattingly, *Well-Tempered Women* 6).

This paradigm for Margaret Cavendish finds parallels in the predicament of my current project of translating and compiling the essays on gender of seven highly regarded post-Mao (since 1976) Chinese writers.[1] The intention of this project is to offer Anglophone critics/readers primary sources in English about Chinese women writers' insights on gender issues. However, the dominant binary theoretical frameworks of academic feminism have created problems in evaluating these essays.

It is perhaps a big disappointment to Western feminists that two of the writers, poet Shun Ting and essayist Han Xiaohui, actually declare they are not feminists. Another novelist, Zhang Kangkang, believes that women's emancipation is not simply a "women's issue" that can be isolated from human issues in a larger social context. Some of these writers propose that criticizing male supremacy does not enhance women's quality of life; a woman needs to look at herself critically to increase female integrity to overcome her sense of sexual inferiority. Although the selected essays are on gender issues, they seem to sound "antifeminist," in conflict with mainstream Euro-American feminist thought, arousing doubts about the credibility of the texts as feminist rhetoric. As a matter of fact, these writers have been criticized for joining the dominant force in maintaining traditional female virtues, the same accusation leveled at Margaret Cavendish. The essays of Zhang Kangkang and Lu Xing'er, prominent Chinese novelists, have been criticized for presenting "female stereotypes and essentialized views on gender".[2]

But these critics did not know that I, an academic trained in the West, had evaluated Chinese writers the same way they did. In the process of assembling these essays, I had used both traditional and feminist criteria to measure the academic merits of these essays. I too had problems with their propositions and thought the way these women wrote was illogical, believing their whims were overriding their reasoning. The critics did not know that I, in fear that these writers would be criticized for their "antifeminist" rhetoric, had almost torn these essays apart in the hope of finding logic and ideas that might appeal to Western academics. My requests to the writers for explanations of their positions were frustrating as well because those who wrote back repeated what they had demonstrated in the essays. As a translator and editor, I was discouraged as well as disappointed because I was not entitled to change the originals, nor did I have the right to tailor Chinese women writers' positions to meet Western conventional rhetorical demands and feminist agendas. My fear now is that because of the dominant theoretical frameworks of gender studies, the rhetorical pieces of critically acclaimed Chinese women writers may be prohibited from reaching Anglophone readers.

If dominant theoretical directives can be considered critics' calling cards, because they shape the academic market of knowledge production and construction, these cards, then, can also give critics authority to export, albeit perhaps unknowingly, contemporary Western feminist theories into the reading of women's rhetorical texts from other time periods and cultural locations. Reflecting upon my difficulties in assessing Margaret Cavendish's and Chinese women's rhetorical works, I feel the cards with which scholars are supposed to call in the academic market are escaping my grasp because the established theories may actually demolish my authority as a Chinese scholar instead. The common practice in scholarship—theory and application—is hardly applicable either to my project or the case of Margaret Cavendish. I am afraid that by these framings and expectations I would be holding a losing hand at the card table before the game begins.

It was after long contemplation that I realized that the essential problem in the evaluation of the rhetoric of Chinese women and Cavendish lay in the tendency to draw upon predominant theories institutionalized by tradition and mainstream academic feminism: the dualistic analytical model in terms of gender identity and virtues. The capacity for rational thinking has been believed to be a positive male trait, and therefore the achievement of human status is construed as the realization of maleness (Hall and Ames 81), but not as the realization of a human potential that women also possess. Conversely speaking (the "reasoning" goes), femaleness bespeaks a lesser human trait; caring indicates a weaker mind for reasoning; and gender equality cannot be achieved through maintaining human differences.[3] Feminist criticism of texts based on these convictions, I have realized, may lead to the reinforcement of patriarchal ideology, by and large privileging traditional norms in rhetorical practices. At the outset of the analytical process, our interpretations of texts and the space for knowledge making are restricted by the straitjacket of these norms, putting the rhetoric of the women under study at stake. To restate the point, the moment we apply binary categories to analyzing women's texts, we are entrapping ourselves immediately in a patriarchal analytical practice. Consequently, the rejecting of Margaret Cavendish's and Chinese women's writings, similar to the disbelief that the historical study of African-American rhetorical women has encountered, may "short-circuit a more inclusive knowledge-making process and limit the impact of challenges . . . to predominant interpretative frameworks" (Royster 254).

Therefore, I propose to begin with an awareness of the contingency and cultural specificity of analytical categories in terms of women's rhetoric, particularly in a global context. As many scholars point out, Chinese rationalization of gender identity, equality, and the capacity for human moral thinking, to a large extent, is not built on a dualism of opposite sexes, but on correlative relationships[4] to a larger social and familial hierarchy which requires more well-rounded, complex analytical insights than those merely based on dichotomies of females against male dominance. For example, in discussing the human capacity for self-cultivation for moral reasoning, the Chinese philosophical tradition seldom puts as much emphasis on oppositional gender traits as on general human nature, without indicating explicitly whether learning and reasoning abilities apply to men only (Raphals 223–226). For this reason, instead of considering male/female as opposite gender traits, we need to take into consideration Chinese gender identity in relation to the concept of human as it is understood in the hierarchical patriarchy directed largely by Confucianism. Instead of separating public from private, we need to look correlatively at the Chinese concept of family and its functions in society, investigating the public in relation to the domestic. In other words, the interpretative frameworks of gender identity and equality should not be built merely on dualistic thinking but on a nondichotomous, relational understanding of the concepts of "human" and "family" in terms of morality and life achievements as conceived in a different culture. The proposed model, by complicating women's dynamic rhetorical approaches, situates itself in the perception of women's human rights in order to address the shared value for women as well as the limiting political/social factors that condition the effective realization of certain mainstream feminist values in certain specific cultural or historical contexts.

Many post-Mao Chinese women writers insist that to address gender equity a woman must be recognized first and foremost as a human being and then as a woman, for example Hu Xin, Shu Ting and Zhang Kangkang. This view indeed creates problems in the understanding of their rhetoric because whether or not women are recognized as humans has hardly been questioned by Western feminists. That a woman is a human is an unarguable, obvious fact in the West. It is recognized without much doubt that "[i]n the dominant strains of the Western tradition, even though a woman must resign her difference to become a person, she can still lay claim to an essential humanity that distinguishes her from her context. Essential human nature is a guarantee. Regardless of how degraded woman's role, she is still potentially and irrevocably a human being" (Hall and Ames 97).[5] The second confusion may be caused by Chinese women writers' persistence as women fulfilling their motherly and wifely responsibilities alongside their professional pursuits. This claim not only sounds essentialist but also goes head on against feminist dichotomies that challenge the traditional motherly/wifely virtues that have confined women to the private domain. In the following, my effort is to show how a correlative understanding of human and family offers a discursive feminist approach to diverse gender politics in a cross-cultural context in the hopes that this analytical model can shed light on the evaluation of the rhetoric of Western historical women, such as Margaret Cavendish.

The Chinese notion of *ren,* human, embodies two facets: the physical person and the cultured person. Though they overlap, the physical existence of a person does not necessarily entail his/her human status, because every person is not born a *ren,* and, therefore, all humans are not born equal. For example, a newborn baby is called *tian ding,* meaning an additional head count in the household. This forms a striking contrast to the Christian understanding that we are all created equal. Confucian ethics teach that the human (*ren*) is a realized person that has established himself/herself socially through self-learning and self-cultivation with full understanding of human relations and the fulfillment of the duties these relationships entail. This means that to be a human involves two stages of life: growing up and becoming *ren.* In other words, a person earns the status of human by growing into an exemplary person, *ren,* who, through education and life experience, is fully aware of the central virtue that asserts "the relationality and interdependence of human beings" (Hall and Ames 84). Therefore, a person without the knowledge and morality required for self-realization through fulfilling civil, communal, or familial duties is not a qualified human. For example, a child without knowledge about human relationships has yet to develop into a human; an uneducated/illiterate person who neglects self-learning in his/her lifetime can hardly be respected as a human; and a person imperfect in temperance or character is not a human.[6] In theory, a woman can become *ren* by fulfilling motherly/

wifely duties in the home, where she establishes herself by leading the family. Indeed, many scholars rightly observe that, in ancient China, women of well-off families became *ren* after they had received private education in reading classics, composing poetry and music, painting, and playing musical instrument as well as having fulfilled wifely and motherly duties. If we think that women are expected by Chinese patriarchy to be dutiful and obedient daughters, wives, and mothers, so are men as sons, husbands, and fathers. Theoretically, both the male and the female are expected to establish themselves as *ren* by accomplishing their life achievements for society and family. This is because the relationship of an individual to society is envisaged in terms of a continuing permeation from the individual throughout the ever-broadening circles of family.

The family, the private zone, is the predominant social and economic institution wherein start relations among individuals as well as the role of an individual in his/her relations with community and society. The Chinese family "traditionally has been defined by its value system: age grading; the generational sequence; the dutiful bonding between parents and siblings; the security brought to its members by a complex but highly effective extended family system" (Slote 38). Additionally, the Confucian teaching that "the ancients who wished clearly to exemplify illustrious virtue throughout the world would first set up good government in their states. Wishing to cultivate their persons, they would first rectify their families. Wishing to cultivate their persons, they would first rectify their minds" (de Bary, *Sources* 129) still dominates contemporary Chinese society and power relations. Epistemologically, public and private arenas remain as an inseparable whole where both genders coexist, making complementary contributions. Therefore, the public stage is *theoretically* no better than the private realm in traditional China,[7] which is believed to be an inherited idea from the primitive characterization of physical labor division, *nan geng nu zhi* (the husband ploughs and the wife weaves), the ideal economic cooperation in family life for maintaining social harmony.

Therefore, the Chinese think of male/female not as oppositional but as complementary and supplementary human traits, like *yin* and *yang*, coexisting and intertwined in both males and females for temperance, balance, and social and familial harmony. In the Confucian tradition, the distinction between genders is believed to be a matter of division of social labor, based on natural human biological conditions with respect for women's leadership in the family, which exerts influence on their husbands' public performances (or labor outside the home) and then children's upbringing, without necessarily implying that domestic affairs take less reasoning power and fewer management skills than those in the public arena. Within the home it is the mother who is the primary force that sustains power, domination, and the centrality of the family (Slote 40–42). "Mother" in Chinese culture is glorified almost as the female sage symbolizing wisdom, altruism, generosity, kindness, the embracing nature, and the warmth of home. The Chinese are familiar with the ancient stories about Mecius's mother teaching him ethics concerning social responsibilities and spousal relations and about the mother of General Yue Fei encouraging him to devote his life to the king and the state. As many scholars rightly observe, the mother or wife in many Chinese households was, and is still, a strong, assertive manager in the domestic realm and a partner in a common enterprise, rather than a meek and passive servant of the male (Hall and Ames; de Bary, *Asian Values* 129). For example, the wife of King Xuan of Zhou (827–782 BC) threw away her jewels to take the blame for the king being late for his court because it was her duty to make sure the king served his people well. Wang Xifeng, in *Hong Lou Meng* (The Dream of the Red Chamber), has the power to make decisions concerning the whole extensive family. In many contemporary urban families, women have the final say regarding financial matters. For example, many husbands hand their total salaries or wages to their wives and receive in return monthly allowances. As for the husband/wife relationship, it often involves reciprocity. The obligations are differentiated but mutual and shared (de Bary, *Asian Values* 17). Mutual affection and respect is stressed on an idealized level, *theoretically and ethically*.

Does this mean that, in the hierarchical family-oriented society wherein the mother, and even the wife, has so much power, Chinese women may not be subject to gender inequality? The answer is no. History has shown that the brutality of sexual suppression of Chinese women was extreme in the form of foot binding, concubinage, forced marriage, and the exclusion of women from civic life in traditional China. Even since the Maoist era (1949–1978), when women were supposedly liberated, with legal protection of their right to education, to work outside home, to enter marriage of their own free will, and to do, literally, whatever men could do physically, women still have been largely excluded from leadership roles in civil services. If the ideal gender relationship illustrated by Confucian theories worked, and if gender equality could be ensured by women's power in the home, Chinese women writers would not raise women's issues in their essays. They would not be concerned about women's economic independence, nor the empowerment of women. So, where exactly do gender politics occur that have been subordinating Chinese women to men ideologically?

Here we again encounter the difficult areas where Chinese women writers' argument that women's issues are part of human issues looks opaque to many Western feminist critics. While Western dualistic gender differentiation still embraces women as humans, in contrast, in China, "[m]ale dominance is a consequence of sexual differentiation into male and female that has tend to exclude the female from the achievement of becoming human" (Hall and Ames 81). In spite of women's power in the family (as many scholars have argued, such as Hall and Ames, de Bary, and others), the traditional Chinese familial and cultural format is rigidly authoritarian, bolstered by an essentially totalitarian social matrix, allowing the legal (not the psychological) power of males and rulers to approach the absolute (Slote 38), thereby limiting women's accesses to civic services and thus the public decision-making mechanisms. True, the wife or the mother in traditional China might have been recognized as *ren* at home, to be obeyed by her children and respected by her husband, but she could not achieve the status of *ren* due to limited civil rights (she was not even allowed to appear in public). For this reason, the dominance of the Chinese family in terms of social structure and women's domestic power does not ensure a full range of women's human rights, because only those recognized as humans can compete for and be chosen to hold public service positions,[8] or administrative positions in contemporary China, to become thus members of the ruling class. Confucius's saying that he who labors with his brain is to rule, and he who labors with his muscles is to be ruled (*lao xin zhe zhi ren, lao li zhe zhi yu ren*) stratifies humans virtually into two social classes: the ruler in charge of public affairs and the ruled in obedience to the ruler. Only the people in the ruling positions are believed to have achieved the status of human. Therefore, by asking society to recognize women as human beings, Chinese women writers are asking for the basic human rights that ensure women's opportunity for education and leadership. They appeal for recognition that the same potential and intelligence required for professional careers, leadership, and upward social mobility exist in women as in men.

Their rhetoric, however, differentiates itself from Western feminist understanding of gender equality, which grows out of the conviction that "the best non-sexual society possible under the continuing hegemony of dualistic categories would be achieved through the promotion of females to the status of *honorary males*" (Hall and Ames 88, emphasis original). To claim that women are the same as men invokes precisely what post-Mao Chinese women writers worry about—gender sameness at the expense of sacrificing a range of female integrity that ought to be retained—because the same rhetoric in the Maoist era made them experience the most tyrannical abuses and grossest violations of human dignity in world history.

From the 1950s to the late 1970s, the slogans "men and women are the same" and "what men can do women also can do" dominated the Maoist women's liberation movement. Although women received equal rights to education and were mandated to participate in socialist construction outside the home, Mao's emancipation of women was based on the logic that women were liberated merely to join men to perform physical labor without intending them to be public leaders (except the very few that were appointed as "décor" to embellish the Maoist women's liberation), so it was legitimate to desexualize women to assimilate them into the male world. This logic kept male standards dominant and the norm, which justified the use of male standards to judge women. Accordingly, a woman had to lose her sexual identity in order to achieve gender equality. Womanhood was thus deemed inferior to manhood, embodying lesser human traits that had to be suppressed. As I have analyzed elsewhere (Wu, "Alternative" 221–22), during the Cultural Revolution from the late 1960s to the late 1970s, female dignity was impaired more than at any other time. Femininity was criticized as "petit bourgeois." Gender-specific apparel was condemned as a symbol of bourgeois lifestyle.[9] Love, beauty, emotion, courtship, gender relations, sexuality, and family life were privatized and thus forbidden to be discussed publicly.[10] Chinese women actually have lived without identity or acknowledged sexual differences for more than four decades (Wang 166). For this long period, China was a society where "woman" as a concept of human was virtually non-existent (Zhang Kangkang 265).

Consequently, having worked alongside men for four decades, particularly during the Cultural Revolution when female teenagers and college students along with their male counterparts were assigned to be factory workers, soldiers, and farmers, post-Mao Chinese women found that they had not only lost the integrity of woman but had yet to achieve the status of human. On the one hand, women's dignity as humans was derogated; on the other hand, there had been little intention to uplift women to the position of leadership,[11] in spite of the fact that women's self-confidence and consciousness of their own professional competence were greatly enhanced (see Zhong, Wang, and Bai *Some of Us*).

Women's condition in the post-Mao period proves that Chinese women writers' concerns are not without reasons. Since the institution of economic reform and the free market in the 1980s, the female body, after regaining its femininity, has been vastly abused for economic and ideological purposes. The tension between the role of liberated women and the traditional ideology about womanhood resurfaces with new problems (for example, see Vincent E. Gil and Allen F. Anderson's "Case Study of Rape in Contemporary China"). While under Mao's regime, urban women were all required to work outside their homes, now, as a way of efficiency, many state-run enterprises lay off women over thirty-five years old who have held low-skilled jobs. Additionally, it is harder for female college graduates to find professional jobs than for their male counterparts, because many female graduates are around the age when a woman is expected to be married and begin reproduction. The state policy that a female employee is entitled to receive paid maternal leave after giving birth works against women. To avoid the liability, businesses simply refuse to hire them. These are some of the reasons that post-Mao Chinese women writers cannot bring themselves to use the dualistic thinking of public/private. To them, liberating women does not only mean women working outside the home or competing with men physically or psychologically.[12] Women's liberation must entail empowerment and emancipation from patriarchal ideology. As Zhang Kangkang says, women "do not want merely to be like men; they want to be different from and more powerful than men" (266). This means to gain and hold decision-making positions, with an emphasis on women's leading roles at home and in public based on the mutual respect and support as well as shared responsibilities between husband and wife.

For these reasons, many post-Mao women's essays are dominated by the ethical consideration of the relationships between and among the individual, the family, the community, and the society. If traditional values are thought of as transmitted on different social levels and in diverse cultural contexts, rather than as cultural baggage constituting fundamental principles, then post-Mao women's essays simply reflect Chinese social values. In other words, if women want to gain public recognition as humans, Chinese women writers must take into account social and familial issues as well as human relations. They must also understand that under an autocratic political system, it is a life risk (not only a political risk), and thus not a realistic goal, to break down the traditional social format but to seek to modify the power structure and transform public attitudes. The concept of *ren* based on humanity and its position in maintaining familial and social harmony thus becomes the major strategy in post-Mao women writers' rhetoric, which sends the message that women's equal rights must be recognized as human rights. This is why their essays emphasize that an ideal society of gender equality is one where men and women live harmoniously on an equal basis with mutual respect and play reciprocal, and not separate, roles.[13]

The moral concerns and strategies in Chinese women's essays can enlighten our reading of Margaret Cavendish's rhetorical pieces.

Considering the specific oppressive culture indoctrinating gender hierarchy into women's minds, we can understand the anxiety displayed in her "Sociable Letters" when Cavendish apologetically offered her notion of eloquence, humbly confessing that she could not prepare orations as skillfully as men because of her limited access to a well-rounded formal education. Her jealous criticism of Aspasia for deviating from womanly roles is more understandable when we take her seventeenth-century audience into consideration. Like the temperance women in nineteenth-century America, she presented her ideas in a manner carefully crafted to appeal to members of high society like her husband who might not have been pleased with nontraditional rhetoric on gender morality. As Mattingly observes, the incorporation of traditional and progressive ideas may be a strategy that scholars often misinterpret as conservative (*Well-Tempered Women* 7). For example, while Cavendish may be read as supporting patriarchal values in the imaginary speeches, she may also be read as criticizing the oppression of women, when she says, "Men are made for Liberty, and women for Slavery, and not only Slaves to Men's Humours, nay to their Vices and Wickednesses . . ." (183). She might not make a commitment to both sides in her imaginary debates on the liberty of women, but she might be practicing arguing from both sides to model a learning experience that many ancient rhetoricians had proposed. If nothing else, it is at least a fact that a historical woman inspired by rhetorical tradition, and probably by Aspasia too, completed a collection of one hundred seventy-six pieces of eloquence. As Cavendish herself said in "To the Readers" (maybe with a sense of competing against men in the back of her mind), "[be]fore I did put this my Book forth, I did inquire, to find whether any Person had Composed and Put out a Whole Book of Pure and Perfect Orations, but I could neither hear of, nor see any such works of any person that Composed and Set forth to the Publick View, a Book of Pure Orations, Composed out of One Orators Own Fancy, Wit, and Eloquence" (4). The question we need to ponder is: If it is unfair for rhetorical patriarchy to exclude her collection of eloquence from its canon because the author was denied the access to the public podium due to her sex, is it fair now to discredit it again because some of her thoughts cannot be cut clean and straight to fit today's feminist dichotomies?

The complexity of the rhetorical reasoning of both post-Mao Chinese women writers and British writer Margaret Cavendish reveals that women's gender identity is neither inherently divisible nor autonomously existent but relational and contextually bound. The rhetorical interpretation of women's texts demands innovative, multiple analytical categories that can possibly initiate active knowledge-making processes in order to offer careful as well as accurate evaluations of their rhetorical practices. Drawing on the Chinese concepts of "human" and "family," my inquiry attempts to approach the questions of what counts in rhetoric and what counts as feminist rhetoric through a contextualized, correlative examination of gender politics reflected in post-Mao women writers' essays. This nondichotomous model tries to negotiate with the predominant, rigid theoretical frameworks for space to include the rhetoric of women of diverse cultural and historical backgrounds. Hopefully, the intricateness of "the phenomenon of Margaret Cavendish" and Chinese women writers' rhetoric can serve as a wake-up call to mainstream academic feminist critics, enabling the latter to realize that the evaluation of women's rhetorics must be firmly grounded in the pursuit of women's human rights and empowerment. Any assessment that separates women's discourses from their material realities and a situated awareness of gender politics would put the archival work on rhetorical women, and thus feminist rhetorical studies, at risk.

NOTES

I am thankful for Professor C. Jan Swearingen's reading of the chapter and supportive feedback.

1. Post-Mao women writers refer to those whose literary works have gained popularity since the end of Mao Zedong's era (1949–1976). Chinese critics also call them post-Cultural Revolution writers, who served as factory workers or farmers or soldiers during the Cultural Revolution from 1966 to 1978. Post-Mao writers usually do not include the writers of younger generations who have emerged after or during the economic reform (since the early 1980) without experiencing Mao's movement of women's liberation and the Cultural Revolution.

2. One of the reviewers of my grant proposal pressed this charge. In addition, on an almost identical note, while many of Cavendish's rhetorical pieces have been considered too short to be taken as serious rhetorical works (Sutherland 262), Chinese women's essays are also judged to be too short based on the standard of the Western essay. The limited space of this chapter, however, does not allow me to include a comprehensive study of this issue.

3. Critiquing these assumptions, some feminist critics have tried to single out the power of women's way of communication by theorizing the coerciveness of traditional public eloquence in opposition to the connectiveness of women's private communication, for example, Foss and Foss's *Women Speak* and the invitational rhetoric proposed by Foss and Griffin. This public/private approach confuses rhetorical discourses with personal writings, or ordinary communication, which men can also accomplish. They have yet to deal with the burden of what constitutes rhetoric (for this question, see Thomas Miller and

Melody Bowden; Hui Wu "Historical Studies" 89), because women now are no longer excluded from participating in civic/public activities. Celeste Michelle Condit challenges their "gender dichotomy approach" with a gender diversity theory, which, in spite of her attempt to transcend the dichotomies by embracing the complexity of race and class as well as male-female connections in shared public spaces, has yet to take into account women's rhetorics in other cultures and historical periods.

Also, gender sensitive critics of moral philosophy have recognized caring as a positive female trait in terms of family and gender relationships, for example, Carol Gilligan, Peta Bowden, and Chenyang Li. The recognition that caring embodies the sense of being responsible for the world, however, does not demonstrate its contributions to society similar to those of public services due to the binary thinking of public/private. The Chinese traditional belief that male public service is no more important than female caring in the home is where Chinese gender studies challenges Western feminism. See reasons in the rest of this study.

4. Chinese understanding of self does not entail such as strong notion of "individuality" as that in the West that is associated with autonomy, equality, liberty, and freedom (Hall and Ames 25). The Chinese self is realized through the consciousness of his/her roles and relationships, writer Hall and Ames. Hence, a Chinese person is "self-conscious, not in the sense of being able to isolate and objectify one's essential self, but in the sense of being aware of oneself as a locus of observation by others" (Hall and Ames 26).

5. Due to this contractual agreement on women's status of human, the identification of women's rights as human rights was delayed in Western feminism until it had been challenged by studies of race, class, and third world women. For the development of and controversy about this issue, see Clair Apodaca, Susan Moller Okin, and Elizabeth Riddell-Dixon.

6. I want to point out briefly that the discrepancy between Christian and Confucian traditions in the understanding of "human" creates communication problems in discussing human rights issues with China.

7. I must point out that Chinese women's material life, to a large degree, does not reflect this idealism in the Confucian tradition (see also Chenyang Li 109–110 and Margaret Wolf). See the following for more on this paradox. At this point of discussion, I prefer, for the purpose of arrangement, to sty on the track of the Chinese understanding of gender identity and virtues.

8. The civic examination designed to select the most talented for state rulership in traditional China (about 26 AC—late nineteenth century) excluded women from participating.

9. A personal note may help explain the extremity of the rhetoric. I remember in the summer of 1966 when I was walking in the neighborhood in a new sleeveless shirt and a pair of shorts in a sky-blue flora design, a middle-aged lady beckoned me to her and then warned me cautiously in a whisper, "Kid, how do you dare to wear such pretty clothes these days? Go back and change, if you don't want to get in trouble." Without her warning, I would have been stripped by the Red Guards on the street.

10. For example, though the Marriage Law protected marriages of personal choice, couples who wanted to get married had to obtain the endorsement of their institutes. Also, an unmarried woman in her late twenties or a divorced woman was often harassed by gossips and suffered from unfair institutional treatment. Many women were married out of family obligations or social pressure. Moreover, married women who gave birth to girls received family disapproval. But these problems were not allowed to be discussed openly.

11. Some women do serve as officials, including some who hold high rank in the state. But in the Maoist period, most of high-ranking women officials or administrators were the wives of top state officials or were considered necessary to orchestrate the Communist Party's political agenda.

12. Chinese history has witnessed their competitiveness on both levels. Hence, many contemporary Chinese women appear self-confident, strong, and independent, especially college educated women professionals.

13. Zhang Qingyun's "The Ideals of Contemporary Women" outlines what a contemporary Chinese woman desires: self-value, a strong character, career accomplishments, center of the family and her own day-to-day life in relation to her husband, the family, and society.

Chapter 13

"Making This Country Great"

Native American Educational Sovereignty in North Carolina

Resa Crane Bizzaro

Over the past ten years, many scholars have called for new examinations of the history of composition and rhetoric and the inclusion of the stories of others to give a more balanced view of the field (see, for instance, Gilyard, Villanueva, and Royster and Williams). As a result, the discipline has broadened to include a number of "new" voices. Inclusion of the stories of Native Americans has been slower to develop than those of African Americans[1]; however, in the recent past, *College Composition and Communication* has led the way in including voices of indigenous peoples, and essays published there have chronicled Native American use of rhetoric and language and the professional development of indigenous peoples.[2] These essays examine Native American sovereignty and social resistance to the dominant culture. To add to this conversation, this essay examines how the Lumbee exerted control (or sovereignty) over their educational system in North Carolina, and—in the process—made substantial contributions in the state.

One of the most salient aspects of the essays published in Native American rhetoric is that they use archival work—oral histories and documents from the past—to substantively change previously accepted histories, in particular that of higher education. In many ways, these essays attempt to change the dominant culture's perception of American Indians, which often has been based upon stereotypes, to a more realistic picture of Native Americans as groups of peoples with distinct histories, cultures, and values who continue to survive in a world dominated by European "invaders." Changing these stereotypes requires that we reconsider and rewrite history to accommodate the perspectives and contributions of indigenous peoples. Unfortunately, these stereotypes are pervasive in our culture and are difficult to eradicate. As a Native American scholar in composition and rhetoric, disrupting these stereotypes has become an important part of my research agenda. Examining history and hypothesizing how things might be for Native peoples, if a more inclusive version of that history is told, allows us to overcome negative and erroneous views and reveals the reality of the contributions of indigenous peoples. In North Carolina, these contributions clearly demonstrate Native Americans' commitment to the early and ongoing education of their people, in general, and their children, in particular. At this preliminary stage of my research, I can't say specifically what an all-inclusive Native pedagogy might privilege today, but it is crucial for scholars to consciously consider which strategies they will use to teach Native American students in a predominantly Caucasian country.

The necessity of revising our current history of education was emphasized to me when I picked up the Greenville (NC) *Daily Reflector* one day in September, 2001, and read an article titled "Legislator Apologizes for E-Mail." The story discusses a message sent by North Carolina Republican Representative Don Davis of Harnett County to all members of the North Carolina House. The message proclaimed that "two things made this country great: white men and Christianity." Like most conscientious people across the state, I was outraged at Davis's blatant racism and his deliberate omission of the many others who made significant contributions to this country's, and North Carolina's, growth and prosperity. After the uproar that ensued from the distribution of this message, Representative Davis apologized and issued the following statement:

> I humbly want to apologize if the e-mail forwarded from my office on Monday night was offensive or disrespectful to anyone in this General Assembly, state or nation. . . . The only reason the document was forwarded to each of you was for information and to show the type of messages that come across the Internet. My purpose in sending out the e-mail was for no other reason and was not intended to be indicative of my personal views. In fact, I made no personal comment with the

> e-mail, it was simply forwarded as information only. I am not now nor have I ever been a racist or white supremacist.[3]

It appeared this statement was intended to excuse Davis's behavior in a public forum; however, reading further in the article, an interviewer quoted Davis, who said, "There's a lot of it that's truth, the way I see it. . . . Who came to this country first—the white man, didn't he? That's who made this country great. . . . There's nothing racist about it."

Shortly after reading this article, and the flurry of responses that followed it, I received a letter in the mail that reported the ethnicities of students enrolled in institutions of higher education. I was not surprised to see that, of the number of PhD graduates in 1999, only two were Native American. I was one of those two.

These two events and my research into the deprivations in the nineteenth-century government schools established solely for American Indians made me wonder how Native peoples survived the American educational system—much less became "educated." But investigating notions of "education" reveals that the term often means teaching minority populations to conform to the dominant social order's notion of knowledge and, more importantly, to conform to behavioral standards. In 1938, Richard Wright described his struggle to educate himself, noting, "[I]t was almost impossible to get a book to read. It was assumed that after a Negro had imbibed what scanty schooling the state furnished he had no further need for books" ("The Ethics"). Lack of books is the least of the problems Wright referred to; history reveals inadequacies in funding, materials, and methods of teaching those materials for many schools whose dominant populations were minority students. No wonder Davis thinks white men made the country great; in many instances minority peoples were prevented from contributing or their works were marginalized.

Wright's statement could describe the education of all minority groups at the time and in the preceding century, as well. His essay also describes the hegemonic attitudes of other African Americans in the early part of the twentieth century. No doubt these attitudes were common among minority groups, since this notion of education seeks to reinforce the dominant group's ideology; that is, "educated" people have been taught to assume and keep their places in the social hierarchy. Certainly Native Americans were not immune to this type of "education." Intentional or not, significant efforts were made over five centuries to eradicate the cultures and languages of indigenous peoples in order to acculturate them to assume their places in the patriarchy in this country. These efforts are well documented (see Elk, Deloria, and others). Many Native Americans believe that the dominant culture's "education" of their children has stripped them of important and necessary cultural values, replacing them with values to keep Native Americans at the mere level of subsistence in a capitalist society and as "noncontributors" in a Caucasian-dominated society.

If we examine the historical record, an inability to contribute might have been enforced by the state of North Carolina. Government officials believed that if "we can teach the Indian boys how to farm and care for livestock they will be better farmers and make more money. If you teach the girls how to cook, how to sew, and how to select their clothes, they will all live better and be more contented" (Eliades and Oxendine 37). In actuality, the "Indian boys and girls" would become more "white," and the educational values taught in the schools encouraged conformity to this patriarchal system. Some scholars may feel that it is inappropriate to assess and criticize history from a much later perspective; however, if we do not reconsider our history from today, the contributions of others will *never* be discovered, acknowledged, and celebrated.[4]

Currently, research reveals that Native students suffer poor performance and high attrition in educational settings (see Hamrick). In colleges and universities there are a number of reasons for high failure and dropout rates among members of the group—including lack of cultural role models and community, institutional racism, underpreparedness, and difficulties with learning styles. These problems also may be exacerbated by the patriarchy's perception that Native Americans have not contributed to society. Native leaders must ask themselves what the low grades of Native students really mean; perhaps they don't indicate poor performance as much as they demonstrate resistance toward accepting a "place" in the social and economic order, a resistance to becoming "better citizens" in a social order that marginalizes them, their heritage, their culture, *and* their contributions.[5] The question that must ultimately be answered is this: What kind of schooling methods would exist today if the evolution of thought about how to educate Native Americans had not been interrupted?[6]

We might point out to Representative Davis that "white men" did not come to this country first. But to attack him for the obvious errors in his statements would be too easy. More to the point, I began to ask myself, "Why is it that our—that is, indigenous peoples'—contributions to the growth and development of this country have been overlooked?" In order to answer my questions—and to potentially reshape the recorded Eurocentric history of education—I began at a basic yet convenient starting point: the educational system in North Carolina. I wondered what, if any, accommodations had been made over the years for indigenous peoples not only to be educated but also to take their rightful places in business and government (positions for which education prepares us). North Carolina has the largest population of American Indians east of the Mississippi,[7] so it would seem that state government would have provided for their education over the years. As I searched through the historical records, I discovered some astounding progress made by Native Americans, in particular the Lumbee,[8] in the mid- to late-1800s. When the state permitted the Lumbee to officially develop and manage their own school, many people believe that indigenous peoples took a step in making significant contributions to the larger society of North Carolina. Although the record is not specific, it appears that for a short time (perhaps twenty years, at most), state-sponsored schools developed and followed their own curricula, so the Lumbee had some flexibility in determining what education their children received. Their school, the Croatan Normal School, developed in 1887, was the first school proposed, financed, developed, built, and—at first—staffed by Native Americans for Native American students.[9]

North Carolina Government: 1585–1979 reveals that, in 1776, North Carolina developed its own constitution, which was modeled after those of other states. This constitution was replete with archaic language, reading much like an ancient legal brief. One glaring omission—for Caucasian residents of North Carolina, at least—was that voting rights were not restricted solely to Caucasians. Any man who was over twenty-one and paid taxes could vote for House of Commons representatives, and any man who was over twenty-one, owned at least fifty acres of land, and paid his taxes could vote for Senate representatives. These laws gave minorities who met the guidelines an opportunity to influence all aspects of North Carolina law. Records show that many minority peoples—particularly Native Americans—were influential in elections and legislation because of their numbers. Their political support could have reversed the white patriarchy in public elections and in a number of land use issues. Although there were no Native American legislators, there were a number of Caucasian sympathizers and supporters for the "betterment" of indigenous groups. In addition, North Carolina's large population of Native peoples could influence legislation to overturn or change the educational system in North Carolina and resist their children's acculturation to the patriarchy, if they chose.

By 1834, however, many Caucasian citizens of North Carolina were dissatisfied with the age and inflexibility of the constitution for a number of reasons, so legislators met in Raleigh to revise it. One of the most heated issues was that of "Negro disfranchisement." According to Hugh Talmadge Lefler and Albert Ray Newsome, many free African Americans were politically allied with western North Carolinians; people from the western part of the state were, largely, intellectual; many westerners were quite liberal in their political views and did not own slaves. In addition, Native Americans across the state sided politically with the western Republicans and supported legislation to improve social conditions for minorities. Caucasian farmers and plantation owners from the eastern part of the state feared a loss of political and social control if support for western Republicans increased, so they introduced an amendment to take away the voting rights of African Americans and, later, of all nonwhites (845).

The resulting elimination of the rights of "Negroes" to vote was significant to more than the African American population. At the time, federal and state censuses placed Native Americans (who were referred to in state documents as "Indians") into the category "free person of color, not white." The amendment of 1834 specifically stated that "No free Negro, free mulatto, or free person of mixed blood, descended from Negro ancestors to the fourth generation inclusive (though one ancestor of each generation may have been a white person) shall vote for members of the senate or house of commons" (*NC Government* 820). Although this amendment did not specifically exclude Native Americans from voting, a later amendment did. The amendment of 1857 excluded Native Americans from participation in the electoral processes, when legislators ratified into law the additional provision that "every free *white* man of the age of twenty-one years . . . shall be entitled to vote" (emphasis added; *North Carolina Government* 823).

As a result of the amendments of 1834 and 1857, the Lumbee lost their rights to vote, bear arms, hold political office, and develop and run their own schools. The loss of educational opportunities was most significant, at least to this argument, since a Caucasian-dominated educational system would not instill Lumbee cultural values in its students; in addition, nontribal schools did not teach respect for Lumbee elders and their authority, a central tenet of Lumbee (indeed, of all Native American) ideology. New schools and instructors would not teach the history, evolution, geography, and importance of family and tribe to their Native students. The Lumbee feared that their loss of control over their children's education would help to eradicate forever the Lumbee as a people. These fears do not seem unfounded when we read firsthand accounts of nineteenth-century Indian schools across the country.[10]

In 1868, some rights were returned to Native Americans by amendments established when the Constitutional Convention allowed the Lumbee who could meet then-current requirements to vote. At that time, North Carolina also permanently established an education system for the state's children between the ages of six and twenty-one. This amendment reads:

> SEC. 2. The General Assembly at its first session under this Constitution, shall provide by taxation and otherwise for a general and uniform system of Public Schools, wherein tuition shall be free of charge to *all the children* of the State between the ages of six and twenty-one years.
>
> SEC. 3. Each County of the State shall be divided into a convenient number of Districts, in which one or more Public Schools shall be maintained, at least four months in every year; and if the Commissioners of any County shall fail to comply with the aforesaid requirement of this section, they shall be liable to indictment. (emphasis added; *North Carolina Government* 863).

The amendment did not specify any division among the races in educational settings; separation was implemented in post-Reconstruction amendments. Apparently, the education offered to Native students would be the same as that offered to privileged Caucasian students; Native—indeed all minority—students would be educated to standards that were intended to teach and reinforce the dominant social order of the state, to "fit them for the duties of American citizenship" (Eliades and Oxendine 22). This step legislated the acculturation of Native American students in North Carolina, another step in disguising the contributions of indigenous peoples to the state's advancement.

The North Carolina Constitutional Convention met again in 1875 and ratified an amendment stating, "[T]he children of the white race and the children of the colored race shall be taught in separate public schools, but there shall be no discrimination made in favor of, or to the prejudice of, either race" (863). Unfortunately, no requirements for funding or maintenance were set out in that document. Obviously, no specific provision was made for the education of Native American children in North Carolina. *Senate Report Number 204* stated that the state government attempted to compel the Lumbee to send their children to the Negro schools, but the Lumbee "preferred to allow their children to grow up in ignorance" (Oxendine 24). The report does not state the Tribal Council's fears that the Lumbee would lose their ethnic identity and the few legal rights they had been able to maintain if their requests for their own schools were denied.

In addition, the report did not mention the subscription schools, or private schools, that the Lumbee had established and continuously maintained since before the Civil War; subscription schools taught and reinforced Lumbee culture and tradition in addition to basic skills, such as reading and writing in English, to children. This instruction was offered to small groups of students who met in their teachers' homes; the teachers were overseen by community elders. The Tribal Council believed reading, writing, and knowing their people's history were essential for Lumbee children, who were growing up in a Caucasian-dominated and controlled state, to survive as individuals and as a people. Also, the Lumbee believed a school would help in their struggle for community identity and opportunity.

Clifton Oxendine, a Lumbee historian, notes that the Lumbee had never been under federal jurisdiction nor had they received any federal aid. As a result, they were ineligible for ongoing federal financial support, so for seventeen years they made unsuccessful efforts to acquire continuing state funds. Their first success came in 1885, with the assistance of Hamilton McMillan,[11] when the North Carolina General Assembly passed an act that gave legal identity to the "Indians of Robeson County" and allowed them to maintain schools of their own. The official bill states:

> Whereas the Indians now living in Robeson County claim to be descendants of a friendly tribe who once resided in eastern North Carolina on Roanoke River, known as Croatan Indians;
>
> Therefore; the General Assembly do enact; That said Indians and their descendants shall be hereafter designated and known as the Croatan Indians.
>
> That said Indians and their descendents shall have separate schools for their children, school committees of their own race and color, and shall be allowed to select teachers of their own choice, *subject to the same rules and regulations for all teachers* in the general school law.
>
> The treasurer shall procure from the County Board of Education the number of children in said county between the ages of six and twenty-one belonging to said Indian race, and shall set apart and keep separate their prorata share of said school funds, which shall be paid out upon the same rules in every respect as are provided in general school laws. (emphasis added; qtd. in Oxendine 25)

Upon ratification, this bill set a precedent for the state. Although the Lumbee had unofficially educated their children in subscription schools, the state of North Carolina was prepared to officially sanction and fund a public school for Lumbee students. Although this seems to be a great step, examining the legislation reveals that the government required Lumbee teachers to be certified by the state. The Lumbee instructors staffing the school would be trained according to then-current state standards, and they would pass on and reinforce the state's curriculum to their students, according to the law. The Lumbee served by the new public school would be educated as if they were Caucasian children, following the same methods used in predominantly Caucasian schools. This "homogenization" of Lumbee children would conceal their cultural identities, obscuring their contributions to the dominant social order.

Two years later, the General Assembly passed another landmark act that specifically mandated the establishment of the "Croatan Normal School." The primary purpose of the school was to educate Lumbee students, preparing them to be state-certified teachers at other primary and secondary Native American schools in the area, where they would teach following the state curriculum. This act reads:

> That W.L. Moore, James Oxendine, James Dial, Preston Locklear, and others who may be associated with them, and their successors are hereby constituted a body politic and corporate, for educational purposes, in the county of Robeson, under the name and style of the trustees of the Croatan Normal School and by that name shall have perpetual succession to have and hold school property, including buildings, lands, and all appurtenances thereto, situated in the county of Robeson, provided such place shall be located between Bear Swamp and Lumber River in said county. (qtd. in Oxendine 25)

This act also set aside five hundred dollars to support the school; however, a stipulation was attached that unless the Lumbee provided a building by the next session of the General Assembly the following year, they would forfeit the state's contribution. Not only did the Lumbee have to accept the Caucasian educational system, they also had to provide the building materials, money, and labor to house that system! The dominant patriarchal system was to be reinforced not only through the establishment of the school and its potential effects on students but also via the building schedule imposed on the school's board of trustees.

Failing to follow through on financial support of the school became characteristic of North Carolina state government. A "shortage of money plagued the institution for years" due to the North Carolina

Bureau of Indian Affairs' refusal to allocate appropriate resources (Eliades and Oxendine 23). Some Caucasian educators at the school worried that this lack of money might have serious consequences—such as decreasing the quality of education and the opportunities of graduates—and urged continuing support to fund school repairs and teacher salaries. These fears continued throughout the years; in his 1916 report, Principal Neal commented on the character of the Lumbee people, in general, noting:

> The Indian is not like the Negro. The Negro takes what we give him and pretends to be thankful whether he is or not, because he knows that is the best thing for him to do. The Indian will not do it. . . . Ninety per cent of the Indians believe the State is not doing its duty by them so far as a school is concerned. They resent it and harbor their resentment because it is the nature of the Indian to do so. But if the State will do a small part of what it should and furnish them a school they will respect, they will patronize it, be benefited by it and benefit us in return. (qtd. in Eliades and Oxendine 37)

Even without adequate resources, the Lumbee were determined to establish the school. In just a few months, the trustees and the Lumbee people raised money by public subscription from Caucasian and Native Americans. This money—along with donations of lumber, materials, and skilled labor—allowed the Lumbee to erect a school building that would have then cost one thousand dollars. The acre of land upon which the school sat was purchased from the Reverend William Jacobs for eight dollars. Clearly, the Native American inhabitants in the late nineteenth century were committed to providing their children an education—an opportunity to move up in the Caucasian-dominated North Carolina society. Their commitment is also a sign of their contribution to the education of *all* state residents, which they believed would have long-term effects on the state's prosperity and the tribe's survival. In addition, "historical developments, sometimes by default, made . . . [the school] the educational, cultural and social center of the Indian community" (Eliades and Oxendine 35). Since there was "no college in the State where the higher branches are taught that is open to the Indians," maintaining the normal school was an absolute necessity for the Lumbee (34).

By the fall of 1887, fifteen students were enrolled in the school, which was run by the Reverend W. L. Moore. Moore was an educator who gave up his job for two years to volunteer his services and help establish the Croatan Normal School in accord with the stipulations of the legislative act. In addition, he gave two hundred dollars of his own to the school's building fund and frequently paid for supplies from his personal account.

Unfortunately, even though the school was designated a "normal" school, no studies were attempted beyond the seventh grade for a number of years. This lack of a complete education stymied the development of teachers for the Native American primary and secondary schools. By keeping the normal school from full operation, the Caucasian citizens of the state reinforced and maintained the educational structure in North Carolina. It wasn't until 1905 that any kind of diploma was given, and that certificate was for completing the Scientific Course of study rather than for completing high school. When D. F. Lowry received this first certificate, he noted that students at the school were allowed to study "anything they could handle," much like the modern Montessori approach to learning. This rather "unstructured" way of learning reflects and reinforces Native American notions of the interconnectedness of all things; there was no need to break learning into artificial "categories" or "disciplines" for students.[12] In 1911, the school's name was changed to the Indian Normal School of Robeson County, but it wasn't until 1912 that the school had its first high school graduate.

In 1913, the North Carolina Legislature once again changed the name of the school, and it became the Cherokee Indian Normal School of Robeson County. The following year, two female students graduated with high school diplomas. For the next twenty-one years, a few students completed high school courses of study—including vocational training for both men and women—and the faculty slowly enlarged. By 1923, four faculty homes and dormitories for both girls and boys were established, and the following year the state high school inspector gave the high school a standard rating, which was an accreditation equal to ratings for Caucasian schools in the area. Although the records do not clearly state the criteria for such a designation, apparently the normal school had achieved the state's goal: to educate in the same manner as Caucasian schools supported by the state and, in the process, eradicate ethnic identities. During that year, the normal school—which was still not in operation—was separated from the high school and moved to another building. All of these activities were supervised and completed by the Tribal Council and Board of Trustees—an exclusively Lumbee group. However, they were still bound by the strictures of the education laws of the time.

In 1926 the first students were enrolled in the normal school, and in 1928 the school received full accreditation as a normal school with no work below the high school level. At that time, the Cherokee Indian Normal School also maintained the only standard high school for the more than 3,500 Native American school children in Robeson County. A few years later, in 1935, the Cherokee Indian Normal School began offering two years of college work in addition to the normal school curriculum, when they also organized a department focused on teaching deaf students. Although the school showed marked success in educating deaf students, the program was discontinued after three years due to expenses and an inability to retain qualified instructors (Eliades and Oxendine 51).

My research indicates several other important dates in the later history of the school. In 1928, the first students in the normal school graduated—apparently well prepared to "teach" their students—and began work in one of the six local high schools for indigenous peoples in Robeson County. More than ten years later, the school was renamed Pembroke State College for Indians, the year after graduating its first class of students with baccalaureate degrees. In 1949, the school's name was changed again, and it became Pembroke State College. In 1953, Pembroke State College permitted Caucasians to enroll after gaining the approval of the board of trustees. In encouraging Caucasian enrollment, it appears that the State Board of Education was issuing its imprimatur of Pembroke State as an officially sanctioned institution enforcing values. The culmination of Pembroke State's enforced conformity can be found in 1972, when it became a constituent of the University of North Carolina Systems and its name was changed to the University of North Carolina at Pembroke.

At this point, most readers would expect information about the various programs at the Cherokee Indian Normal School. According to common research practice in language studies, that information must be extracted and interpreted from the archives at what's now known as The University of North Carolina at Pembroke. The information available will need scrutiny by a careful eye, but I believe it will indicate continuing conformity. In fact, this method of research and its presentation is a commitment to the educational patriarchy, and I'm not sure there is value for indigenous people (or other minority groups) in following a pedagogical or research strategy that does not allow for all-inclusive ways of knowing. In addition, following the Caucasian-dominated investigation of history overshadows contributions made by others, including native peoples.

My next step in this research will be to visit the archives on campus, where I can investigate programs and their evolution. I believe we will find that Native American education in this state, much like that across the country, has been and continues to be dominated by the Caucasian educational system—which may not be the best way to educate Native American students. But that assumption is based upon my notion of education, which obviously is much more liberal and inclusive of a variety of learning styles than that of eighteenth- and nineteenth-century North Carolinians. Influenced by Vine Deloria's commentary on Native ways of learning and perceiving (see *We Talk, You Listen*), my notion of education—which requires teaching students to critically analyze processes, texts, and appearances—allows for a much fuller, more inclusive perspective on what constitutes learning *and* contribution than Representative Davis allows.

I'm certain that if I were to investigate North Carolina's state archives, I would find a number of areas in which Native Americans, African Americans, and other minority peoples have made equally great achievements and contributions to the development of the state and country. Unfortunately, those achievements are evaluated by the standards of the patriarchy and its representatives, including Don Davis of Harnett County, which means that these contributions can be further marginalized and ignored. It's unfortunate that there are still people like Don Davis, an elected public official who demands that we look through the limited confines of his historical perspective—what William Blake would call the "narrow chinks of his cavern" (33). Davis sees the part and fancies it the whole. Perhaps Harnett county voters will support Davis's opponent in the next election, and the patriarchal culture in their county will become more inclusive, recognizing the contributions of *all* its citizens.

NOTES

A very early draft of this chapter was presented at a featured session titled "Scholars for the Dream Tenth Anniversary Session: Connecting Our Pasts, Shaping Our Futures" at the 2002 CCCC in Chicago, IL.

1. Perhaps inclusion of these histories has been slow because of the low numbers of Native American scholars in composition studies: .46 of one percent by Villanueva's count. See "The Tree and the Woods: Racism in Multiculturalism."

2. See Lyons, Powell, and Crane Bizzaro.

3. Ironically, the source of Davis's original note was a website called "God's Order Affirmed in Love." The web address is *www.melvig.org*, and search engines list this site, and many others, under the category of "Hate Groups."

4. This notion of reception is forwarded by Hans Robert Jauss; for insight into this dilemma, see *Toward an Aesthetic of Reception.*

5. Indigenous peoples' social resistance and insistence upon survival is termed "survivance"; see Powell for a discussion of this term and its applications.

6. Obviously, this same question should and must be asked about African Americans and other minority groups.

7. The largest tribes include the Lumbee and the Cherokee.

8. The Lumbee have been known by a variety of names—including Croatan and Cherokee—over the past two centuries, but I will refer to them as Lumbee for consistency's sake.

9. Currently, this school is known as the University of North Carolina at Pembroke.

10. See Luther Standing Bear's firsthand accounts for examples of nineteenth-century Sioux education.

11. Hamilton McMillan was the Democratic state representative from Robeson County in the General Assembly; he originated the theory that the Lumbee are descendants of Sir Walter Raleigh's Lost Colony and the Croatan nation.

12. This approach to education was also followed at Black Mountain College in the 1940s.

Part III

(Re)Forming Analytical Paradigms

Chapter 14

Say What?

Rediscovering Hugh Blair and the Racialization of Language, Culture, and Pedagogy in Eighteenth-Century Rhetoric

David G. Holmes

All of my interests in the field of rhetoric and composition—black preaching, the cultural literacy debate, and civil rights movement rhetoric—converge at the places where the evolution of race ideology and the development of meaningful pedagogy meet. I have also remained intrigued with Hugh Blair, who in 1762 became the first professor at the University of Edinburgh whose title appended the phrase "Belles Lettres" to "Chair of Rhetoric." Given my interests, I wonder why rhetoric-composition scholars have rarely considered how canonical rhetoricians' ideas might contribute to current pedagogies that inadvertently exclude people of color. We should continue tracing the evolution of intellectualized racist discourses, wherever they might be uncovered, so that we might see more clearly the extent to which these discourses continue to impact theory and pedagogy.

James Berlin, Sharon Crowley, and W. Ross Winterowd acknowledge that both Blair's appointment and title illustrate a cultural shift in rhetorical history, one that Scottish academics enacted, as they became gradually more concerned with the art, rather than the science, of rhetoric.[1] They posit in particular that Blair's focus on fine writing contributed to the privileging of literature over composition and laid the groundwork for current traditional rhetoric. Moreover, they indicate that Blair, in the tradition of George Campbell, trivialized invention, contending that the rhetorician should be concerned primarily with negotiating the task of persuasion. Other scholars, such as Lois Agnew, argue conversely that while Blair's treatise centers on belles lettres, it does so to serve a public function. That is to say, Blair's treatise may not be as consumed with the individual writer's imagination as Winterowd, for example, assumes. Still, many scholars agree that Blair redirected if not restricted rhetoric beyond the obvious transition from oral to written discourse. I argue, however, that not only was the practice of rhetoric restricted, the practitioners were also restricted. In other words, Blair has left quite a legacy to composition, and we are obligated, therefore, to fully examine the implications of Blair's work, including its implications for teaching writing to students of color.

For instance, Hugh Blair's enterprise in his second lecture in the collection on belles lettres entails an ethnocentric standardization of taste. I am concerned with exposing the correlation between racist assumptions about the innate intellectual inferiority of people of color and the concurrent emergence of a style-centered view of written rhetoric. Put another way, when contemporary rhetoric and composition scholars read Blair, they should be able to recognize his participation in the widely accepted racialized discourses of his time and to understand more clearly the connections between rhetorical theory and the racist ideologies of the eighteenth century.

Substantial work has already been done that documents the history of African-American rhetorical practices. Shirley Wilson Logan's *We Are Coming* and Jacqueline Jones Royster's *Traces of a Stream* come to mind. Similarly, Keith Gilyard and Victor Villanueva have exposed salient interconnections among the past exclusion of peoples of color from rhetorical narratives and the contemporary politics of literacy. There exists a need to more closely examine icons of rhetoric, such as Blair, through these lenses.

A STORY WORTH RETELLING: MECHANISTIC RACISM IN THE EIGHTEENTH CENTURY

Henry Louis Gates Jr., among others, has traced the inception of "blackness as the ultimate signifier of nothingness" to the eighteenth century. For Gates, science and religion were not the only disciplines used to justify denigrating African Americans; art was as well. According to Gates, the need to condone slavery, specifically between 1730 and 1830, resulted in a fastidious critique of black literature unmatched until the Harlem Renaissance:

> After Descartes, *reason* was privileged, or valorized, among all other human characteristics. Writing, especially after the printing press became so widespread, was taken to be the *visible* sign of reason. Blacks were "reasonable" and hence "men," if—and only if—they demonstrated mastery of the "arts and sciences," the eighteenth century's formula for writing. (*Loose Canons* 54)

Race hypotheses, proposed during the eighteenth century, revolved around two ideas: (1) token deference to religious ideology, and (2) concession to the idea of hereditary inferiority of blacks, despite the so-called "natural rights" of all men, a gender-exclusive designation to begin with. Some of the founding fathers were deists; not all were theists. Yet the Christian God and the Old Testament are consistently employed to establish a given writer's credibility. For example, notwithstanding his affirmation that the African's inferiority was largely cultural, Thomas Jefferson actually accepted the notion of the African's innate inferiority, as suggested in his *Notes on the State of Virginia.* The religious ethos and the scientific ethos of the time period functioned as uneasy rhetorical allies to disenfranchise blacks, until the latter took center stage during the mid-nineteenth century.

Given the mechanistic racism of the eighteenth century, Blair's views on race and rhetoric should not be surprising. We would expect Blair to make the following problematical statement about people of color in his lecture on taste:

> I begin by observing, that if there is no such thing as any standard of taste, this consequence must immediately follow, that all tastes are equally good; a position, which, though it may pass unnoticed in slight matters, and when we speak of the lesser differences among the tastes of men, yet when we apply it to the extremes, presently shows its absurdity. For is there any one who will seriously maintain that the taste of a Hottentot or a Laplander is as delicate and as correct as that of a Longinus or an Addison? (Golden and Corbett 42–43)

Here, Blair focuses on the "deviations" from taste "in its most improved and perfect state." One of the characteristics of this most cultivated state of taste Blair calls "delicacy." For Blair, "delicacy" involves a degree of discernment that escapes the "vulgar eye" of someone from "one of the rude or unrefined nations" (Golden and Corbett 41). Delicacy includes the capacity to apprehend "the true merit of a work" and is mostly a "gift of nature" (Golden and Corbett 41–42).

Earlier in this lecture, Blair began addressing the nature and nurture polarity to illuminate his take on taste. To an extent an inclination toward taste is inborn:

> Taste, in the sense in which I have explained it, is a faculty common in some degree to all men. . . . Even in the deserts of America, where human nature shows itself in its most uncultivated state, the savages have their ornaments of dress, their war and their death songs, their harangues and their orators. We must therefore conclude the principles of taste to be deeply founded in the human mind. (Golden and Corbett 38)

On the other hand, taste is cultivated through education and culture and partly assessed through reason. For our purposes as rhetoric composition scholars, Blair views taste as a sensibility to be exercised by studying the great stylists and, as a result, improving one's own prose:

> Precisely in the same manner, with respect to the beauty of composition and discourse, attention to the most improved models, study of the best authors, comparisons of lower and higher degrees of the same beauties, operate towards the refinement of taste. (Golden and Corbett 39)

Both this passage and the one referring to Longinus and Addison demonstrate how nurture contributes to the evolution of taste; yet these passages also tout genetic superiority. Blair considers Longinus one of the classical models for delicacy. Hence, Longinus and Addison are juxtaposed with a Hottentot and a Laplander. Laplanders are geographically Europeans, residing in a land in the extreme north of the continent, but not culturally or ethnically Europeans. Of central Asiatic descent, most Laplanders were nomads, hut dwellers, or farmers.

COLLIDING CULTURAL CONSTRUCTS: COLORIZED PHYSICAL AMBIGUITY AND RACIALIZED LINGUISTIC DIFFERENCE

By the middle of the eighteenth century, Europeans were quite familiar with the people they called "Hottentots." This accounts for why allusions to the "Hottentot" pervade a wide array of texts during the eighteenth century. Georges Buffon's remarks in his *Natural History: General and Particular* are telling. Like Thomas Jefferson and a host of other eighteenth century thinkers, Buffon embraced the environmental explanation for the African's complexion. Buffon contends that the tropical heat, presumably more intense in western Africa than in either eastern or southern Africa, explained why the first group was generally darker than the second two groups. This observation lays the foundation for Buffon's depiction of the Hottentots, who hailed from South Africa. The Hottentots had yellowish skin and, hence, were of lighter complexion than the western Africans, whom Buffon and other eighteenth-century thinkers deemed "real Negroes."

Winthrop Jordan argues that Hottentots were deemed by some to be more savage than West African blacks, and that European travelers negatively associated the former group with the latter one. Conversely, since race, partly manifested by complexion, was a measure of intellectual capacity, other eighteenth-century European thinkers, such as Buffon, might deem racially mixed blacks brighter than the "pure" ones. Consequently, both Buffon's specific and general references to the Hottentots may signify the slightly less damning regard with which the eighteenth-century mind assessed the racially mixed group.

Additionally, Buffon's explication of "the real Negroes" may provide insight into Blair's statement about the Hottentots. True, the term *Hottentot* has been employed either to describe a people of color that once dwelled in South Africa or as a general epithet connoting savagery. However, that the Hottentots were not visibly *Negroid* to the same degree as western Africans is significant. Linda E. Merians agrees:

> According to Philip Curtin, the Restoration and eighteenth century mark the time when "culture prejudice . . . slid off easy toward color prejudice." Ironically many travelers at this time described the skin color of the people of the Cape in relation to whiteness and compared it with English and European skin tones. Indeed, the confusion over the skin color of the people of the Cape would be one of the reasons for their racial classification as Hottentot rather than "Negro." (129)

Merians further claims that some eighteenth-century descriptions of the Hottentots suggest that although their lips, noses, and hair were similar to those of western Africans, "their Skin is naturally as White as ours" (129). Hence, Blair places Hottentots at the bottom of his cultural chain of being, but that is considerably higher than where he might place Nigerians, for example. Like West Africans, however, and unlike Longinus and Addison, for Blair and other Europeans of his time, Hottentots are also a faceless group signifying cultural inferiority.

But Blair's myopic assessment that the Hottentots, and by extension other Africans, could not fully appropriate European style evinces more than Eurocentric standardization and cultural elitism. His assessment mirrors a larger practice of conflating language and genetics. In fact the name *Hottentots* illustrates this practice. Seventeenth-century Dutch settlers and other Europeans initially used "Hottentot" to pejoratively describe the language of the Khoikhoin people. To these settlers' untrained ears, the Khoikhoin dialect sounded like clicking.[2] The term *Hottentot* translates loosely from Dutch "stammers" and "stutters." The more accurate name *Khoikhoi* means "men" of "men." And although the expression "men" of "men" would hardly be appropriately inclusive for contemporary times, it demonstrates the strength that these South African nomads ascribed to themselves and, by extension, to their language.

Since the members of the Edinburgh literati revered English culture, it is not surprising to find the British also associating the name *Hottentots* with this group's cultural and linguistic inferiority:

> What was spoken by the people of the Cape, the English refuse to recognize as language; what was worn, they could not consider as clothing; what was danced and sung to, they did not see as worthy of religion; and the food or shelter that sustained existence, they could not judge according to its appropriateness. (Merians 127)

This is not to say that all depictions of Hottentots by Europeans were entirely derisive. Indeed, James P. Carson notes that eighteenth-century novelist Tobias Smollett actually critiques the cultural assumptions Blair, Buffon, and others embraced. Carson argues that Smollett's "abolitionist sentiments" compelled him to challenge the widespread tendency to construct British culture as ideal by contrasting it to the obviously *inferior* African culture.

Carson notes, however, that Smollett does his own juxtaposing of Africans and Europeans, specifically the Hottentots and the Scottish Highlanders (Western Islands of Scotland). Interestingly, Smollett focuses on similarities rather than differences. Many of the similarities were customs the Scottish Highlanders practiced for which Africans were denigrated as savages. For example, some British travel writers during the eighteenth-century deemed the Hottentot "delicacy" of animal "entrails boiled in blood" as a definitive sign of savagery. Smollett counters by discussing Scottish haggis, which "contains various innards and is boiled like a pudding" (Carson 485–88). Beyond these eating habits both groups, as pastoral people, "wrap themselves up in" their respective "garments for sleeping" (Carson 489). Likewise, both groups lived in huts with "an open hearth in the middle and no chimney except for a hole in the center of the roof" (Carson 489).

By underscoring these similarities, then, Smollett destabilized the geographical space between Europe and Africa; and thereby blurred the Enlightenment spatial binary of savagery and civilization. He further exposed the hypocritical dichotomy Merians noted that Europeans established "to separate the people of the Cape from their rich landscape" (Carson 127). Hence, eighteenth-century Scots needed not to brave the tumultuous tides of the Atlantic to *civilize* the *savages*; the Scots needed only to scale the hills of their homeland.

Granted, Blair would dissociate himself from the customs and speech of the highlanders, not to mention those practiced by the Scottish residents from his town of a lower-class station. But this is precisely the point. Blair and other members of the Edinburgh literati possessed a driving obsession to maintain the linguistic status quo, an obsession that, according to Paul Bator, pitted "strong Scottish patriotism" against "an earnest desire . . . to adopt plain English idiom and to remove Scotticisms from practical discourse"(41). Consequently, an almost irreconcilable tension emerged in which Blair and others of his ilk strove "to assert a national pride that was inextricably bound to their linguistic heritage" (41). During this period of strong nationalism, the rhetorical models in the Scottish universities shifted from classical to British.[3] As a representative of the Scottish elite, then, Blair would co-opt his homegrown dialect for the pottage of British standardization. Ideally, this strategy would enable Scots to avoid the fate of the Irish. Merians explains:

> There is great resemblance between late sixteenth and early seventeenth century English representations of the native Irish and the people of the Cape, and in some cases, the association is made quite directly. Once again Thomas Herbert can be our source. He found similarities, for example, between the native Irish language and people of the Cape: "their pronunciation is like the Irish: their customs not much unlike the rude ones of antique times." (130)

The above quote underscores two points about sixteenth- and seventeenth-century European perspectives on what we would now refer to as ethnicity and culture. First, the passage foreshadows how European perspectives on race would evolve during the eighteenth century and be codified during the nineteenth century. By the late eighteenth century the term *race* would be used to differentiate between groups of people we now call "white," including the Irish, Scots, and English. Secondly, Africa became a spatial metaphor for cultural deficiency; the farther a given country moved away from privileged European customs and practices, including speech practices, the closer that country descended toward Africa.

Descriptive, rather than prescriptive approaches to language study, reveal the folly of linguistic ethnocentrism generally and distorted views of phonology particularly. Producing sounds for speech involves a manipulation of airflow, partly with the lungs but mostly with the tongue, teeth, and lips. As Victoria Fromkin observes, English, and most of the world's languages for that matter, are "pulmonic egressive." "Pulmonic" refers to the lungs as the source of air for speech, while "egressive" refers to expulsion of that air. Whenever the air in the mouth is "sucked in" rather than expelled, as is the case for the Khoikhoi among other cultures, "ingressive sounds, like implosives and clicks, are produced" (223).

TALKING THE WALK: STANDARDIZED VOICE, VERNACULAR, AND THE COMPOSITION CLASSROOM

Whether or not Blair was aware of the etymology of the term *Hottentot,* he nevertheless participated in a larger, evolving trend to ignore the right of people of color to name themselves and privilege their language. And this constitutes the same type of thinking that led some nineteenth-century linguists to espouse the "thick lips theory" in order to explain reductively the phonology of African American Vernacular English. From the early nineteenth to early twentieth centuries, not only academicians, but also artists, using plantation fiction and minstrel shows among other media, employed orthographic distortions to codify African American linguistic diversity. More recently, the 1996 Ebonics controversy illuminates the American ethnocentric impulse to openly critique AAVE as deficient and to tacitly condemn its users as dim-witted.

That standards for language and literacy are largely controlled by the dominant culture is not a new theme within rhetoric-composition studies. Indeed our profession has been on the forefront engaging in cultural critiques of canonized discourses. Somehow Blair has escaped our, to borrow from Jacqueline Jones Royster and Jean C. Williams, "critical gaze" in this regard. Although Blair's biased statements about Khoikhoi, therefore, should hardly surprise us given the historical context, the tendency of rhetoric composition scholars to ignore the import of these statements for our profession is both surprising and troubling.

More broadly speaking, we have not allowed ourselves to challenge what Royster and Williams have called "officialized narratives." In their article, Royster and Williams argue that our American histories of rhetoric-composition have been canonized inadvertently in that they either exclude the voices of scholars of color or fail to fully allow those voices to articulate in their own ways. Royster and Williams challenge the profession to "resist" the impulse toward "primacy" of certain mainstream composition histories.

The myopia Royster and Williams wish to avoid in American histories of rhetoric could and should be applied to global histories of rhetoric. And both Blair's lecture on taste and our tendency to deify his work, albeit tacitly at times, attest to this need. To read Blair without setting a "critical gaze" on his depiction of the Khoikhoi is to avoid what insight might be found, borrowing from Royster and Williams, "in the shadows."

Writing teachers, therefore, should, ideally, expose their students to the South African rhetoric of the Khoikhoin people of Blair's time, as well as the multiple rhetorics of other African regions, peoples, and places. Composition rhetoricians would do well to begin with works such as Molefi Asante's *The Afrocentric Idea,* for a strong introduction to the contrasting rhetorics of eastern, western and southern Africa. Maulana Karenga's, "Nommo, Kawaida, and Communicative Practice: Bringing Good into the World," traces the ethical and communal aspects of African American discursive practices back to ancient African/ Egyptian rhetoric. And Henry L. Evans's, "An Afrocentric Multicultural Writing Project," explores how an Afrocentric worldview would broaden our understanding of African American students' learning styles and, thereby, could inform our composition pedagogy. Blair's discussion of the Khoikhoin people can serve as a starting point for such discussions.

Obviously, these discussions evince the necessity of including both African American and Euro-American critiques of Blair. As I noted earlier, many rhetoric composition scholars explicitly or implicitly critique occupation with fine style, among other features of Edited American English, as one of the foundations for current-traditional rhetoric. These types of critique are long-standing practices within our profession. Consider Sharon Crowley's *The Methodical Memory* and *The Students' Right to Their Own Language,* to cite a couple of examples.

Our students, however, still need to be encouraged to explore the evolution and implications of both the theories and the critiques. We should not feign historical amnesia but consider the assumptions upon which theories were based and how they have been used to enact and inscribe oppressive agendas, such as the racist discourses that were prevalent during Blair's era. The Scottish philosopher David Hume, for example, appropriated Aristotle's claim that some people are better suited for labor to justify African enslavement. So, while we may continue to value rhetoricians, such as Aristotle, in this case, and Blair, there is much to be acknowledged, interrogated, and critiqued.

Closer critical engagement with rhetorical icons allows both liabilities and benefits to become visible. Some of Blair's ideas, for instance, remain useful. Agnew argues that Blair could not have predicted the rhetorical practices in our composition classrooms, which for the most part center on writing, giving virtually no attention to speech. As a result, Agnew deems many of our criticisms of Blair to be off mark. For Agnew, Blair did not see taste as an end in itself. Rather, taste was a criterion for measuring discourse that would serve the purpose of "civic" communication. Agnew claims that Blair's lectures privilege oral discourse. This claim actually suggests a similarity between Blair's views and historical African American views on language. From its inception during the eighteenth century to the present, discussions on African American language, literature, and literacy have been framed within the tension between the spoken word and the written word, with the oral side being privileged generally. In those cases when the written word appears at the forefront, those texts must evince a respect for African American orality.

Curiously, Jacqueline Bacon and Glen McClish have argued that during the 1820s and '30s, African Americans founded literary societies in Philadelphia, in which the rhetors "appropriated" and "reinvented" the rhetoric of Hugh Blair and George Campbell (22–23). This fact takes on greater significance when one remembers the wide popularity of Blair's lectures among white Americans during the nineteenth century.

William Whipper, a businessman from Pennsylvania who was born free, serves as one of Bacon and McClish's striking examples. A founder of Philadelphia's Colored Reading Society, Whipper utilized and taught Blair's rhetoric with a new twist. He adopts Blair's view that orators can improve their sense of taste by studying great models of oratory and literature, yet Whipper opens that canonical space to include authors of African descent. Similar to Frederick Douglass and a host of other African American men and women, Whipper exemplifies two key points about African American rhetors, that they are at once capable of mastering and reshaping standardized European discourse.

The goal in reexamining iconic figures in our field is to clarify and deepen historical knowledge and also to lay a better foundation from which to develop better pedagogical uses for this knowledge. We must challenge students, including students of color, to critique Blair and others, to analyze ideological contexts, and to analyze purposes and consequences as well. Whether we see Blair as the progenitor of current-traditionalism or of fine oral style, the effort is neither to dismiss traditional contributions to the history of rhetoric nor to idolize them. We must take seriously all dimensions of this work and clarify the impacts and consequences of it for contemporary theory and practice. As a disciplinary field, what we cannot afford is canonization without well-deliberated critique. Our field boldly asserts that we value critical questioning. We should demonstrate this value in casting a more critical gaze on figures such as Blair.

NOTES

1. Paul Bator's essay traces Blair's emergence as Chair of Rhetoric and Belles-Lettres. Worthy of note is Bator's detailed analysis of the cultural factors that led to both Blair's appointment and his title.

2. For a fairly extensive discussion consult Bernard Makhosezwe Magubane's *The Political Economy of South Africa,* chapter 2.

3. Winfred Horner makes this observation in her introductory essay on eighteenth-century rhetoric in *The Present State of Scholarship in Historical and Contemporary Rhetoric* as well as in *Nineteenth Century Scottish Rhetoric,* which includes an extensive discussion of the eighteenth century.

Chapter 15

"By The Way, Where Did You Learn to Speak?"

Black Sites of Rhetorical Education

Shirley Wilson Logan

For centuries, curious observers have asked black speakers and writers, "How did you learn to use the English language so effectively?" Determined to answer this question, eighteen of Boston's leading citizens put Phillis Wheatley through an extensive oral examination and pronounced her, even though "brought an uncultivated Barbarian from Africa," sufficiently "qualified to write" her 1773 *Poems on Various Subjects.*[1] The authenticating documents accompanying slave narratives represent later attempts to answer this question. William Lloyd Garrison, in his preface to Frederick Douglass's *Narrative,* wrote that Douglass had written it in "his own style, and according to the best of his ability" and that it was "entirely his own production." These same kinds of supporting documents surround the narratives of Harriet Jacobs, Sojourner Truth, and others whom the white reading public felt the need to authenticate. A twentieth-century fictional version of this question is asked in Ralph Ellison's *Invisible Man* (1947) when the protagonist, after inciting a riot by addressing a crowd at the scene of a Harlem eviction, flees the scene followed by Jack, a member of the brotherhood. When Brother Jack catches up with him, he says, "You know, I haven't heard such an effective piece of eloquence since the days when I was in—well, in a long time. You aroused them so quickly to action, I don't understand how you managed it. If only some of *our* speakers could have listened!" He goes on finally to ask, "By the way, where did you learn to speak?" When the invisible man answers, "Nowhere," Brother Jack responds, "Then you're very talented. You are a natural. It's hard to believe."[2]

I use the term *rhetorical education* here to mean those combinations of experiences influencing proficiency in communication. This rhetorical education did not always include explicit training in rhetorical theory, but the application of theoretical principles occurred nonetheless. Aristotle writes in his introduction to the *Rhetoric* that "ordinary people" make use of rhetoric, "either at random or through practice and from acquired habit," adding that it is possible to inquire the reason why some speakers succeed through practice and others spontaneously" (1354[a] 6–11).

So, to return to a paraphrased version of Brother Jack's question, "Where *did* they learn to speak?" What were some sites of black rhetorical instruction, especially in the nineteenth century? Recognizing that some sites may turn out to be less significant than others, that all are not uniquely "black" sites, and that new sites will emerge, I offer the following eight: (1) imported African oral traditions of storytelling; (2) church-affiliated singing, preaching, and teaching; (3) sewing circles or "at homes"; (4) literary, benevolent, and debating societies and lyceums; (5) self-education, including private lessons in oratory and elocution; (6) political gatherings; (7) pamphleteering and the black press; and (8) formal instruction in black schools and colleges. I discuss only the first five, identifying some manifestations of rhetorical training in these sites. I close with an invitation to consider some of their implications for contemporary rhetorical education. I draw on the experiences of such black intellectuals as Frederick Douglass, Frances Harper, Charles Chesnutt, and Ida Wells, as well as those of less well-known rhetors like Mary Virginia Montgomery and Elizabeth Johnson Harris, making some tentative and cautious generalizations from their experiences to a wider population. In future research, I hope to discuss the rhetorical training embedded in all of these settings.

IMPORTED AFRICAN ORAL TRADITIONS OF STORYTELLING

First, it is important to remember that many enslaved Africans were brought to the Americas already literate, able to read and write in their native languages. They were "illiterate" only to the extent that they lacked facility in the oppressors' languages. Many literate Muslim slaves left documents in Arabic and transcribed English into Arabic (Matory).

They also brought with them oral traditions of storytelling that preserved cultural wisdom and enabled memory and delivery, the last two rhetorical canons. Sterling Stuckey writes of this tradition in *Slave Culture.* He points out that the tradition of storytelling prevailed among enslaved Africans in Connecticut as well as in the deep South, that it was a primary method of teaching important lessons and further that many of the storytellers during the last half of the eighteenth century were, in fact, first generation Africans, who, as such, told those stories drawn directly from "African cultural resources"—often in their native tongues (78). He observes that recognizing the facility with which children on the sea islands of Georgia mastered the ring-shout dance traditions of their ancestors enables an understanding of how other cultural traditions, such as the gifts of improvisation, oratory, and song, were transmitted as an "unconscious ornament of the child's inheritance" (88). One example that this practice continued late into the nineteenth century can be found in the handwritten autobiography of Elizabeth Johnson Harris. Harris, the daughter of former slaves, recorded memories of growing up in post–Civil War Augusta, Georgia. On long winter nights, her grandfather told her of "wonderful and terrible happenings during the days of slavery—including Ghost Stories, which he said all were true and many experienced by himself" (Harris 11).[3] She admitted that although the tales frightened her she "liked to *hear* him tell them" (11; emphasis added). The joy derived from the sound of the telling pleased her most. The oral tradition of storytelling among the enslaved instilled respect for the spoken word and preserved ancestral wisdom and culture. Many slaves who could not read committed these stories to memory. Preachers often impressed audiences with their ability to recite long chapters from the Bible and the Catechism.

RELIGIOUS SINGING, PREACHING, AND TEACHING

From secret worship services in slave assembled "hush harbors" and camp meetings to publicly held and carefully prescribed services of such religious bodies as Richard Allen's African Methodist Episcopal Church, religious singing, preaching, and teaching provided many opportunities for rhetorical performance and education.

Frederick Douglass's experiences as a class leader, exhorter, and licensed preacher in New Bedford's A. M. E. Zion Church may have been the greatest influence on his polished oratory. To become an exhorter, Douglass had to pass an examination and deliver a mini-sermon or exhortation in the presence of the congregation and various church officials. He was first licensed as an exhorter in 1839; however, the license had to be renewed annually. As Gregory Lampe has pointed out, although it is not clear how often Douglass exhorted the congregation, church guidelines required that exhorters be allowed to speak frequently (39–40). These regular required performances contributed to the rhetorical education of many young *men* such as Frederick Douglass. One author notes, however, that during the antebellum period, at least in the Bethel A. M. E. Church of Baltimore, even though women outnumbered men more than two to one, women never held the position of class leader, exhorter, or minister (Phillips 135).[4]

In her memoirs, Harris recalled the religious gatherings or "old-time Bush meetings," held in bush harbors built in open fields: "[D]uring summer seasons . . . hundreds would attend from near and far. Many came to the early morning service, and would remain until the last services at night." During these gatherings there were many opportunities for exhorting, testifying, preaching, and other forms of oral expression. In the antebellum South, by law in some states, blacks were forbidden to assemble in groups of more than five, providing added incentive for these "hush harbor" or "brush harbor" meetings. Albert Raboteau notes that slaves devised a number of methods to avoid discovery, meeting in secluded places in woods and thickets, huddling behind quilts and rags dampened to absorb the sound of their voices, kneeling in a circle in order to speak over a vessel of water, placing an iron kettle in the center of the group to catch the sound. They frequently did not need a preacher because everyone wanted to say something (215-18). That these antebellum rhetors took such risky steps simply to have the opportunity to speak, shows the extent to which oral expression was valued and nurtured.

SEWING CIRCLES OR "AT HOMES"

I named this site "sewing circles" to represent those parlor spaces where black women and frequently men gathered privately in homes to discuss matters of common interest. In 1871, Frances Harper wrote of engaging in private conversations with poor women in post–Civil War Greenville, Georgia. At the other end of the social scale, Anna Julia Cooper wrote excitedly of her early years in Washington, D.C., and the regular weekly get-togethers in her home with Charlotte and Francis Grimké, Edward Blyden, Mrs. Frederick Douglass, and others to discuss art, politics, literature, and religion. She describes these gatherings as "systematic and enlightening but pleasurable and progressive intercourse of a cultural and highly stimulating kind" (Lemert and Bhan 311). Sites of domestic rhetorical activity were also re-created in black women's fiction. For example, in "The Sewing Circle," a chapter from Pauline Hopkins's novel *Contending Forces,* women gather at the Smiths' boarding house to sew and to debate "events of interest to the Negro race." In Hopkins's account these "parlor entertainments" were frequently held to raise money for specific events. Once the sewing tasks had been assigned, the business meeting convened with a review of the past week's events and closed with a talk by a prominent senior woman of the community. At one gathering, a Mrs. Willis spoke on "[t]he place which the virtuous woman occupies in upbuilding a race." Only after the close of the business meeting were the men invited to join them for socializing (143–48). Frances Harper's novel *Iola Leroy,* devotes one chapter, "Friends in Council," to a *conversazione,* in this case a gathering of "some of the thinkers and leaders of the race to consult on subjects of vital interest to our welfare" (243). Both men and women assembled to consider such matters as black emigration to Africa, patriotism, the education of mothers, and the moral progress of the race. Each speaker opened with a prepared paper on the topic followed by extended critical discussions. It is worth noting that the two women present at the meeting in Harper's novel, Iola Leroy and Lucy Delany, participated in these discussions on equal footing with the men.

Rhetorical performances that took place in parlor rooms rather than in so-called "public" spaces gave participants the opportunity to hone their rhetorical skills in more intimate settings and ultimately in alternative public spheres.[5] Lauren Berlant points out that by being "performatively democratic," these gatherings helped make counterpubic spheres "more permeable by women and the ethnic and class subjects who had been left out of aristocratic privilege." She adds that they learned "to construct a personal and collective identity through the oral sharing of a diversity of written ideas" (237). Thus, such meetings existed as sites of rhetorical education.

LITERARY, BENEVOLENT, AND DEBATING SOCIETIES AND LYCEUMS

African Americans also formed a number of societies designed first for self-improvement and subsequently for general racial uplift, variously called literary, educational, benevolent, and debating societies or lyceums. Their development paralleled but rarely intersected with the history of the predominantly white American lyceum movement, which always had a community orientation, in that lectures, plays, and debates were held in public spaces. Opportunities to speak on such occasions provided valuable practice for many who later became lecturers for the antislavery cause. Carl Bode links the rise of the lyceum movement to the Age of Jackson, around 1828 when Andrew Jackson was elected president. The first American lyceum was established in 1826 for the purpose of providing a practical and inexpensive education for youth, information to the community generally, and practical applications of the sciences (Bode 11–14). Organizations such as the Philadelphia Free African Society, organized in 1787, prefigured this rise. These societies established libraries, discussed books, and debated current issues, giving participants practice in public speaking. Douglass, for example, was the only enslaved member of the East Baltimore Mental Improvement Society, and Ida Wells, soon after moving to Memphis, joined a literary club that met weekly for recitations and debates. She described these meetings as a "breath of life," reminding her of grade school oratoricals (Decosta-Willis 33–34).

In an 1881 speech, "Advantages of a Well-Conducted Literary Society," delivered at a meeting of the Normal Literary Society of Fayetteville, North Carolina, Charles Chesnutt stressed the importance of learning to speak coherently and convincingly through practice. One of the chief advantages of a literary society, he observed, is that it teaches the rules of argument and helps one to develop self-confidence to stand "without trepidation before a real audience, and discuss questions of public moment" (*Essays* 18). With this statement, Chesnutt links rhetorical training to social action, later adding that oratory has never been an art practiced primarily for its own sake but is always associated with some cause. He ends this speech with the rule that the goal of oratory is "truth, and not victory" (23).

Later in the century, Kelley Miller, Alexander Crummell, and W. E. B. DuBois helped to establish the Negro Academy to counter the racist discourse in documents such as Frederick Hoffman's 1898, *Race Traits and Tendencies of the American Negro*, purporting to demonstrate the genetic inferiority of blacks. The academy provided a site for the production of a range of rhetorical responses to such claims.

SELF-EDUCATION, INCLUDING PRIVATE LESSONS IN ORATORY AND ELOCUTION

Because oratorical performance was valued highly in the nineteenth century, many ordinary citizens, not preparing to be lawyers, preachers, or public servants, took private elocution lessons to improve themselves. Elocution was also taught regularly as a school subject that prescribed rules governing posture, gesture, facial expression, and movement. At the Watkins Academy for Negro Youth, Frances Harper was trained in elocution. Wells took intermittent elocution lessons depending upon her finances, expressing disappointment when lack of funds prevent her from going out "not even to take a lesson" (Decosta-Willis 44). Hallie Quinn Brown, an older contemporary of Wells, was a practicing elocutionist and professor of elocution at Wilberforce College. Brown authored three books on elocution, *Bits and Odds: A Choice Selection of Recitations* (c. 1880); *Elocution and Physical Culture* (c. 1910), a textbook; and *First Lessons in Public Speaking* (1920). Extolling the value of elocution, she wrote in *Bits and Odds* that it "gives mental and moral strength, great power, and a wide social influence to all who will take the time and patience to master it" (qtd in Donawerth 346). She also wrote that elocution was a source of empowerment for women: "Thanks to elocution, the sickly, young lady with her puny form and wasp waist, is being supplanted by the strong, vigorous woman, who is to preside in the home and to move to and fro over the land as a queen among men" (qtd. in Donawerth 344).

Mary Virginia Montgomery's diary reveals a practice that best fits the definition of self-education as regular, disciplined approaches to rhetorical education, initiated and carried out for self-improvement. I offer first the diverging examples of Ida B. Wells and Charles Chesnutt.

Always a voracious reader, Wells's rhetorical training was influenced by the Bible and such writers as Charles Dickens, Louisa Alcott, Charlotte Bronte, and William Shakespeare. She wrote that during her early years she "never read a Negro book or anything about Negroes" (Duster 22). Wells's interest in public oral performance led her to take elocution lessons from a Mrs. Thompson at two dollars a session, even when she had little money. She was sharply critical of the preaching style of one minister because his sermon lacked the reverence required in "dealing with holy things" being too similar to a public lecture he had given earlier (39).[6] Wells's comment here marks a preference for clear distinction between what rhetorician Hugh Blair, author of a popular nineteenth-century rhetoric text, called the eloquence of the popular assemblies and the eloquence of the pulpit and the bar (Golden and Corbett 99).[7] Later in the diary, however, she questions why many preachers did not give people the kind of practical information needed for everyday living, information usually associated with the eloquence of popular assemblies.

Certain entries in the *Journals of Charles Chesnutt* provide an unusual record of the daily actualities of black schooling in the postbellum South. Chesnutt, fiction writer, essayist, and public speaker, mentions that he had been studying Quackenbos's *Composition and Rhetoric* and writing practice essays. Chesnutt had accomplished a great deal "largely through a strenuous self-education regimen" (*Essays and Speeches,* xxv), assisted by access to a local citizen's well-stocked library. Without a high school diploma, at the age of sixteen he taught at and was subsequently principal of the Fayetteville Colored Normal School. An October 1878 journal entry is actually a précis of Lecture X: "On Style—Perspicuity and Precision" of Hugh Blair's *Lectures on Rhetoric and Belles Lettres* (1783), a standard text in American schools in the eighteenth and nineteenth centuries.

Another Mississippian who also kept a diary some thirteen years before Wells began hers was Mary Virginia Montgomery. Born in 1849, Montgomery spent the first sixteen years of her life in slavery on a plantation near Vicksburg, Mississippi, run by Jefferson Davis's brother. Given certain opportunities not usually afforded to slaves, Montgomery's father helped to run the plantation and for a short period hired a tutor for Mary Virginia. After the war ended, her father purchased the property and Davis Bend developed into a thriving black community even during the turbulent years of Reconstruction. Frances Harper, an older contemporary, commented on the lifestyle she observed in Davis Bend during a 1871 visit there. Harper was especially impressed with the kinds of work women such as Mary Virginia and her mother performed, writing that they were "one of the most interesting families I have ever seen in the South" (Still 774–75).

Information on her rhetorical education comes primarily from portions of a diary, covering the period from January 17, 1872, to December 28, 1872. The diary also provides a rare account of the daily activities of a young black woman, living a relatively comfortable but busy life, on a postwar former Mississippi slave plantation. Montgomery maintained a rigid schedule of household responsibilities, work at the family store, and an ambitious self-education project, reading at every spare moment and before retiring. Although this reading was no doubt based on her hopeful anticipation of matriculation at Oberlin College, it is also clear that she enjoyed it.

For one entry, she wrote, "Beautiful morning. I have so much to do that I hardly know how to begin (1/17).[8] She sewed, played the piano, and worked in her mother's flower garden, but her ultimate pleasure seems to have been reading. She notes at the close of one early entry that she has decided to "forgo book pleasure" because of illness (1/26). Among the material she particularly enjoyed reading over this twelve-month period were two works titled "Self Education" and "Self-Culture." She does not mention an author and might have been referring two different works since "self-education" and "self–culture" were often used interchangeably to refer to self-improvement of the mind.[9] Montgomery also read the Ten Commandments, books on phrenology, mineralogy, the Punic Wars, zoology, chemistry, United States history, and parallel histories of the construction of Babel. She enjoyed reading Cowper's "The Task" and Plutarch, whom she found "difficult for fast reading" (6/20). She also read Tennyson, Dryden's translation of Virgil, Byron, and Darwin's *The Origin of the Species*, noting that "[i]t bids to be interesting and will entertain me many nights" (4/16). Calling reading a "great recreation," she enjoyed the *New York Times*, *Harper's Bazar* [sic]:*A Weekly Journal of Fashion*, and *Demorests' Monthly Magazine.*

Montgomery also wrote her own compositions and critiqued the written and oral productions of others. She practiced and studied Parker's *English Composition* in the evenings.[10] On an unexpected day off she began an essay on the "situation and requisites of the colored people everywhere" (4/26). Another source of ideas and inspiration was Maturin Ballou's compilation *Treasury of Thought*, an encyclopedia of quotations, which she noted would "serve as a reference when engaged in composition" (10/1).

Diary entries also demonstrate attention to public speaking and politics. She read a great deal of history during the summer months and followed in the *New York Times* the divisiveness surrounding the election of Congressional representative George McKee. After hearing one political speech, she commented regretfully that the speaker was "intellectually unable to do the subject justice" (10/16). The family often discussed their readings together. Once she enrolled at Oberlin, her reading relates to class assignments, with other study time devoted to grammar lessons, recitations, and rhetorical exercises. Montgomery returned to Davis Bend in 1874 and taught school.

Ida Wells, Charles Chesnutt, and Mary Virginia Montgomery were typical of many nineteenth-century black rhetors who relied on self-education, along with various levels of formal training, to improve their rhetorical skills.

SOME CAUTIONS

It should be clear then that I have not been describing an idyllic time, chock with opportunities for rhetorical education. At the close of the nineteenth century, the vast majority of Southern blacks were classified as illiterate. In 1900, the total number of black college graduates in all the Southern states was 131, with none listed in my current home state—Maryland (Anderson 112). Still, W. E. B. DuBois, in his sociological study the *Philadelphia Negro*, reported that in 1896, while some 18 percent of all black Philadelphians were categorized as totally illiterate—neither reading nor writing—this percentage was far below that of five other ethnic groups, including Italians (64 percent), Russians (42 percent), Poles (40 percent), Hungarians (31 percent), and Irish (26 percent) (92).

Throughout this chapter I have offered examples of both men and women who acquired varying levels of rhetorical education in a number of ways. The apparent randomness of examples may belie significant gender differences that complicate these narratives further. While I set out to consider black sites of rhetorical education *in general*, these differences cannot be ignored. My examples draw heavily on the experiences of the nineteenth-century black women I study. But black women's acquisition of rhetorical skills in the United States came almost always at a greater price and with greater challenge to the status quo. Enslaved women, with stronger ties to children, were less free to move about than were enslaved men such as Frederick Douglass, who could barter for literacy on the Baltimore docks and ultimately escape North. Frances Harper and Sara Parker Remond were not typical of most Northern antebellum black women struggling to make a living. One disadvantage of putting forward such women is that, while their accomplishments were significant and need to be remembered, they do not represent the experiences of most ordinary women, who never delivered addresses or left written records. But the same can be said of the men. Further, after emancipation, attitudes toward the education of women shifted. The passage of the Fifteenth Amendment in 1870, granting black men the vote, signaled the first major gender distinction made among blacks by the government. Society during the 1880s and '90s grew increasingly patriarchal, and black men fully internalized the concepts associated with Victorian manhood, glorifying homemaking and encouraging women to educate themselves for lives of domesticity. Thus, while to some extent the sites of rhetorical education for black men and women were similar, gender differences must not be dismissed.

In addition, I do not mean to argue that literacy—an essential component of rhetorical training—only comes in communities with schooling, although formal schooling is an effective source of mass literacy, for that has clearly not been the case. Nor do I subscribe to what Harvey Graff calls the literacy myth, the belief that literacy is the most potent driving force in social change. Douglass never attended school; Frances Harper's formal schooling at the Watkins Academy for Negro Youth ended when she was thirteen; the assumption is that Mary Ann Shadd Cary never received any formal education although some sources say that she was educated in a Quaker school from the age of ten to sixteen. Charles Chesnutt, a writer and lecturer, received a solid education at the Howard School in Fayetteville, North Carolina, until he turned sixteen and began to teach at a similar school in Charlotte; at sixteen, Ida Wells also began teaching in a country Mississippi school after attending Rust College in Holly Springs; Fanny Coppin, a graduate of Oberlin, became head of a Philadelphia school for black youth; and Alexander Crummell, an Episcopal priest, received the BA degree from Queen's College, Cambridge at the age of thirty-four. Thus, in these eight rhetors we have a broad range of educational backgrounds. While they all used language to effect, their rhetorical skills were shaped by an impressive array of educational influences, and they are still not representative of the whole.

For us today, "Where did you learn to speak?" is not merely, then, what one graduate student called "a white question," prompted solely by curiosity. Rather, it is driven by urgent contemporary educational exigencies. Robin D. G. Kelley, in his foreword to *White Architects*, summarizes their salient features:

> A crisis-ridden public education system characterized by massive budget cuts, crumbling buildings, overcrowded classrooms, and a curriculum that measures success by standardized tests. A book arguing for a correlation between race and intelligence (guess who has the lowest IQ?) on the best seller list. The swift dismantling of affirmative action programs, especially on college campuses. A *Democratic* welfare "reform" law that excludes higher education in its definition of work or "training programs" and, instead, limits welfare recipients to vocational programs. (xii)

My hope is that this chapter will reshape our understanding of U.S. rhetorical education then and now. We need to recognize the various ways in which people can acquire and have acquired rhetorical knowledge. A broader definition of rhetorical education might help us answer important questions: What are the sites of rhetorical education today? What new sites have replaced those no longer in existence? How confidently can we as teachers and scholars of rhetoric and composition answer the question, "Where and how will our students learn to speak?"

NOTES

1. The full text of the letter "To the Publick," prefacing Wheatley's volume, reads as follows:

> We whose names are under-written, do assure the world, that the poems specified in the following page, were (as we verily believe)

> written by PHILLIS, a young Negro Girl, who was but a few years since, brought an uncultivated barbarian from Africa, and has ever since been, and now is, under the disadvantage of serving as a slave in a family in this town. She has been examined by some of the best judges, and is thought qualified to write them. (Gates and McKay 167)

2. The parallels between Ellsion's invisible man and Frederick Douglass are worth noting. The invisible man was employed in the service of the Brotherhood specifically because of his facility with language in much the same way that Douglass was used as an instrument of the antislavery movement, with William Lloyd Garrison as Brother Jack. Further, like Douglass, the invisible man escapes to the North and "freedom" where the Brotherhood attempts to control what he can say, just as Garrison's attempt to censure Douglass led to his separation from Garrison's organization.

3. The appendix to Harris's memoirs contains one of these stories, "The Calf and the Ghost" In the story, one afternoon, Grandpa, a young boy, fell asleep under a tree and was late completing his last chore, bringing the calf back to the pen. With night approaching, he started out to retrieve the calf and discovered that he was being accompanied by a" black calf" with red eyes. This "black calf" followed him home, where Grandpa collapsed in fright. No doubt, for his young listener, the tale carried a strong warning against procrastination in completing chores (Harris, Appendix 4).

4. Phillips notes that between 1825 and 1853, Bethel A.M.E. enrolled 873 women and 407 men; during that same period, thirty-six men became class leaders.

5. The term *alternative public spheres* resists the notion of one privileged white male–dominated public and recognizes instead the always already existence of many publics. The issues acknowledged as "public" in the nineteenth century were those articulated, recorded, and perpetuated by property-owning, literate white males, who had the ability to endow them with salience. An issue had the potential to become of "public" interest, that is, to be debated openly, when it appeared to affect the lives of those in power. A black counter-public emerged, in part, in response to exclusion from such public deliberations, but only in part. Sites of black political activism provided not only an alternative space, but a much needed separate space in which to deliberate about "race matters" and to develop strategies for entering and thereby disrupting mainstream discourse.

6. Wells's notion of purpose-driven delivery is reflected in later remarks to Douglass. While both were waiting backstage to speak before an 1894 meeting in Providence, Rhode Island, Douglass asked her why she was not as nervous as he was. She replied: "That is because you are an orator, Mr. Douglass, and naturally you are concerned as to the presentation of your address. With me it is different. I am only a mouthpiece through which to tell the story of lynching and I have told it so often that I know it by heart. I do not have to embellish; it makes its own way" (*Crusade* 231).

7. Hugh Blair, in *Lectures on Rhetoric and Belles Lettres* (1783) asserted that the eloquence of popular assemblies, though based on logic, was the most animated form of public speaking, a form easily arousing passion.

8. Quotes from Montgomery's diary are taken from excerpts in Dorothy Sterling's collection *We Are Your Sisters* and from the original document in the Montgomery Family Papers in the Library of Congress. Month and day of entry are enclosed in parenthesis following each quote.

9. Since Montgomery was engaged in a project of self-improvement, it is possible that these were how-to manuals for self-education. Given her interest in phrenology, she may have been reading about the possible connections between this pseudoscientific belief that the human mind can be divided into several organs or regions, each controlling various mental faculties, and mental development, a subject covered, for example, in Orson Squire Fowler's 1841 book *Phrenology and Physiology Explained and Applied to Education and Self-improvement.* The book dealt with mental discipline, the cultivation of memory, and methods of increasing and decreasing the phrenological organs.

Following one period of reading "Self-Culture" Montgomery remarks "I must say it is an excellent book for the mind." (2/26) and later notes that her father enjoyed reading "Self Culture" as much as she. Montgomery was possibly referring to William Ellery Channing's "Self-Culture: An Address Introductory to the Franklin Lectures" delivered at Boston in 1838 to the Mechanic Apprentices' Library Association. Such series of lectures flourished during the 1830s and 1840s and were established to educate working-class people. Channing (1780–1842), emphasizing the need for mental improvement for persons from all stations of life, defines self-culture as "the care which every man owes to himself, to the unfolding and perfecting of his nature" (11). Although in other writings Channing opposed slavery on the moral grounds that it degraded the slave, removing from him the ability to cultivate moral and intellectual faculties; he argued that the institution should be eradicated without violence or condemnation of the slaveholder. It is clear that the essay "Self-Culture" was addressed to working-class white men. Reading it in 1872, Montgomery may have been more interested in his views on self-improvement than his implied views of slavery (for a critique of "Self-Culture," see Broaddus 82–83).

"Self-Education" could refer to *Self-Education: or, The Philosophy of Mental Improvement* (1847) by William Hosmer, also author of *Slavery and the Church* (1853), in which he argues against the claim that Christianity sanctions slavery.

10. Possibly Richard Green Perkins's *Progressive Exercises in English Composition* (1832).

Chapter 16

Rhetorical Tradition(s) and the Reform Writing of Mary Ann Shadd Cary

Ann Marie Mann Simpkins

> The passage of the odious Fugitive Slave Law has made a residence in the United States . . . dangerous in the extreme—this consideration, and the absence of condensed information accessible to all, is my excuse for offering this tract to the notice of the public. The people are in a strait—on the one hand, a pro-slavery administration, with its entire controllable force, is bearing upon them with fatal effect: [*sic*] on the other, the Colonization Society, in the garb of *Christianity* and *Philanthropy*, is seconding the efforts of the first named power, by bringing into the lists [*sic*] a vast social and immoral influence, thus making more effective the agencies employed. Information is needed.
>
> —Mary A. Shadd, *Notes of Canada West*

In recent discussions of the history of rhetoric and composition, Shirley Wilson Logan's *We Are Coming* (1999) and Jacqueline Jones Royster's *Traces of a Stream* (1999) have theorized the writing practices of black women who were previously omitted from the rhetorical canon. Logan's compelling argument regarding the significance of traditions of oratory practiced by nineteenth-century black women orators such as Maria Stewart, Frances Ellen Watkins Harper, and Victoria Earle Matthews illustrates how the women blended practices employing classical Western topoi with distinctly Afrocentric rhetorical strategies. In addition to Stewart, Matthews, and Harper, Logan also considers the rhetorical strategies of Mary Ann Shadd Cary. Logan, however, focuses primarily on Shadd's work as an abolitionist orator. Jane Rhodes in *Mary Ann Shadd Cary: The Black Press and Protest in the Nineteenth Century* (1998) and Jim Bearden and Linda Jean Butler in *The Life and Times of Mary Shadd Cary* (1977) focus primarily on writing biographies of Shadd's life and work, and each positions her primarily as an abolitionist journalist. Royster notes that Shadd was both a contributing writer to the *Anglo-African Magazine* and editor and publisher of an abolitionist newspaper, the *Provincial Freeman*. To this ongoing conversation about black women's persuasive discourse and Mary Ann Shadd Cary, in particular, I would like to focus attention on the rhetorical practices of black women publishers specifically, and on Shadd's discourse in particular, as I discuss her texts as evidence of previously undocumented reformist rhetorical practices. In this chapter, I will discuss Shadd's knowledge of varied abolitionist audiences and her use of intertextuality as rhetorical strategies. Shadd employed her knowledge of complicated abolitionist audiences and intertextuality to address dissent specific to abolitionist émigré settlements in Ontario, Canada. The existence of Shadd's protest pamphlet and her own description of Canadian contexts in letters she wrote to the American Missionary Association make it possible for me to draw from her testimony in order to construct an implied theory of rhetoric for this aspect of Shadd's reformist writing. Her writing in *Notes* presents a dual narrative consisting of a subtext that juxtaposes the subtle presentation of counterhegemonic strands of argument with apolitical, almanac information including discussions of the Canadian climate, livestock, and clearing land. Shadd's juxtaposition of her own rational appeals with arguments taken from official documents, such as Canadian school law, constitutes her rhetorical strategy of creating an intertext. This intertext provided one line of argument to abolitionist émigrés in Ontario and another to abolitionist audiences in the United States who did not share concerns such as the lack of housing or jobs in Ontario.

In *Notes*, Shadd makes no attempt to disguise her textual identity, and rhetorical markers recognizing dissent are in plain view for émigré audiences in Windsor and Sandwich who are familiar with the struggles over schools and land to see. Intertextuality and a developing concept of audience that came to distinguish significant differences in emigrationist ideology characterize Shadd's rhetorical practice. Shadd depended heavily upon the use of intertext alternating the descriptive almanac information with an intertext of dissenting argument to enter the public forum of abolitionist reform writing in which few émigré black women offered written response advocating reform to either school policy or émigré settlement policy governing the émigrés' acquisition of land in Ontario.

Mary Ann Shadd Cary addressed audiences consisting of abolitionist reformers in the United States as well as freeborn and fugitive ex-slave émigré abolitionists in Ontario. She emigrated from the United States to Ontario in 1851. A good deal of Shadd's writing called for reform of the policy set forth by various émigré settlement organizations in Ontario. According to Logan, black women orators were "keenly aware of their ability to reach wider audiences through reprints in newspapers" (2000). A review of Shadd's writing suggests that black women's opportunities to take the podium during the nineteenth century may have been more infrequent than their opportunities to write, edit, and publish about civic issues in public forums. The texts Shadd produced shortly after immigrating to Canada reveal how she came to rhetorical power within those Canadian émigré settlement communities through her control of a printing press and specific rhetorical strategies that often proved effective in Ontario and within certain nineteenth-century abolitionist emigrationist circles in the States.

Gary French (1978) notes that the written activism of more obscure black petitioners such as Paolo Brown and J. C. Dutton who sought the means to establish protected settlements in Canada and to also govern affairs within these communities dates back to at least 1829. Better-known protest pamphlets espousing abolitionist reform include *Narrative of the Proceedings of the Black People, During the Late Awful Calamity in Philadelphia* (1793), written by Absolom Jones and Richard Allen, David Walker's *Appeal to the Coloured Citizens of the World* (1829), and Martin Delany's *The Condition, Elevation, Emigration, and Destiny of the Colored People of the United States* (1852). Like Shadd, these earlier émigrés in Canada resisted the lure of American Colonization Society claims.[1] Following the 1829 enforcement of Ohio Black Codes,[2] the black colonization society in Cincinnati, Ohio, to which Brown and Dutton belonged petitioned Sir John Colborne, lieutenant governor of Upper Canada, for asylum. Their petitions won the support of approximately five hundred black Americans who purchased eight hundred acres of land in Ontario and left Ohio to occupy the Oro Township Canadian émigré settlement in 1831. This early settlement was short-lived because the émigrés had difficulty sustaining themselves after relocating. Nevertheless, the practice of petitioning Canada, specifically, for asylum on grounds of racial and ethnic persecution was a writing practice familiar to black Americans and other abolitionists who proposed emigration in response to slavery and other forms of racial oppression. Shadd's discursive practices, therefore, joined a larger tradition of abolitionist reform writing. Shadd joined this tradition to advance her arguments for reforms in educational policy and émigré settlement land acquisition.

Shadd's early civic activism was born out of her activities as a teacher; it is therefore necessary to discuss the context that informed her knowledge of challenges facing black émigrés in Ontario. Shadd first emigrated from New York City to Toronto in early 1851 and then relocated from Toronto to Sandwich, Ontario, where she founded a school. By October 1851, Shadd had moved her school to Windsor and extended admission to include anyone who wished to attend, regardless of their standing as an émigré or non-émigré, or of their ability to pay her for academic instruction. When it became clear that community support for her school did not include sufficient funding, Shadd began to petition the American Missionary Association (A.M.A) for financial support through quasi-public correspondence, which she addressed to the A.M.A. Corresponding Secretary George Whipple.

Shadd's arguments for self-governance and financial independence in social policy related to the schools and land acquisition are presented in the protest pamphlet that she published in her own name in 1852, *Notes of Canada West in its Moral, Social, and Political Aspect: with Suggestions Respecting Mexico, West Indies, and Vancouver Island for the Information of Colored Emigrants.*[3] Like the Oro Township émigré settlers who fled the Ohio Black Codes, Shadd also attributes her own decision to emigrate to the passage of the Fugitive Slave Bill of 1850.[4] Deciding how groups and individuals could acquire land and create employment opportunities for themselves were critical issues for black émigré communities in Ontario, and provided lines of argument for those who could both write and envision how settlements could be organized and governed to meet the needs of residents and to help ensure the community's survival.

On one level, *Notes,* served a community of prospective black émigrés by providing essential information about the social, political, and economic climates in Ontario; geography, including descriptions of land favorable for harvesting timber; agricultural prospects; and opportunities for other skilled laborers. On another rhetorical level, however, *Notes* indicated to audiences Shadd's official affiliation with the prestigious A.M.A., which had begun funding part of her teaching salary in 1851. More significant is the fact that *Notes* signaled Mary Shadd's self-appointed entry into the echelons of Ontario's small cadre of émigré, policy-making elite. In *Notes,* Shadd's rhetorical style applies familiar appeals common to abolitionist discourse as it also introduces counterhegemonic strands of argument specific to tension regarding policy affecting civic life for freeborn and fugitive abolitionist émigrés in Ontario.

In *Notes,* audience needs, particularly, determine Shadd's choice of arguments and the order in which she presents these along with apolitical almanac information. The audiences that Shadd addresses in *Notes* included: potential émigrés to Canada West (skilled fugitive and freeborn men who were farmers, trade laborers, store keepers and clerks), and current Ontario residents of fugitive ex-slave and freeborn origin who opposed certain émigré settlement practices, which too closely resembled the exploitation that the émigrés experienced in the States.

Shadd's disclosure of otherwise covert émigré settlement practices and Canadian school law was itself an argument achieved through a strategy of intertextuality for the purpose of maintaining an independent émigré school in order to protect her own employment as a teacher. Shadd also sought to further develop alternative abolitionist émigré forums. For Shadd, the concept of audience was complicated by contextual factors including a (mainly) unlettered and impoverished primary émigré audience that could not afford to purchase her plea. Shadd compensated for this fact by fashioning a discourse that could be delivered orally (with modification to adjust the text for both lettered and unlettered audiences) by literate preachers, politicians, teachers, and other civic leaders who, in accordance with the charge of uplift, would steer their "flocks" away from a land of persecution. Those uplift leaders who were not repelled by Shadd's criticism of the "imported prejudice" of Canadians not sympathetic to abolitionist causes and the separatist tendencies of black émigrés who did not quickly adjust to Canadian contexts disseminated the message contained in *Notes.*

More similarities than differences exist among Shadd's conceptions of her audience. For example, Shadd distinguishes primary, secondary, and tertiary levels of audience but does this through her arrangement of arguments regarding school law, for example, rather than by naming her audiences explicitly in *Notes.* The importance of Shadd's discussion of school law, in *Notes,* is equal to that concerning émigré land acquisition and both, according to Shadd's testimony, are more central to struggles facing Shadd's fugitive ex-slave audience than farming techniques. Shadd arranged arguments in *Notes* so that information most vital to discussion of dissent among the émigré audiences in Ontario appears in the middle and near the end of the text, which may have diminished its significance to the general abolitionist reader. Ostensibly, Shadd's primary audience consists of prospective émigrés. The secondary audience consists of

Canadian émigrés committed to opposing certain émigré settlement practices. The tertiary audience consists of abolitionists in general. Shadd's use of intertextuality is achieved in *Notes* when she strategically invokes the school law from British Parliament and the constitution and bylaws from various settlement organizations in order to present the strongest appeals to varied audiences.

In order to effectively contextualize her arguments for intercommunal émigré audiences on the subject of schools, Shadd reprinted "that portion of [Canadian] school law governing the formation of schools in the provinces." This information was clearly intended to inform émigrés who had a strong desire for formal education. To differentiate social policy mandated by Black Codes in the States from black émigrés' practice of self-imposed "exclusivity," Shadd appeals to her primary audience of fugitive ex-slave émigrés by supplementing the law with her own argument clarifying social policy regarding the parents' right to petition for separate government schools privileging exclusivity based on race or religion. Shadd's strategic intertext clarifies that school "exclusivity" should result from the émigré parents' activism and that it should not result from guidelines developed by émigré settlement organizations wishing to control the public sphere and to divert government funds to support émigré settlement school initiatives.

> There are no separate schools: at Toronto and in many other places, as in the churches, the colored people avail themselves of existing schools; but in the western country, in some sections, there is a tendency to "exclusiveness" [Shadd emphasis]. The colored people of that section petitioned, when the School Law was under revision, that they might have separate schools: there were counter petitions by those opposed [who] . . . by following a prescribed form, demand a [separate] school for their children; but if other schools, under patronage of Government, exist, (as Catholic or Protestant,) [*sic*] they can demand admission into them. . . . (*Notes* 19)

Though aware of her powerful audience members, such as those affiliated with the A.M.A., Shadd's subtext of argument does not address this group directly. Instead, she appeals to the majority émigré audience consisting of her adult students and the parents of children enrolled in her day and Sabbath schools. Shadd's notion of audience in *Notes* constructs the majority of émigré community as a group capable of determining the future of the Canada Mission school through their advocacy facilitated by a better understanding of Canadian school law. This law, according to Shadd, did not require that black émigré children be educated in separate government schools. The émigrés' understanding of this law was, therefore, critical to establishing the Canada Mission as a government school in order to prevent available school funds from being diverted to support émigré settlement schools.

Shadd creates an intertext when she invokes actual school law enacted by Parliament. Shadd invokes the law in the following passages to strengthen her claim that, provisions already existed in school law to establish separate schools based on differences in race and religion and upon request of at least twelve families, therefore, her argument implies, such requests are most appropriately initiated by parents and need not be initiated by abolitionist émigré settlement organizations. Shadd quotes directly from the Canadian school law, which read in part:

> And be it enacted, That [*sic*] it shall be the duty of the Municipal Council of any township, and of the Board of School Trustees of any city, town or incorporated village, on the application in writing of twelve or more resident heads of families, to authorize the establishment of one or more separate schools for Protestants, Roman Catholics or colored people. . . .

An interesting paradox exists in another of Shadd's intertexts when she invokes legislation endorsing the exclusivity of race and religion when it is endorsed by Canadian law. Critical to this rhetorical strategy is the way that Shadd invokes school law to reveal that exclusive schools, like other government-sponsored schools, will receive monies from the school fund. Shadd uses this strategy of invoking official discourse to reveal the primary goal of some R.H.S. émigré settlement organizers to divert government funds to support settlement operations.

> Provided that each separate Protestant, or Roman Catholic, or colored school, shall be entitled to share in the school fund according to the average attendance of pupils attending each such separate school,

Shadd continues to build upon her strategic use of intertextuality when building her case against émigré settlement organizers whom she identified as activists willing to place the needs of their organizations above the general welfare of vulnerable, newly arrived freeborn and fugitive ex-slave émigrés. The civic ideal promoted in the following argument restates Shadd's desire to see schools and churches in Ontario serve as rhetorical sites that were free of the encumbrances that exclusive practices in public space create. If schools and churches in Toronto are integrated, Shadd reasons, then those in Sandwich and Chatham should also be integrated.

> [T]he facilities for obtaining a liberal education, are ample in the large towns and cities. In Toronto, students of all complexions associate together, in the better class schools and colleges. The operations of missionaries being chiefly among colored [émigrés], they have established several schools in connection with their labors, yet they are open to children without exception. The colored common schools have more of complexional character than the private, which, with no exception that I have heard of, are open to all.

Shadd invokes the Act of Parliament regarding school law to clarify her primary argument: that existing Canadian legislation already provides equable facilities for instruction to everyone and, therefore, additional settlement-specific policy governing émigré schools were unnecessary.

By reprinting the school law in *Notes* Shadd assured émigrés that the separate race-based schools advocated in some émigré settlement bylaws were a choice reflecting émigré policy rather than a government mandate. When Shadd argues for schools, she uses her knowledge of audience and intertextuality to persuade readers to support the maintenance of the Canada Mission school in Windsor, which she founded. Her argument is designed to prevent the transfer of A.M.A. financial support away from the Canada Mission.

Shadd also consistently creates an intertext privileging émigré self-governance within a British parliamentary framework rather than émigré settlement policy, which, Shadd argued, would better protect émigré interests. Throughout her text, Shadd's critique of constitution and bylaws governing the fugitive ex-slave émigrés' acquisition of land on properties owned by one abolitionist settlement especially, called the Refugees Home Society (R.H.S.) versus the purchase of land from the Canadian government are quite instructive in understanding her arguments for self-governance and fiscal independence by freeborn and fugitive ex-slave émigrés of African descent.

Shadd invokes the R.H.S. constitution in order to define the organization and better represent R.H.S. émigré settlement development policy. Embedded in her argument is Shadd's critique of the inequities that characterize settlement policy. She argues, covertly, that the émigré community can ill afford to foster intercommunal division among free-born and fugitive ex-slave émigrés.

> The Refugees' Home is the last of the settlements of which I may speak in this place. . . . This Society is designed to appropriate fifty thousand acres of land for fugitives from slavery, *only*. . . . The plan is to sell farms of twenty-five acres, that is, to give five acres to actual settlers, with the privilege of buying the adjoining twenty acres at the market value—one-third of the purchase money constitutes a fund for school and other purposes; and ten years are given to pay for the twenty acres, but no interest may accumulate.

Shadd references intercommunal dissent as she alludes to the long-term implications of R.H.S. policy for acquiring land that divides émigrés through their status as propertied or unpropertied settlers. Through this intertextual strategy, Shadd publicly voices the dissent among black émigrés, freeborn and fugitive ex-slaves alike. Through this intertextual strategy, she challenges the party line, offered by more than one émigré settlement organization, which insisted that refugees to Canada who were fugitive ex-slaves were necessarily in agreement with settlement policy articulated in constitution and bylaws. In fact, Shadd's testimony regarding her knowledge of unlettered émigrés who were fugitive ex-slaves reveals that this audience often did not necessarily believe that émigré settlement policy had been written with their best interests in mind.

> This society may now be considered in operation . . . and the results to be looked for from it, from the extent of the field operations, will have an important bearing on the colored people who are now settled in Canada, or who may emigrate thither. The friends of the society, actuated by benevolent feelings towards victims of oppression and the odious Fugitive Law, are sanguine as to the success of the measure, *but not so universal is the opinion in its favor, even among those designed to be benefited; in fact, all the objections raised against previously existing settlements, hold good against these, with the additional ones of greater magnitude.* (emphasis mine)

Shadd identifies R.H.S. policy as some of the most egregious of émigré settlement practice because she claimed that it was inconsistent with abolitionist values. Shadd embeds this criticism of the R.H.S. in her intertextual argument. She suggests that R.H.S. abolitionists have merely codified their constitution and bylaws with the logic governing plantation practices that forbade interactions between freeborn and formerly enslaved émigrés.

> [T]hey arrive in Canada destitute . . . but may not settle on the land of the Refugees' Home, from the accident of [their freeborn status]. . . . Again, the policy of slaveholders has been to create a contempt for *free* [Shadd's emphasis] [black] people in the bosom of their slaves, and pretty effectually have they succeeded.
>
> Their journey to Canada for liberty has not rooted out that prejudice, quite, and reference to a man's birth, as free or slave, is generally made by colored persons should he not be as prosperous as his better helped fugitive brethren. Thus, discord among members of the same family is engendered: a breach made, that the exclusive use by fugitives of the society lands is not likely to mend.

Shadd references the nominal freedom of freeborn black émigrés as she articulates her discursive aims central to abolitionist dissent regarding R.H.S. land purchases. As a freeborn émigré, Shadd uses *Notes* as a rhetorical site in which a conversation occurs articulating multiple positions codified by class distinctions among émigrés that are directly related to one's status as freeborn or fugitive ex-slave, lettered or unlettered. Through her textual strategies of intertextuality and audience analysis Shadd positions herself with all disenfranchised black émigrés from the States whose agency regarding the acquisition of land, which is required for British citizenship and all the benefits it affords, is severely limited by émigré organization settlement policy. Freeborn émigrés, Shadd, argued, could not compete with any settlement organization for the purchase of government land. Fugitive ex-slaves, she continues through her intertextual strategy, found their potential land acquisition to be constantly under threat because the judgment of émigré settlement agents could, at any time, accuse them of intemperance or some other offense that could serve as grounds for having the accused offender default on the agreement to purchase the land. In either case, Shadd argues, if land were purchased directly by émigrés from the government, then the émigrés' position would be strengthened.

> Again, the society, with its funds, is looked upon in the light of a powerful rival, standing in the way of poor *free* [empha-

> sis Shadd's] men, with its ready cash. . . . [P]oor men who would have bought on time, and as an able purchaser from the government, the society must have first choice. The objections in common with other settlements, are: 1) the individual supervision of resident agents, 2) and the premium indirectly offered for good behavior. (*Notes* 24–25)

Shadd proceeds to further contextualize articles in the R.H.S. constitution and bylaws in order to clarify specific articles barring freeborn black émigrés from acquiring lands purchased by the society, even when the purchasing power of the R.H.S. made it more difficult for individuals to compete when attempting to acquire lands from the government. Shadd combines her previous claim of inconsistent abolitionist practice and ideology with her most incriminating accusation, which ascribes motive to R.H.S. written policy. In the argument that follows, Shadd accuses the R.H.S., and other émigré settlement organizers of eliminating freeborn émigrés from the pool of those eligible to acquire land from the society in order to eliminate those most likely to possess lettered literacy skills from contexts in which they might be able to challenge the process through which lands are actually purchased.

> Article 11. This society shall not deed lands to any but actual settlers, who are refugees from southern slavery, and who are the owners of no land.

In conclusion, Shadd's knowledge of varied abolitionist arguments and intertextuality are strategies specific to her identity as a black woman with a sharply attuned critical view of abolition, freedom, and social and political empowerment. Arguments to support Shadd's discursive aims run parallel throughout the series of varied texts that Shadd produced. The flexibility of rhetorical structures employed by Shadd, in *Notes,* lies in her ability to embed rhetorical intertextual strategies that were necessary for her to address varied audiences within her abolitionist forum.

The impact of Shadd's rhetorical choices illustrates the extent to which her writing in *Notes* promoted reform within émigré communities despite her positioning as a petitioner writing outside the abolitionist mainstream. Through her written strategies, Shadd's polemic invokes law from British Parliament in order to question émigré settlement policy. To this end, Shadd initiates discourse in *Notes* that suggests that alternative policy regarding school policy and land acquisition would prove more egalitarian and inclusive and, therefore, make possible equal access to land purchase and other resources. Through her knowledge of abolitionist émigré audiences and construction of intertextual rhetorical strategies, Shadd advocates reform to position émigrés of African ancestry as people with greater agency and potential for economic, social, and political reform.

NOTES

I want to thank Jacqueline Jones Royster, Nan Johnson, and Janice Lauer for reading and commenting on this chapter.

1. Shadd had reason to be wary of both the Democratic, pro-slavery administration of U.S. president Franklin Pierce and of the American Colonization Society (ACS) according to Henry Graff (1997). In 1821 the ACS purchased the title to Liberia in order to create an annexed territory for African American émigrés. Shadd was accurate in her assessment that Liberian colonization was a colonization scheme intended to better secure the institution of slavery in the States by concentrating the free black population in an area the ACS controlled (Franklin 242). For this reason, Shadd warned prospective black emigrationists against the alluring arguments made by the ACS and similar organizations who addressed them "in the garb of Christianity and Philanthropy."

2. Black Codes were laws most often associated with the North American South, but that actually varied from state to state and were not limited to the South. This body of laws codified the unequal treatment of black Americans.

3. Richard Almonte republished *Notes* in an edition that studies Shadd's text through the critical framework offered in the philosophy of Walter Benjamin.

4. In 1793 the United States passed the first Fugitive Slave Law. According to John Hope Franklin (1963), this legislation permitted the "master of an interstate fugitive to seize [her] wherever found, carry [her] before any federal or state magistrate . . . and with oral testimony of claimant or affidavit and without trial by jury . . . to return [her] to the state from which [she] allegedly fled." In the quote that begins this article, Shadd implies that the U.S. Fugitive Slave Bill of 1850 was a more virulent version of even the legislation from 1793 and that it posed even more of a threat to black Americans as it read, in part, "[J]udges of the circuit and district courts of the United States, . . . shall grant certificates to such claimants, upon satisfactory proof being made, with authority to take and remove such fugitives from service or labor, . . . to the State or territory from which such persons may have escaped or fled." The Fugitive Slave Bill of 1850 then, in effect, increased the trafficking of all black people, freeborn and fugitive ex-slave alike, in the United States and across the border in Canada through its promise to grant "certificates . . . upon satisfactory proof being made" authorizing their removal from lives lived as free persons. We may equate the role of claimants referenced in the 1850 act with that of the contemporary trafficker. And French (1978) points out, that in the 1800s, only the

trafficker's word against that of the captured or the act of violent capture itself constituted "satisfactory proof." Paramount in nineteenth-century Canadian émigré settlement contexts, therefore, was not only the purchase of land for settlement, but also the adoption of settlement laws to protect residents from falling victim to kidnapping by traffickers crossing the U.S.-Canadian border in search of black people to capture and sell.

Chapter 17

Toni Morrison and "Race Matters" Rhetoric

Reading Race and Whiteness in Visual Culture

Joyce Irene Middleton

> 86% of white suburban Americans live in neighborhoods that are less than 1% black.
>
> —Cornel West, 1993

> [The] immense fear of "the black" next door is one reason that the United States is so densely segregated. Only two percent of white people have a black neighbor, even though black people constitute approximately thirteen percent of the population.
>
> —Patricia Williams, 1997

> [Some African Americans] reinforce wishful beliefs that society has reformed, in spite of the the marginalization of masses of African Americans who live lives largely separate and remote from the majority of white Americans.
>
> —Kimberly Crenshaw, 1997

> . . . just make sure you move to a blue state [a reference to the 2000 election map delineated by red and blue states].
>
> —Political Science Colleague, 2001

In *Seeing a Colour-Blind Future: the Paradox of Race*, a series of lectures given for the prestigious Reith Lectures for the BBC, legal scholar Patricia J. Williams carefully examines the narratives of contradiction associated with arguments about race and white identity. Williams admits that, like the desire of many people she encounters, it would be nice to live in the "milk and honey" land of colour blindness (51). But we're not "there" yet, as she argues by examining the "quieter forms of racism" (61), or what she also describes as "the small aggressions of unconscious racism, rather than the big-booted oppressions of bigotry" (61). Although Williams's primary audience for her lectures was British, her American readers may certainly recognize the problems with audience that she must have faced as a black woman talking about race. The liberal goals of color-blind rhetoric combined with the claim that we now live in a postracial society (so we don't need to talk about race) are increasingly persuasive to more and more Americans, especially in the visual rhetoric that appeals so strongly to American youth. But the epigraphs that open this essay help to graphically illustrate a critical paradox for those who believe in color-blind rhetoric. Race doesn't matter, on the one hand, but on the other, race is an essential fact for naming one's American identity.

The geographic spaces described in the introductory epigraphs illustrate a racialized divide that is a material reality and not simply a debate instigated and sustained by political discourse in American society. In fact, analyzing race and religion in the geographical realignment among American voters from 1986 to 2000, political analysts David O. Sears and Nicholas A. Valentino demonstrate that "partisanship has undergone a profound sectional realignment, with Republicans coming to dominate the South, and Democrats, the Northeast, the upper Midwest, and the Pacific Coast" (Sears). The authors find that "this realignment is intimately associated with the longstanding and continuingly unresolved racial conflicts in American society" (Sears).

Talking about race in the academy—that is, as an intellectual proposition—is situated in a "paradox" that on one hand persistently affirms the ideology of whiteness (and the racist oppression that results from this) while, on the other, resists, denies, and silences a truly in-depth investigation of that ideology and its link to race and racism (in addition to Williams's description of a "paradox" for talking about race, see Morrison, *Race-ing ix*; Middleton, *Innovations*, 2004). In response to this academic problem, I have been formulating what I describe as a "race matters" rhetoric which I define in relation to work primarily by Toni Morrison but also by Cornel West and Patricia Williams. After I describe some of the elements of this rhetoric, I will use it to analyze a diverse range of illustrations and issues in visual culture, especially in Hollywood films, and to interrogate the elusive problems of racial metaphors in popular culture. This essay is part of a larger project on visual rhetoric.

Rhetorically speaking, the simple phrase "race matters" has generated a huge national conversation about historical and contemporary constructions of race and white identity (see Lubiano). Much of this rhetorical force may be attributed to Cornel West's publication *Race Matters* with its strong, continuing commercial success and with both academic and broad popular appeal. But while the origins of this rhetoric would seem to derive from West's publication, its intellectual beginnings may also be traced to Toni Morrison's lecture, "Black Matters," the first chapter from *Playing in the Dark: Whiteness and the Literary Imagination.* A kind of translation from "black matters," "race matters" has become a signature phrase used to counter the liberal claims and rhetorical force of the color-blind paradigm in the American racial consciousness (Crenshaw 1997; Middleton 2000; Ratcliffe 2000).

An important emphasis for Morrison's "race matters" rhetoric (one that is not as dominantly present in West's arguments) is that the subject of race is always self-reflexive. Morrison writes: "The fabrication of an Africanist persona is reflexive; an extraordinary meditation on the self" (17). "It seems both poignant and striking how avoided and unanalyzed is the effect of racist inflection on the subject" (11). "My project is an effort to avert the critical gaze from the racial object to the racial subject; from the described and imagined to the describers and the imaginers; from the serving to the served" (90). In "Home," a later essay, Morrison's rhetorical articulation about race and whiteness is a significant reminder of her earlier arguments in *Playing in the Dark*, as she asserts, "I have never lived, nor has any of us, in a world in which race did not matter" (3). Strategically in her analyses, Morrison examines both the racialized object and the racializing subject simultaneously, with a greater emphasis on the racializing subject, to explore the effects of racism and the act of racializing on white people. This element of the self-reflexive racial analysis—the text that says as much about the racial subject as it does about the racial object—is a crucial element in what I call a "race matters" rhetoric, and it is too easily ignored when talking about race in our teaching, scholarship, and lived experiences (consider, for example, a writing assignment that interrupts students' traditional and historical thinking about race by asking them to develop an essay on the dominating effects of slavery on white people after reading Douglass's *Narrative* or any slave narrative for the first time). Without examining what the racialized subject says about white identity, or what white identity says about racism, arguments about race continue to maintain a dominant focus on racialized, nonwhite bodies as the only victims of racism, while whiteness maintains its politically privileged, yet silent, invisible status that appears to be nonparticipatory and/or unaffected by racism (on the importance of whiteness studies, see Liu, "The Unbearable Being of Whiteness").

A few quick examples from American popular culture will help to illustrate how this self-reflexive element in "race matters" rhetoric works. When Tiger Woods won the Masters Tournament in 1997, the media proclaimed that he "broke the race barrier," and, indeed, many Americans of color (including white Americans) celebrated the significance of the moment. But this description of Woods's "accomplishment" effectively avoids noting who created the racial barrier in the first place. Our focus on race, then, is on the triumph of the racialized body but not on the meaning of the event for the racializer. This moment reflects one problem of whiteness that rhetoric and composition scholar Thomas West analyzes in "The Racist Other." He observes that "subjectivities are . . . rarely reflected on in-depth" (7), but instead "are generally built around silences about the cultural significance of whiteness" (5). Is it possible then, that this silence allows for another celebration linked to the silence and normalcy of whiteness—the myth of racial transcendence? Questions about this myth and its contradictions are the basis of a substantial discussion for historian Thomas C. Holt in his book, *The Problem of Race in the 21st Century*. Like Tiger Woods, other Americans of color and black Americans such as Oprah Winfrey, Michael Jordan, and Colin Powell have become paradoxically e-raced personalities by effectively transcending race. The racial contradictions that Holt observes about Colin Powell may be multiplied when we think about the myth of racial transcendence. Holt writes: "[W]hat is most interesting about the Powell phenomenon ["as a viable Republican challenger for the presidency"] is its anomalous relationship to the conditions of life and the life chances of most black people" (5). After he elaborates on the significance of these contradictions, Holt concludes that "[t]he simultaneous idealization of Colin Powell and demonization of blacks as a whole (especially the politically motivated demonization of large numbers of black women as 'welfare queens' by members of Powell's own party) is replicated in much of our everyday world" (6).

More recently in two political debates, the absence of the self-reflexive rhetorical element for talking about race reveals how flawed arguments, rooted in the normalcy and silence of whiteness, nonetheless effectively win audiences. During the 2000 presidential election campaign, the NAACP ran an advertisement in selected commercial outlets that exploited the vicious lynching of James Byrd in Texas. The advertisement was designed to persuade Americans to vote against George W. Bush because he did not support hate crime legislation in Texas. While the basic claim of the advertisement was irrefutable, several neoconservative African American commentators, Armstrong Williams and J. C. Watts among them, used the news media to condemn the NAACP and the advertisement, claiming that it encouraged a racial divide. Yet these commentators who condemned the NAACP were effectively silent about George Bush Sr.'s Republican campaign use of the "Willie Horton ad" that was not only a gross and disgraceful misrepresentation of Willie Horton, but also exploited the racial polarizing elements that these African American commentators condemned in the NAACP's political ad. (Needless to say, the current media access of black conservatives is highly controversial; according to political analyst Michael C. Dawson, African American political conservatives "have remarkably little mass support" compared to their dominant visibility in "mainstream (white) American media" [281].)

Thomas Holt analyzed some of the rhetorical effects of the "infamous Willie Horton ad." He acknowledged that some viewers of the commercial were persuaded that it was "simply about preserving law and order," but he also recognized that for others, the ad was "saturated with discourse about the black-beast-rapist-on-the-loose used a century earlier to justify lynching" (40). The statistics from the opening epigraphs may help us to draw some inferences about which audience was which. In addition to Holt's description of the pathos of that ad, Kathleen Hall Jamieson's powerful rhetorical analysis of the racializing language that George Bush Sr.'s Republican campaign used in the Willie Horton ad illustrates how so many false claims were constructed, especially by the delivery of the ad in the media (5–10). Her analysis demonstrates how the evidence of a new rhetoric of racism works. Jamieson carefully examines the metaphors of race, which have "become more powerful than biological race ever was" (Morrison, *Playing* 63).

Another example of faulty, slippery arguments about race that focus only on raced bodies—and not on the racializer—may be demonstrated by examining David Horowitz's arguments offering ten "reasons" against reparations for slavery in America. Oddly enough, even the rhetorically infamous Bill O'Reilly (who debated reparations with Horowitz) has demonstrated a tolerance for listening to reparations arguments. Making a rather absurd claim, Horowitz argues forcefully to his audiences that the slave trade was, in fact, a good fortune for African Americans who are as a group some of the wealthiest descendants of Africans in the world as a result of being tranplanted in the United

States. But the self-reflexive element in a "race matters" rhetorical analysis would ask whether the same argument could be made both for many white people in America individually and for the foundations of wealth in America more generally. On the wealth of whiteness in America, however, Horowitz is predictably silent.

"Race matters" rhetoric investigates a difficult intellectual terrain because it begs the question from its audience to affirm or reject its relevance in the academy (Morrison, "Home" 7). Clearly, for too many Americans in the twenty-first century, a negative response prevails, even if it is a seemingly neutral response—that race doesn't matter (or that it matters to some whites but not to others; see Hale 295–96). Within our own field of rhetoric and composition, talking about race too often lacks the self-reflexive element that helps to shift the gaze from black bodies to whiteness. An important example of this is in Catherine Prendergast's Braddock Award winning article, "Race: the Absent Presence in Composition Studies." Prendergast provides a very impressive analysis of critical race theory and its usefulness to rhetoric and composition studies. Yet the term *whiteness* is used only once in the entire essay, and even then the term is used in the conclusion as a kind of afterthought, summarizing the significance of her analysis: "The present challenge for composition is to develop theorizations of race that do not reinscribe people of color as either foreign or invisible, nor leave whiteness uninvestigated; only through such work can composition begin to counteract the denial of racism that is part of the classroom, the courts, and a shared colonial inheritance" (51). But Prendergast's readers can too easily read race as "other" without thinking about whiteness as a racialized subject at all by the conclusion of her article.

Readers of Helen Fox's problematic text, *When Race Breaks Out*, may also question, by its conclusion, where and how whiteness fits into a discussion of race, which is too often confused with ethnicity, but is clearly and consistently oppositional to whiteness. In fact, Fox's readers who are not white may be humored by her implicit references to them as white. In one example, while she discusses white privilege and pedagogy in the classroom, Fox writes: "White students should be prompted by the [Peggy MacIntosh's] article to see how their whiteness or apparent whiteness adds to any other privileges they have. Model this by mentoring a few of your own privileges" (121). In my own reader response to Fox's statements, I'm puzzled and thinking, "so, I'm white?" The political, historical, essentialist, and rhetorical problems of Fox's book directly contrast with Prendergast's carefully articulated argument, which speaks to a central problem in Fox's pedagogy: "The idea that socialization of itself will create a level-playing field is inherited from liberalism, and like liberalism itself, it has become a casualty of the post-civil-rights-era backlash" (51). Indeed, there are still too many analyses that construct a racial subject as if it belongs only to the racialized and not also to the racializer (which continues to describe the dominant status of race studies in the academy—that is, as a subject that is optional for whites or, even more, as a subject that is met with outright hostility).

If whiteness continues to be an unracialized, unpoliticized subject matter, then we should consider the range of inferences that may be suggested by Ian Marshall and Wendy Ryden's valuable dialogue, when Marshall points out that the majority of teachers in rhetoric and composition studies are white (252). In fact, in "The Racist Other," Thomas West also raises numerous questions about the dominant presence of white identity in rhetoric and composition studies. He acknowledges, importantly, that "identities are not fixed and stable but constantly negotiated and produced through dialogue and reflection" (9). But people who believe they are nonracist actually limit the range of investigation of whiteness, and West argues that "speaking from a perspective that imagines itself outside of critique ultimately perpetuates oppressive practices since the critical perspective itself often remains unexamined" (9). West argues to white readers as his primary audience that "denying implication in structures of domination because we feel guilty puts those we would hope to help resist discriminatory practices in great peril" (9). Indeed, in workshops and group discussions, I have found that most white teachers find it extremely difficult to utter the words "my white identity" when they are talking about race, even for those who willingly participate in seminars on race and white identity. While teachers and classrooms are clearly the most visible site of whiteness in rhetoric and composition, many journals, books, bibliographies, graduate programs, and innovations in our discipline continue to reflect a lack of serious investigation about the persistence of a dominant white presence in this discipline (again, as if race does not matter and, more importantly, as if white is not a race).

Addressing the problem of talking about whiteness as a racialized category, a "race matters" rhetoric with its self-reflexive element has generated considerable, admirable, interdisciplinary investigations. Much of this recent work explicitly acknowledges Toni Morrison's claims in *Playing in the Dark* about the inescapable reality of racial inflection in American discourse. As a practice of literary criticism, Morrison's "race matters" rhetoric helps to articulate relationships between race (the Africanist presence) and white identity that could not exist without the construction of a racialized other. Morrison demonstrates her most provocative use of "race matters" rhetorical inquiry when she speaks in interviews about her own work. Many of her white interviewers arrive, inevitably, at the question about when or whether Morrison plans to write a novel that includes substantially developed white characters (many of us may recall her response to Charlie Rose after the publication of *Paradise*). In a more recent interview, *Toni Morrison Uncensored*, Morrison responds to this question by asking her interviewer to think about the problematic invisibility of whiteness when talking about raced characters:

> You can't understand how powerfully racist that question is, can you? Because, you could never ask a white author, "when are you going to write about black people?" Whether he did or not, or she did or not, even the inquiry comes from a position of being in the center and being used to being in the center, and [asking], is it ever possible that you'll enter the mainstream? It's inconceivable that where I already am is the mainstream . . .

While Morrison's rhetorical inquiry is literary and linguistic, her claims may be easily appropriated in film analyses and discussions of visual rhetoric (see Willis 3–4; McKee 1–30).

For example, given the overwhelming American desire for the color-blind paradigm to succeed, it is no wonder that most American audiences were baffled, frustrated, very uncomfortable, or even outraged by Spike Lee's film, *Bamboozled.* The film not only challenged the dominant Hollywood color-blind formulas that cultivate the American viewing public, but it also criticized contemporary African American participation in the production of those formulas. In a critical interview on the film and its context, Lee said: "I'm not saying there's a wealth of opportunities available to black performers today, but no one is going to the poor house if they turn down some of this stuff" (Crowdus 6). Despite the film's flaws (for example, does the film work successfully as a satire, or is it too easily read as a contemporary film about the history of blackface in Hollywood?), Lee who was awarded an Honorary Doctorate from Princeton University in spring 2002, represents a highly informed, cultural voice when he questions representations of African Americans in contemporary Hollywood film. He uses "race matters" rhetoric in his film analyses by focusing on both subject and object when he asks who is speaking for whom. His brilliant, narrative framing of *Girl 6* with a black female (Theresa Randle) in auditioning scenes with two white male film directors, Quentin Tarantino and Ron Silver, provides a metaphorical lens for reading race and whiteness in this film. In the opening scene, Tarantino tells the unnamed black woman, that he is "making the greatest romantic African American film ever made, directed by me [Tarantino], of course, told from the point of view of an African American woman." Lee's perpetual experience of the Hollywood double standard regarding race, both as a film director and in the subject matter of his films, makes his own analysis of race, whiteness, and representation in film inherently self-reflexive.

After Toni Morrison offered her analysis of the Africanist presence in early American literary traditions in *Playing in the Dark*, she suggested areas for further critical investigation: "We need to analyze the manipulation of the Africanist narrative . . . as a means of meditation . . . on one's own humanity . . ." (53), she argues. "Criticism of this type will show how that narrative is used in the construction of a history and a context for whites by positing history-lessness and context-lessness for blacks" (53). Many recent films may come to mind easily as we think about Morrison's call for cultural inquiry (*Forrest Gump* and the recent *Monster's Ball* among them—note Hilton Als's brief film review), but Lee's argument in *Bamboozled* asks his audience to think about these problematic contexts that Morrison has framed as they have appeared and persist in film and television into the twenty-first century. Looking more broadly at the current Hollywood scene (and implicitly demonstrating a "race matters" self-reflexive critique), Lee talks about the recent appearance of the "magical nigger mystique" in films such as *The Green Mile, The Family Man, The Legend of Bagger Vance*, and *What Dreams May Come.* All of these films have these "magical Negroes who appear out of nowhere and have these great powers but who can't use them to help themselves or their own people but only for the benefit of the white stars of the movies" (Crowdus 5). This kind of "Disneyfication of history" (Holden 1) creates visual rhetorical texts that are riddled with racial contradictions, but that satisfy the American spectator's (read "white" for "American") belief in the color-blind paradigm (Morrison, *Playing* 47). Spike Lee's film analyses demonstrate a cultural and critical problem that "not talking about race" promotes.

In his interview with Donna Haraway in *Women Writing Culture*, rhetoric and composition scholar Gary Olson asks Haraway to elaborate on her idea about our reliance on easy closed narratives (in feminist, antiracist, or anticolonial discourses), which creates the problem of "not knowing how to build affinities, knowing instead how to build oppositions" (60). Whoopi Goldberg's voice might be the last that some would cite in arguments about race and white identity, but she created a brilliant moment during the 2002 Oscar awards ceremony that used humor to subversively interrupt Hollywood's tradition of sustaining historically built racial oppositions (not only demonstrating the powerful significance of Haraway's observations, but also illustrating a "race matters" self-reflexive analysis). While the auditorium was still highly animated by Halle Berry's success and Sidney Poitier's receiving an honorary award (and awaiting the announcement of the winner in the Best Actor category, for which two African American men had been nominated), Goldberg challenged the audience to think about the persistent problem of "othering"—racializing and whiteness—even as the Academy was congratulating itself. First, Goldberg briefly acknowledged and congratulated Halle Berry for her success and for "breaking the race barrier." But then, Goldberg continued, announcing:

> I also would like to say that I'm personally so pleased for Robert Redford [who was also given an honorary award]. . . . I felt so moved by what he had to say. . . . But . . . I was a little freaked out that I wasn't included in his "package." . . . Because . . . when we were talking about Sidney we got every black actor in the world to talk about him. No white people, just a whole lot of black people, which was great. And apparently none of us have anything to say about Bob . . . and you know his influence on us has been so profound. . . . I will never forget "The Way We Was" . . . not to mention, "The Stang" . . . and "Bitch Cassidy"—my whole neighborhood rocked when they saw that . . . "Ordinary Peoples" . . . "Jemima Johnson" . . . and, of course, the classic, my favorite, "Out of Africa" which apparently we all were. Now, my next nominated film. . . .

While Goldberg's audience roared with laughter, the paradox of the racialized space that Goldberg created surely lingered right alongside that laughter. Goldberg cautioned the Academy in Hollywood that it is still very much haunted by its deeply rooted practice of segregation in the history—indeed, the inception—of American filmmaking.

Alice Randall, author of the highly controversial novel *Wind Done Gone,* has given us yet another way to think about "race matters" rhetoric. At a Tennessee Book Festival in 2002, she told her audience that "today [in America], it is not about who is black and who is white. It is about who is putting the shackles on, who is taking the shackles off, and who is too distracted to see. And that third category of people who are far too distracted to see the shackles are the most dangerous category of all" (Book TV). Randall's third category may be used to describe people who are so deeply committed to the color-blind paradigm that its rhetoric both verbal and visual may be used as a distraction for not seeing the harmful effects of the shackles and other symbols of historical racial oppression that are oddly reappearing in visual, popular culture. For example, Randall's reference to shackles has clear allusions to the shame of early American slavery through the late nineteenth century. Yet, basketball player Charles Barkley appeared in broken shackles on the cover of an issue of *Sports Illustrated* magazine in the early twenty-first century. The image of Barkley's shiny, sweaty, half-naked body with shackles on his neck, wrists, and ankles, appeared over the caption, "Charles Unchained: Living Large and Holding Forth on Everything from his Gold, Money, and Politics to Michael Jordan, TV Sports and Enron." But, race doesn't matter. Chris Rock appears in a pose of symbolic lynching, his stylishly clothed body draped on one hanger, his name visually hanging from another, and both are hanging on a portable closet on the cover of the June 2002 issue of *GQ Magazine.* The caption reads "Hangin' with Chris Rock." Again here, race doesn't matter. Halle Berry who attracted much media coverage for baring her breasts in the movie *Swordfish,* attracted no such coverage for a controversial scene in the same film where she is effectively "lynched." The camera gazes on her body, suspended, swinging, and struggling in the air until it is released, briefly, and then shot and apparently killed (the camera, again, lingers over her dead body). In the history of filmmaking, lynching black bodies is a very powerful, signifying image. But again, race doesn't matter in our color-blind post-racial society. These images are all debatable. They are also disturbing. If popular culture is where the new pedagogy is, as bell hooks has argued (1996, 1997; see also Giroux, 1997, 2002), then we must develop strategies in our research and teaching that empower our colleagues and students to refuse the passive position of Alice Randall's third category. "Race Matters" rhetoric with its crucial self-reflexive element offers a wide range of support for our future investigations of visual rhetoric, for reading race and whiteness in popular culture, and for furthering the real work of antiracism.

Last Words

Jacqueline Jones Royster

A VIRTUAL REALITY

We, the contributors to this collection, imagine ourselves in a well-lighted space, open, airy, pleasing to the eye. We are surrounded by others who have set the conversation in ways that are neither accommodating to our insights and interests nor invitational to our voices. They speak to each other as if we are not there, suggesting that we are intruders, or even worse that we are imperceptible to them—too far away, perhaps, or maybe too close. How can this be? We are here. We have been here. Others, like us, were here before us. We are not intruders. We are not imperceptible.

In small acts of resistance, we speak as our intellectual ancestors have done, amplifying our voices, presenting ourselves one by one, each in her or his own turn, tossing our cards about the room, claiming space, creating visibility—without microscope, without telescope—for the naked eye. Amid such boldness, we see each other and recognize, as Alice Walker predicted, joy in resistance. We grab chairs, draw closer, clustering as we like, rearranging the furniture—a bit, disrupting the scene—a bit, setting our belongings in plain sight. We find ways to speak our minds and our lives. We share our written words, and then we speak, an opportunity for a few last words.

> ROYSTER: Now that you see your thoughts in the company of the others in this volume, this amplification of our work, what stands out most?
>
> ESPINOSA-AGUILAR: When I first read through this collection, I said—about 130 pages in—What the hell? How are

these pieces at all related? Why are there so many textual analyses of various works by people of color? Where is the advice, cautionary tale, guides, and maps for those engaging in this kind of work? When I got to Hui's piece, it was like a light clicked on. . . . Jackie writes, "We need to imagine a world for rhetorical studies that is global, flexible, and specifically aware of its own complicity in the deploying of systems of dominance and oppression." . . . When I read Hui's piece, I must admit that I was completely surprised by how ignorant I am of the culture of more than a billion people on the planet. Here, I claim to be such a student of cultural studies but I've confined that study to the context of the United States. No wonder we are hated on such a global scale. Similar thoughts arose for me when I read Akhila's piece.

RAMNARAYAN: My best friend got married this past week, the ceremony a braid of Hindu, Buddhist, and Christian traditions. The wedding took place—improbably—on board the *Santa Maria* [a replica of Columbus's Santa Maria anchored in Columbus, Ohio]. Throughout the evening, I wondered if other people noticed the rather obvious irony of an Indian woman (from India) marrying a European American man on board a replica of the ship that brought Columbus to America. I also thought about a gay male friend in India—a close friend of the bride—who had had to leave this country because of visa restrictions, despite the fact that his partner of longstanding hails from the United States. At the same time that this friend was outlawed from U.S. soil and estranged from his partner, the bride and groom on the *Santa Maria* were entering into marriage, perhaps the most legitimate union of all in the eyes of the U.S. government and the law. . . . This collection represents all our struggles with categories that alternately confine and liberate us, giving us both our sense of where we come from, and where we feel impelled to go. And so we create an intricate braid much like the wedding ceremony I was part of, each strand a different color, length, texture, and density, representing diverse and divergent experiences.

L'EPLATTENIER: These chapters remind me that subjectivity is about examining the multitudes contained within ourselves, the people/topics we study, and our interactions with them and the work—that subjectivity is and will always be an incredibly complex and slippery topic. . . . Walt Whitman reminds us all; "I am large. I contain multitudes."

LEE: We are poor rural white, upper-caste Brahmin, first generation Italian male, black feminist lesbian, North Carolinian Native American, and a multiplicity of other contingent and contested identities. Most of us have never met, but from reading what we all wrote, we apparently are all bound in an overdetermined academic culture that we want to transform.

SIMPKINS: In *Calling Cards*, we collapse the borders of the binary constructed by what Valerie Lee appropriately describes as an overdetermined academy. Through our theory we resist the predictable path in which one hegemony merely replaces another, insisting instead upon inclusion, expansion, and theoretical revision. We are a diverse collective, drawing from our unique positioning in the world and our interdisciplinary knowledge to frame the questions that serve as forays into academic inquiry. Susan Krouse's reflection upon a culture's selective memory regarding the contributions of American Indian women in the United States led me back to Mary Shadd as she bore witness to migrations of discursive hegemonic practice as documented in abolitionist newspapers. Shadd's constituencies were inclusive—women and men, African, American Indian, and European descent: All were textual activists, members of a lettered, disenfranchised caste.

CRANE BIZZARO: One of the best things about these essays is that they broaden my understanding of the oppressive effects of culture, and they reinforce to me my own argument (and that of many of the authors here) that we must revise the history of our discipline in order to make others understand how debilitating this oppression can be.

WU: Research is not simply for research's sake nor for the sake of talking only to those within the academy, but for imparting transformations to society, in Renee's words, to "combat the forces" through "countering, counterdiscourses, counter knowledge" . . . we have no choice but to defy the current, available theories and research practices because they tend to put our research into a straitjacket, endangering the lives of the marginalized groups we want to honor and celebrate.

KROUSE: We are scholars with pens not afraid to use them to challenge received notions. . . . If we had not centralized one or all of these constructs—race, gender, culture—our work would have been very different from what it is, and perhaps would not have happened at all. . . . I am an American Indian woman who researches the lives of American Indian women. And I think that what I have to say matters. . . . What matters more is that in many cases it is only women of color who are researching and writing about the lives and words of women of color. I do not mean to suggest that we should segregate these research topics, but rather to honor those women and men who have chosen to focus on the often unheard voices of their own communities. I want to encourage the idea of indigenous scholarship because it includes a perspective that can only come from inside.

HOLMES: We may have our own agendas, and these are betrayed in the metaphors that we appropriate, as Barbara cogently argues. Nevertheless, this collection succeeds in part not because of the particular agendas, or even the inquiries the essayists posit, but because of what I believe are the common denominators for this collection—less of a focus on the *whys* of theories and practices related to race, gender and culture, and more on the *hows,* and also on the collective motives that govern both agendas and inquiries. This collection wrestles with blurring boundaries, most of which materially disenfranchise, while recognizing the rhetorical potential for social and political enfranchisement in these boundaries.

MORENO: I am reminded how painful it really is to confront and then embrace contradictions—remembering that, while being "welcome," we are also rejected . . . it is so important to look to this contested space as one, like academe, that is both hopeful and troubling. . . . For too long the academy has functioned as a community of those who listen only to themselves. So many of us have said that we were struck by the valuable things written in the collection, the issues named . . . but also how these things get ignored, not read, certainly not cited!

L'EPLATTENIER: Since a "complete" history can never be told, my questions become: How can we move into "mainstream history" without sacrificing the uniqueness of our subject area? Can we? Can that be done? What does it take to change a historical paradigm? What does a new, multiple perspective history look like?

BIZZARO: I'd want to argue that history is the history of individuals, not just of institutions. Much of the success of this collection rests in the narratives people have shared, narratives that reflect the history of individuals.

LOGAN: I do worry, as Barbara and many others have indicated, about how we can re-center the conversations. How do we share our histories without othering them? Are we simply reinforcing the old hierarchies? I was struck by Barbara's questions. They are good ones, especially if we think of this not so much as a "move into" as a highlighting of our *always already* presence in mainstream history. I don't always feel like saying, "Me, too; me too." I want to point out how my history has been there all the time. Toni Morrison, right Joyce? And the segregation issue, well everyone in one way or another studies or writes out of her own experience; it just seems that when it's not the experience of dominant culture, it is marked, othered, and categorized as different. But alas, I have no answers. I just wish that the double-consciousness that DuBois talked about, "always measuring ourselves against amused onlookers" wasn't so true.

ROYSTER: What about language and rhetoric?

CARLACIO: No one of us could have imagined how we would all, in some uncanny yet fortuitous way, reflect upon what I see as the need to take responsibility for the ways we use language. . . . It wasn't until I had written through my work on Stewart, for example, that I realized that I needed a new working definition of both rhetoric and of rhetorical history. I have discovered that the "guiding" light of the Western rhetorical tradition blinded and numbed me to what has been there all along. . . . I acknowledge the difficulty I have had in discerning my motives [as a white woman] for "speaking to and with" Maria Stewart. I believe that, far from being asked to stand aside in this collection, I have been invited to question the rigidity of the categories that ostensibly separate us—Stewart and me—materially, historically, culturally, and politically.

WU: I noticed that almost all the contributors chose the first-person pronoun, I, to address the issues and problems, making their positions strong, and perspectives clear. Perhaps, this is because in our research processes, we felt severe restrictions in institutionalized academic writing that required us to use the third-person point of view, which is supposed to establish the writer as an authoritative figure. But it would have distanced those of us in this collection from the situation we wanted to analyze and experiences we wanted to share. If I had not used "I," my essay would give the impression of pretense, remoteness, and indirectness. Yet, the emphasis on the "I" in this collection can be said to be the enemy of self-promotion, or egocentric discourse. To a large degree, the "I" in these essays is not deployed to promote self-interest or enhance self-image. It connects the contributors to the community and society to which they claim alliance, building the bond between the authors and the groups they study . . . the impact this collection may have in a market, where pure research without consideration of its social and ethical consequences has long been esteemed, is to re-steer the direction of academic research. It may draw scholars' attention to the connection between academic research and its potential sociopolitical impact.

BIZZARO: I'm a white male who grew up in a poor Italian section of Buffalo. I went to state universities and managed to get a scholarship to play football at one of them in New York. Having said that, I felt I did not have the language to say what needed to be said about class issues and male feminism. . . . Ann Green's essay helps me understand that, perhaps, the very language I need in order to say what needs to be said about class issues and men's relationship with feminism just does not yet exist. . . . I was also conscious of the fact I did not address my whiteness in my essay, at least not directly. . . . Valerie Babb's wonderfully clear essay fills in many of those problematic gaps for me . . . those essays make mine more sensible than it would be outside the language and context of what others in this collection have thought and written.

BABB: As Pat cautions, though, "If we don't consider how these matters of theory dangerously lead us into confrontation in the world off-campus, we have done little more, in the end, than pose." These collected essays crystallized for me, once again, something that has become second nature. My "calling cards" have allowed me to contribute to a discourse empowered to shape thought and, with luck, subsequently lay the basis for real social change . . . to carry on such a discourse is vital.

ROYSTER: To carry on a discourse, we have no choice but to be fully present, speaking, listening, ever-ready, as Burke suggests, to dive into conversations that we did not always start but still want to transform. So, race, class, gender, the politics of other locations can actually be instructive then?

LEE: As a department chair, I now see that much of what I thought was my adopted administrative style was probably no more than a reflection of my own working-class values. That I am "interruptible," probably has more to do with having shared a bedroom with a sister for eighteen years. That I didn't panic over budget cuts probably has more to do with having spent most of my life with unemployed and underemployed people than with any fiscal management on my part. Although I've told various racialized and gendered narratives about my life, as an academic, I've been selective about the class narratives that I tell. A new car at age sixteen and a sophomore year spent in Europe make the narrative. But until I read Ann Green's essay, I had conveniently forgotten about a father and uncles drinking beer, curing tobacco, shucking oysters, and hunting squirrels and deer in Southern Maryland.

ROYSTER: Critical engagement with identities—and experiences—are indeed instructive, especially when that engagement includes ourselves.

SIMPKINS: I have spent my life learning daily from the activism of my own father, and from my uncles too, that many ardent supporters of gender equality are African American men with daughters. These men substitute critical reflection for patronizing and debilitating paternalism. In this collection, Pat's resistance to paternal models—and his strategies for constructing a method of mentoring other men—brings conscious attention to ways that we can learn and that gender equality can extend advocacy with more action into a professional realm.

MOODY: I hadn't expected to learn as much as I have from this volume! (Don't ask me why.) . . . I learned many different things, and I learned *about* many different things. In my own essay, I stress that I have been fumbling these past years to train myself as an interdisciplinary scholar. So, I was delighted that other contributors have studied in interdisciplinary programs and departments to become interdisciplinary scholars, and that others still, apparently feel much more comfortable than I do with their scholarly locations in multiple disciplines and their capabilities as interdisciplinary scholars.

ROYSTER: What's left to be said?

ESPINOSA-AGUILAR: Jackie writes, "What has become more visible, therefore, is that when the ideologies are naturalized in mainstream constructs, they go unnoticed and uninterrogated; when they go against the mainstream grain, they are deemed problematic, contentious, or even 'unnatural.' " What strikes me about this is that I feel like this is the crux of my essay, and to some extent those of others. It is BECAUSE we are different that we are noticed. We go against naturalized constructs of what authoritative faculty look, act like, etc. from the minute we walk through the door. And we can't help it because we aren't likely to be "naturalized" until there are a hell of a lot more of us not just hired but retained and tenured throughout academe.

L'EPLATTENIER: Something that stands out for me is the fact that sexuality has been left fairly unexplored as an issue that affects subjectivity within our field—both in historical methodology and pedagogy (Queer theory, of course, makes it a primary focus and so do queer histories). Like whiteness, heterosexuality is simply assumed the norm. Joycelyn is the only one who specifically mentions how her "sexuality identities matter in/to the scholarship [she] undertakes." I think I'm pretty safe in assuming that it has also affected the reception of that scholarship within her university (I know that I worry about that issue myself). . . . Including sexuality in our methodological frameworks might reveal other insights and aspects of our analyses—for example, in rhetorical studies, about rhetorical ability/understanding, about the performativity of gender roles, an aspect of subjectivity, about our rhetorical subjects, and also about ourselves as scholars and researchers.

MIDDLETON: I often feel concerned about work in feminism that does not reflect a strong or broad range of readings by women of color on feminism, which posed, again, problems for me with this collection.

LOGAN: Joyce reminds us to be careful about location as we discuss ourselves, our work, and our students. Where do we locate ourselves with respect to whiteness? Are we guilty of privileging whiteness? Do we need to make sure our essays center on the "us" (however defined) rather than the "them"? Do we need to articulate more explicitly the unspoken default of invisible whiteness?

GREEN: If we're taking on (and have taken on) this ethical work of changing the world by looking hard at race, gender, and culture, who is the audience?

ROYSTER: Good question. . . . Who's listening? Who should be listening? How does audience matter?

MORENO: We do this work because it really is a matter of life or death, of being heard or not being heard. . . . The essays, this conversation opens up the inquiry to many different and wise voices . . . we all have something meaningful to say . . . I find myself being helped along . . . you all just have no idea or maybe you do.

BABB: As Barbara says in her essay, "I don't simply come to call and leave quietly." I don't believe any of us do. Our work

> is much too much important for that. . . . Listening to NPR this morning, I heard a story noting that racism is again on the rise, much of it directed against people of Muslim origins. I went back to *Calling Cards* for solace, reread the responses for encouragement, and realized that our work will never be done, that we are means to an end and not the end.

CODA

Alas, we are not in an open, airy, well-lighted space. We are in a virtual one, on-line, communicating across space and time. Technology has helped us to accomplish what we would not have been able to do otherwise—carry on a conversation—too quick, too preliminary, but necessary nonetheless. It is indeed innovative, and it is also renovative. We have transformed our possibilities—a bit, creating an unreal space amid real world issues to reflect, share, and speculate as scholars/researchers in textual studies about things that matter. We speak in the company of others. We learn. We hope that what we have done is instructive to others.

Works Cited

Adams, Bluford. *E. Pluribus Barnun: the Great Showman and the Making of U. S. Popular Culture.* Minneapolis: U of Minnesota P, 1995.

Adams, Katherine. *A Group of Their Own.* Albany: State University of New York P, 2001.

Adu-Poku, Samuel. "Envisioning (Black) Male Feminism: A Cross-Cultural Perspective." *Journal of Gender Studies* 10:2 (July 2001): 157–68.

Agnew, Lois. "The Civic Function of Taste: A Re-assessment of Hugh Blair's Rhetorical Theory." *Rhetoric Society Quarterly* 28 (1998): 25–36.

Ahmad, Aijaz. *In Theory: Classes, Nations, Literatures.* New York: Verso, 1992.

Alcoff, Linda. "The Problem of Speaking for Others." *Cultural Critique* 20 (Winter 1991–92): 5–32.

Allen, Paula Gunn. *The Woman Who Owned the Shadows.* San Francisco: Spinsters Ink, 1984.

Allen, Theodore W. *The Invention of the White Race. Volume One: Racial Oppression and Social Control. Volume Two: The Origins of Racial Oppression in Anglo-America.* London: Verso, 1994.

Allison, Dorothy. "Mama." *Calling Home: Working-Class Women's Writings, An Anthology.* Ed. Janet Zandy. New Brunswick: Rutgers UP, 1990. 138–47.

———. *Skin: Talking About Sex, Class, and Literature.* Ithaca: Firebrand Books, 1994.

Almonte, Richard. *A Plea for Emigration Or Notes of Canada West.* Toronto: The Mercury, 1998.

Als, Hilton. "More Harm Than Good: Surviving the N-Word and Its Meanings." *The New Yorker.* 11 February 2002: 82–88.

Anderson, James D. *The Education of Blacks in the South, 1860–1935.* Chapel Hill: U of North Carolina P, 1988.

Andrews, William, ed. *Sisters of the Spirit: Three Black Women's Autobiographies of the Nineteenth Century.* Bloomington: Indiana UP, 1986.

74th Annual Academy Awards. Host, Whoopi Goldberg. 24 March 2002.

Apodaca, Clair. "The Effects of Foreign Aid on Women's Attainment of Their Economic and Social Human Rights." *Journal of Third World Studies* 17:2 (2000): 202–27.

Appadurai, Arjun. "Grassroots Globalization and the Research Imagination." *Public Culture* 12:1 (2001): 1–19.

Apter, Emily. "On Translation in a Global Marker." *Public Culture.* 13:1 (2000): 1–12.

Aristotle. *The Rhetoric and the Poetics.* New York: Modern Library, 1984.

Arnold, Martin. "A New Imprint is Dedicated to Black Readers." *New York Times,* 23 May, 2002.

Arthos, John Jr. " 'My Voice Is Bound to the Mess of My Own Life': Private and Public Boundaries in Feminist Rhetoric." *The Southern Communication Journal* 63 (Winter 1998): 113–30.

Asante, Molefi. *The Afrocentric Idea.* Philadelphia: Temple UP, 1987.

Babb, Valerie. *Whiteness Visible: The Meaning of Whiteness in American Literature and Culture.* New York: NYUP, 1998.

Bacon, Jacqueline and Glen McClish. "Reinventing the Master's Tools: Nineteenth-Century African-American Literary Societies of Philadelphia and Rhetorical Education." *Rhetoric Society Quarterly* 30 (September 2000): 19–47.

Badger, Reid. *The Great American Fair: The World's Columbian Exposition and American Culture.* Chicago: Nelson Hall, 1979.

Bahri, Deepika and Vasudeva, Mary. "Transnationality and Multiculturalist Ideology: Interview with Gayatri Chakravorty Spivak. *Between the Lines: South Asians and Postcoloniality.* Eds. Deepika Bahri and Mary Vasudeva. Philadelphia: Temple UP, 1996. 64–92.

Baldwin, James. "A Talk to Teachers." *The Graywolf Annual Five: Multicultural Literacy.* Eds. Rick Simonson and Scott Walker. Saint Paul: Graywolf Press, 1988. 3–12.

Bambara, Toni Cade. "The Lesson." *Gorilla, My Love.* New York: Random House, 1972.

Bamboozled. Dir. Spike Lee. Perf. Damon Wayans, Savion Glover, Tommy Davidson, Forty Acres and a Mule Films, 2000.

Barksdale, Richard and Keneth Kinnamon. *Black Writers of America: A Comprehensive Anthology.* New York: The Macmillan Company, 1972.

Bator, Paul G. "The Formation of the Regius Chair of Rhetoric and Belles Lettres at the University of Edinburgh." *Quarterly Journal of Speech,* 75 (1989): 40–64.

Bauer, Dale. "The Other 'F' Word: The Feminist in the Classroom.' *College English* 52: 4 (1990): 385–96.

Bearden, Jim, and Linda Jean Butler. *The Life and Times of Mary Shadd Cary.* Toronto: NC Press, Ltd., 1977.

Belenky, Mary Field, et al. *Women's Ways of Knowing: The Development of Self, Body, Mind.* New York: Basic, 1986.

Bell, Betty Louise. *Faces in the Moon.* Norman: U of Oklahoma P, 1994.

Berger, Maurice. *White Lies: Race and the Myths of Whiteness.* New York: Farrar Straus and Giroux, 1999.

Berlant, Lauren. *The Queen of America Goes to Washington City.* Durham: Duke UP, 1997.

Berlin, Ira, Marc Favreau, and Steven F. Miller. *Remembering Slavery: African Americans Talk About Their Personal Experiences of Slavery and Emancipation.* New York: The New P, 1998.

Berlin, James. *Writing Instruction in Nineteenth-Century American Colleges.* Carbondale: Southern Illinois UP, 1984.

Bernardi, Daniel, ed. *Classic Hollywood, Classic Whiteness.* Minneapolis: U of Minnesota P, 2001.

Bizzaro, Patrick. *Responding to Student Poems: Applications of Critical Theory.* Urbana: NCTE, 1993.

Bizzaro, Resa Crane. "Making Places as Teacher-Scholars in Composition Studies: Comparing Transition Narratives." *College Composition and Communication* 53:3 (February 2002): 487–506.

Bizzell, Patricia and Bruce Herzberg, eds. *The Rhetorical Tradition: Readings from Classical Times to the Present.* 2d ed. New York: Bedford/St. Martin's, 2001.

Black Elk Speaks: Being the Life Story of a Holy Man of the Oglala Sioux. Lincoln: U of Nebraska P, 1979.

Black Women in America: An Historical Encyclopedia. Vol. 1. Eds. Darlene Clark Hine et al. Blacks in the Diaspora Series. Bloomington: Indiana UP, 1993.

Blackman, Margaret B. *During My Time: Florence Edenshaw Davidson, a Haida Woman.* Revised and enlarged edition. Seattle: U of Washington P, 1994.

Blake, William. "The Marriage of Heaven and Hell." *English Romantic Writers.* David Perkins, ed. 2nd ed. Fort Worth: Harcourt, 1995.

Blewster, Kelly. "Oprah Winfrey: Testifying to the Power of Books." *Biblio* (January 1998): 22–28.

Bloom, Lynn Z. "Freshman Composition as Middle-Class Enterprise." *College English* 58:6 (October 1996): 654–75.

Bock, Gisela. "Challenging Dichotomies: Perspectives on Women's History." *Writing Women's History: International Perspectives.* Eds. Karen Offen, Ruth Roach Pierson, and Jane Rendall. Bloomington: Indiana UP, 1991. 1–24.

Bode, Carl. *The American Lyceum: Town Meeting of the Mind.* New York: Oxford UP, 1956.

Bonilla-Silva, Eduardo. *Racism Without Racists.* Lanham, MD: Rowman and Littlefield, 2003.

Book TV. "Forum: *The Wind Done Gone* [Randall, Alice, author] and *Finn: a Novel* [Olshan, Matthew, author] Southern Festival of Books." C-Span.org. Nashville. 13 October 2001.

Bowden, Peta. *Caring: Gender Sensitive Ethics.* New York: Routledge, 1997.

Boynton, Robert S. "Out of Africa, and Back." *New York Times,* 12 April 2002.

Broaddus, Dorothy C. *Genteel Rhetoric: Writing High Culture in Nineteenth-Century Boston.* Columbia: U of South Carolina P, 1999.

Brodkey, Linda. *Writing Permitted in Designated Areas Only.* Minneapolis: U of Minnesota P, 1996.

Brown, Elsa Barkley. "African-American Women's Quilting: A Framework for Conceptualizing and Teaching African-American History." *Signs* 14:4 (Summer 1989).

———. "Negotiating and Transforming the Public Sphere: African American Political Life in the Transition from Slavery to Freedom." *The Black Public Sphere: A Public Culture Book.* Ed. The Black Public Sphere Collective. Chicago: U of Chicago P, 1995. 111–50.

Bruffee, Kenneth. "Collaborative Learning and the Conversation of Mankind." *College English* 46:7 (November 1984): 635–52.

Buffon, Georges. "The Geographical and Cultural Distribution of Mankind." Reprinted in *Race and the Enlightenment.* Ed. Emmanuel Chukwudi Eze. Cambridge: Blackwell, 1997. 15–28.

Burke, Kenneth. *A Rhetoric of Motives.* Berkeley: U of California P, 1969.

———. *A Grammar of Motives.* New York: Prentice-Hall, 1952.

———. *Language as Symbolic Action.* Berkeley: U of California P, 1966.

———. *The Philosophy of Literary Form: Studies in Symbolic Action.* Berkeley: U of California P, 1973.

Burkett, Nancy H., and John B. Bench, eds. *Under Its Generous Dome: The Collections and Programs of the American Antiquarian Society*, 2nd ed., rev. Worcester: American Antiquarian Society, 1992.

Burstein, Andrew. *The Inner Jefferson: Portrait of a Grieving Optimist.* Charlottesville: UP of Virginia, 1991.

Bustamante, Jorge A. "International Migration and Human Rights." Institute for Latino Studies, University of Notre Dame, 2002.

Butler, Melvin A., et al. "Students' Right to Their Own Language." *College Composition and Communication* XXV (Fall 1974): 1–32.

Campbell, George. 1963. *The Philosophy of Rhetoric.* Carbondale: Southern Illinois UP, 1963.

Campbell, Karlyn. *Man Cannot Speak for Her: A Critical Study of Early Feminist Rhetoric.* Vol. 1. Westport: Praeger, 1989.

Carlacio, Jami. "In Their Own Words: The Rhetorical Practices of Maria Stewart and Sarah Grimké." Unpublished Dissertation. U of Wisconsin-Milwaukee, 2001.

Carr, Carolyn Kinder, and George Gurney. *Revisiting the White City: American Art at the 1893 World's Fair.* Washington, DC: Smithsonian Institution, 1993.

Carson, James P. "Britons, 'Hottentots,' Plantation Slavery, and Tobias Smollett." *Philological Quarterly* 75: 4 (Fall 1996): 471–99.

Catano, James V. "The Rhetoric of Masculinity: Origins, Institutions, and the Myth of the Self-Made Man." *College English* 52 (1990): 421–36.

Cavendish, Margaret. *Orations of Divers Sorts Accommodated to Divers Places: Written by the Thrice Noble, Illustrious and Excellent Princess, the Lady of Marchioness of Newcastle.* London: Anno Dom, 1662.

Channing, William E. *Self-Culture: An Address Introductory to the Franklin Lectures.* Boston: Dutton and Wentworth, 1838. Reprint. New York: Arno, 1969.

"Characteristics of Recipients of Doctorates, 1999." *The Chronicle of Higher Education* XLVIII:1: 24. August 31, 2001.

Cheney, John L., Jr., ed. *North Carolina Government 1585–1979: A Narrative and Statistical History.* Raleigh: North Carolina Department of the Secretary of State, 1981.

Chesnutt, Charles W. *Essays and Speeches.* Eds. Joseph McElrath, Robert Leitz, and Jesse Crisler. Stanford: Stanford UP, 1999.

Christian, Barbara. "The Race for Theory." *Cultural Criqique* 6 (1987): 335–45. Reprinted in *African American Literary Theory: A Reader.* Ed. Winston Napier. New York: New York UP, 2000.

The Chronicle of Higher Education. "Number of Full-Time Faculty Members by Sex, Rank, and Racial and Ethnic Group, Fall 1997." 31 August 2001.

Clark, Gregory, and S. Michael Halloran, eds. *Oratorical Culture in Nineteenth Century America: Transformations in the Theory and Practice of Rhetoric.* Carbondale: Southern Illinois UP, 1993.

"College Enrollment by Racial and Ethnic Group, Selected Years." *The Chronicle of Higher Education* XLVIII:1: 20. August 31, 2001.

Condit, Celeste Michelle. "In Praise of Eloquent Diversity: Gender and Rhetoric as Public Persuasion." *Women's Studies in Communication* 20 (Fall 1997): 91–116.

———, and John Louis Lucaites. *Crafting Equality: America's Anglo-African Word.* Chicago: U of Chicago P, 1993.

———. "The Rhetoric of Equality and the Expatriation of African-Americans, 1776–1826." *Communication Studies* 42 (Spring 1991): 1–21.

Condon, William. "Virtual Space, Real Participation: Dimensions and Dynamics of a Virtual Classroom." *The Online Writing Classroom.* Eds. Susanmarie Harrington, Michael Day, and Rebecca Rickly. Cresskill, NJ: Hampton Press, 2000.

Conley, Dalton. "The Universal Freckle, or How I Learned to Be White." *The Making and Unmaking of Whiteness.* Ed. Birgit Brander Rasmussen, Eric Klinenberg, Irene J. Nexica, and Matt Wray. Durham: Duke UP, 2001. 25–42.

Connors, Robert J. "Teaching and Learning as a Man." *College English* 58 (1996): 137–57.

———. *Composition-Rhetoric: Backgrounds, Theory, and Pedagogy.* Pittsburgh: U of Pittsburgh P, 1997.

Cooper, Anna Julia. *A Voice from the South.* The Schomburg Library of Nineteenth-Century Black Women Writers. New York: Oxford UP, 1988.

Crenshaw, Kimberle Williams, et al., eds. *Critical Race Theory: the Key Writings that Formed the Movement.* New York: New P, 1995.

———. "Color-Blind Dreams and Racial Nightmares: Reconfiguring Racism in the Post-Civil Rights Era." *Birth of a Nationhood.* Eds. Toni Morrison and Claudia Brodsky Lacour. New York: Pantheon Books, 1997. 97–168.

Crevecoeur, J. Hector St. John de. *Letters from an American Farmer.* New York: Dolphin-Doubleday, 1963.

Crowdus, Gary, and Dan Georgakas. "Thinking about the Power of Images: An Interview with Spike Lee." *Cineaste* (May 2001): 4–9.

Crowley, Sharon. *The Methodical Memory: Invention in Current-Traditional Rhetoric.* Carbondale: Southern Illinois UP, 1990.

———. *Composition in the University: Historical and Polemical Essays.* Pittsburgh: U of Pittsburgh P, 1998.

Culler, Jonathan. *On Deconstruction: Theory and Criticism After Structuralism.* Ithaca: Cornell UP, 1982.

Cultural Criticism and Transformation. Video Interview with bell hooks. Media Education Foundation, 1997.

Daily Reflector. "Legislator Apologizes for E-Mail." (Greenville, NC) 23 August 2001.

Dash, Joan. *We Shall Not Be Moved: The Women's Factory Strike of 1909.* New York: Scholastic, 1996.

Davies, John. "Phrenology: Fad and Science." *A 19th-Century American Crusade.* New Haven: Yale UP, 1955.

Davis, F. James. *Who Is Black? One Nation's Definition.* University Park: Penn State UP, 1991.

Dawson, Michael C. *Black Visions.* Chicago: U of Chicago P, 2001.

de Bary, William Theodore. *Asian Values and Human Rights: A Confucian Communitarian Perspective.* Cambridge: Harvard UP, 2000.

———, ed. *Sources of Chinese Tradition.* New York: Columbia UP, 1960.

Decosta-Willis, Miriam, ed. *The Memphis Diary of Ida B. Wells.* Boston: Beacon, 1995.

Delany, Martin Robison. *The Condition, Elevation, Emigration, and Destiny of the Colored People of the United States.* Salem, NH: Ayer Company, 1998.

Delany, Sarah L. and A. Elizabeth Delany. *Having Our Say.* New York: A Dell Book, 1993.

Delgado, L. Elena and Romero, Rolando J. "Local Histories and Global Designs: An Interview with Walter Mignolo. *Discourse* 22:3 (Fall 2000): 7–33.

Delgado, Richard, and Jean Stefancic, eds. *Critical White Studies: Looking Behind the Mirror.* Philadelphia: Temple UP, 1997.

DeLombard, Jeannine. "Getting (The) Man Off (Our) Eyeball: White Critical Discourse and African-American Literature." *Minnesota Review* 52–54 (Fall 2001): 341–46.

Deloria, Vine Jr. *Custer Died for Your Sins: An Indian Manifesto.* New York: Macmillan, 1969.

———. *We Talk, You Listen: New Tribes, New Turf.* New York: Macmillan, 1970.

Delpit, Lisa, and Joanne Kilgour Dowdy. *The Skin that We Speak: Thoughts on* Language and Culture in the Classroom. New York: New P, 2002.

Dennett, Andrea Stulman. *Weird and Wonderful: The Dime Museum in America.* New York: New York UP, 1997.

Dent, Gina, ed. *Black Popular Culture: A Project by Michele Wallace.* Seattle: Bay Press, 1992.

Devi, Mahasweta. *Imaginary Maps: Three Stories.* Trans. Gayatri Chakravorty Spivak. New York: Routledge, 1995.

Dillard, J. L. *Black English: Its History and Usage in the United States.* New York: Vintage, 1973.

Dippo, Don, and Steven Gelb. "Making the Political Personal: Problems of Privilege and Power in Post-Secondary Teaching." *Journal of Education* 173:3 (1991): 81–95.

Dirlik, Arif. *The Postcolonial Aura: Third World Criticism in the Age of Global Capitalism.* Boulder: Westview Press, 1997.

Dominguez, Virginia. *White by Definition: Social Class Stratification in Creole Louisiana.* New Brunswick: Rutgers UP, 1986.

Donawerth, Jane. "Textbooks for New Audiences: Women's Revisions of Rhetorical Theory at the Turn of the Century." *Listening to Their Voices: The Rhetorical Activities of Historical Women.* Ed. Molly Meijer Wertheimer. Columbia: U of South Carolina P, 1997. 337–56.

DuBois, W. E. B. *The Souls of Black Folk.* New York: Gramercy Books, 1994.

———. *The Philadelphia Negro.* Millwood, NY: Kraus-Thomson, 1994.

DuCille, Ann. *Skin Trade.* Cambridge: Harvard UP, 1990.

Duyfhuizen, Bernard. "Textual Harassment of Marvell's Coy Mistress: The Institutionalization of Masculine Criticism." *College English* 50 (1988): 411–23.

Early, Gerald. "A Place of Our Own: My Brilliant Career." *New York Times.* 12 April, 2002.

Easton, Hosea. "A Treatise on the Intellectual Character, and Civil and Political Condition of the Colored People of the United States." *Negro Protest Pamphlets.* Ed. Dorothy Porter. New York: Arno, 1969.

Edelman, Gary. *Solidarity Forever: Rose Schneiderman and the Women's Trade Union League.* New York: Arno Press, 1982.

Edwards, Ishmell Hendrex. "History of Rust College 1866–1967." Unpublished Dissertation. University of Mississippi, 1994.

Ehrenreich, Barbara. *Fear of Falling: The Inner Life of the Middle Class.* New York: Harper Perennial, 1989.

Elbow, Peter. *Writing Without Teachers.* New York: Oxford UP, 1973.

Eliades, David K., and Linda Ellen Oxendine. *Pembroke State University: A Centennial History.* Columbus, GA: Brentwood UP, 1986.

Ellison, Ralph. *Invisible Man.* New York: Random House, 1952.

Ellsworth, Elizabeth. "Why Doesn't This Feel Empowering? Working Through the Repressive Myths of Critical Pedagogy." *Harvard Educational Review* 59:3 (August 1989): 297–324.

———. "Double Binds of Whiteness." *Off White: Readings on Race, Power, and Society.* Ed. Michelle Fine, Lois Weis, Linda C. Powell, L. Mun Wong. New York: Routledge, 1997. 259–69.

Evans, Henry L. "An Afrocentric Multicultural Writing Project." *Writing in Multicultural Settings.* Eds. Carol Severino, Juan C. Guerra, and Johnnella E. Butler. New York: Modern Language Association, 1997. 273–86.

Evans, Mari. "Status Symbol," *I Am a Black Woman.* New York: William Morrow, 1970.

Finn, Patrick J. *Literacy with an Attitude: Educating Working-Class Children in Their Own Self-Interest.* Albany: State U of New York P, 1999.

Fitzgerald, Kathryn. "A Rediscovered Tradition: European Pedagogy and Composition in Nineteenth-Century Midwestern Normal Schools." *College Composition and Communication* 53:2 (2001): 224–50.

Fitzmaurice, James. *Margaret Cavendish: Sociable Letters.* New York: Garland, 1997.

Flynn, Elizabeth. "Composing 'Composing as a Woman': A Perspective on Research." *College Composition and Communication* 41.1 (1990): 83–91.

———. "Composing as a Woman." *College Composition and Communication* 39.4 (1988): 423–35.

———. 1995. "Feminism and Scientism." *College Composition and Communication* 46:3 (1995): 353–68.

———. "Learning to Read Student Papers from a Feminine Perspective, I." *Encountering Student Texts.* Eds. Bruce Lawson, Susan Sterr Ryan, and W. Ross Winterowd. Urbana: National Council of Teachers of English, 1989. 49–58.

Flynn, John. "Learning to Read Student Papers from a Feminine Perspective, II." *Encountering Student Texts.* Eds. Bruce Lawson, Susan Sterr Ryan, and W. Ross Winterowd. 131–38.

Foner, Philip. *History of Black Americans: From the Emergence of the Cotton Kingdom to the Eve of the Compromise of 1850.* Westport, CT: Greenwood P, 1983.

Fontaine, D. C., and S. P. Greenlee. "Black Women: Double Solos in the Workplace." *The Western Journal of Black Studies* 17:3 (1993): 121–25.

Foss, Sonja K., and Karen A. Foss. *Women Speak: The Eloquence of Women's Lives.* Prospect Heights, IL: Waveland, 1991.

Foss, Sonja K., and Cindy L. Griffin. "Beyond Persuasion: A Proposal for an Invitational Rhetoric." *Communication Monographs* 62 (1995): 2–18.

Fox, Helen. *When Race Breaks Out: Conversations about Race and Racism in College Classrooms.* New York: Peter Lang, 2001.

Frankenburg, Ruth. *Displacing Whiteness: Essays in Social and Cultural Criticism.* Durham: Duke UP, 1997.

———. *White Women: Race Matters: The Social Construction of Whiteness.* Minneapolis: U of Minnesota P, 1993.

Franklin, John Hope. *From Slavery to Freedom.* New York: Knopf, 1963.

Fraser, Nancy. *Unruly Practices: Power, Discourse and Gender in Contemporary Social Theory.* Minneapolis: U of Minnesota P, 1989.

———. *Justice Interruptus: Critical Reflections on the "Postsocialist" Condition.* New York: Routledge, 1997.

Freire, Paulo. *Pedagogy of the Oppressed.* New York: Continuum, 1970.

———, and Donaldo Macedo. Literacy: Reading the Word and the World. South Hadley, MA: Bergin and Garvey, 1987.

French, Gary E. *Men of Colour: An Historical Account of the Black Settlement on Wilberforce St. in Oro Township, Simcoe Cty. Ontario, 1819–1849.* Ontario: Dyment-Stubley Printers, 1978.

Fromkin, Victoria, and Robert Rodman. *An Introduction to Language.* Fort Worth: Harcourt Brace, 1998.

Gallos, Joan. "When Authority = She: A Male Student Meets a Female Instructor." *Journal of Management Development* 14:2 (1995): 65–76.

Gates, Henry Louis, Jr. *Black Literature and Literary Theory.* New York: Metheun, 1984.

———. *Loose Canons: Notes on the Culture Wars.* New York: Oxford UP, 1992.

———, and Nellie Y. McKay, eds. *The Norton Anthology of African American Literature.* New York: Norton, 1997.

Gibson, Michelle, Martha Marinara, and Deborah Meem. "Bi, Butch, and Bar Dyke: Pedagogical Performances of Class, Gender, and Sexuality." *College Composition and Communication* 52:1 (September 2000): 69–95.

Gil, Vincent E. and Allen f. Anderson. "Case Study of Rape in Contemporary China." *Journal of Interpersonal Violence.* 14 (1999): 1151–71.

Gilligan, Carol. *In a Different Voice: Psychological Theory and Women's Development.* Cambridge: Harvard UP, 1982.

Gilyard, Keith. *Voices of the Self: A Study of Language Competence.* Detroit: Wayne State UP, 1991.

———. *Let's Flip the Script: An African American Discourse on Language, Literature and Learning.* Detroit: Wayne State UP, 1996.

Girl 6. Dir. Spike Lee. Perf. Theresa Randle, Spike Lee, Isaiah Washington, A Forty Acres and a Mule Film, 1996.

Giovanni, Nikki. "Alabama Poem." *The Selected Poems of Nikki Giovanni.* New York: William Morrow, 1996.

Giroux, Henry. *Breaking in to the Movies: Film and the Culture of Politics.* Malden, MA: Blackwell P, 2002.

———. "Racial Politics and the Pedagogy of Whiteness." *Whiteness: a Critical Reader.* Ed. Mike Hill. New York: New York UP, 1997.

Glenn, Cheryl. *Rhetoric Retold.* Carbondale: Southern Illinois UP, 1997.

———. "Remapping Rhetorical Territory." *Rhetoric Review* 13:2 (1995): 287–303.

Golden, James L., and Edward Corbett, eds. *The Rhetoric of Blair, Campbell, and Whately.* Carbondale: Southern Illinois UP, 1990.

Goldman, Anne E. " 'I Made the Ink': Literary Production and Reproduction in *Dessa Rose* and *Beloved.*" *Feminist Studies* 16 (1990): 313–30.

Gossett, Hattie. "who told you anybody wants to hear from you? you aint nothing but a black woman!" *This Bridge Called My Back: Writings by Radical Women of Color.* 2nd ed. Eds. Cherríe Moraga and Gloria Anzaldúa. New York: Kitchen Table P, 1983. 175–76.

Graff, Gerald. "A Pedagogy of Counterauthority, or the Bully/Wimp Syndrome." *Changing Classroom Practices: Resources for Literary and Cultural Studies.* Ed. David B. Downing. Urbana: NCTE, 1994. 179–93.

Graff, Harvey J. *The Literacy Myth: Literacy and Social Structure in the Nineteenth-Century City.* New York: Academic P, 1979.

Graff, Henry F. *The Presidents: A Reference History.* New York: Macmillan Library, 1997.

Green, Ann E. "My Uncle's Guns." Susan Naomi Bernstein. *Teaching Developmental Writing: Background Readings.* New York: Bedford/St. Martins, 2001. 35–44.

Green, Rayna. "The Pocahontas Perplex: The Image of Indian Women in American Culture." *Massachusetts Review* 14 (1976): 698–714.

Guinier, Lani, and Gerald Torres. *The Miner's Canary: Enlisting Race, Resisting Power, Transforming Democracy.* Cambridge: Harvard UP, 2002.

Gutierrez, Kris D., Patricia Baquedano-Lopez, and Jolynn Asato. " 'English for the Children': The New Literacy of the Old World Order." *Bilingual Research Journal,* 24: 1–2 (2000): 87–112.

Hale, Elizabeth Grace. *Making Whiteness: The Culture of Segregation in the South, 1890–1940.* New York: Pantheon Books, 1998.

Hall, David, and Roger Ames. *Thinking from the Han.* Albany: State U of New York P, 1998.

Hamilton, Alexander, John Jay, and James Madison. *The Federalist: A Commentary on the Constitution of the United States.* New York: Modern Library, 1982.

Hamilton, William Baskerville. *Holly Springs, Mississippi, to the year 1878.* Holly Springs: Marshall County Historical Society, 1984.

Hamrick, Florence, Nancy J. Evans, and John H. Schuh. *Foundations of Student Affairs Practice: How Philosophy, Theory, and Research Strengthen Educational Outcomes*. San Francisco: Wiley, 2002.

Haney-Lopez, Ian F. *White by Law: The Legal Construction of Race*. New York: New York UP, 1996.

Harasym, Sarahjed. *The Post-Colonial Critic:* Interviews, Strategies, Dialogues. New York: Routledge, 1990.

Harding, Vincent, Robin D. G. Kelley, and Earl Lewis. "We Changed the World: 1945–1970." *To Make Our World Anew: A History of African Americans*. Eds. Robin D. G. Kelley and Earl Lewis. New York: Oxford U Press, 2000. 445–542.

Harper, Frances E. W. *Iola Leroy or Shadows Uplifted*. Boston: Beacon P, 1987.

Harris, Elizabeth Johnson. Life Story, 1867–1923. African-American Women, Digital Scriptorium Projects, Duke University Rare Book, Manuscript, and Special Collections Library. http://scriptorium.lib.duke.edu/harris/harris-indx.html.

Harris, Susan K. "Responding to the Text(s): Women Readers and the Quest for Higher Education." *Readers in History: Nineteenth-Century American Literature and the Contexts of Response*. Ed. James L. Machor. Baltimore: Johns Hopkins UP, 1993. 259–82.

Hartman, Saidiya. *Scenes of Subjection: Terror, Slavery, and Self-Making in Nineteenth-Century America*. New York: Oxford UP, 1997.

Harvey, Joan C., and Cynthia Katz. *If I'm So Successful, Why Do I Feel Like a Fake? The Impostor Phenomenon*. New York: St. Martin's, 1985.

Hedin, Raymond. "Probable Readers, Possible Stories: The Limits of Nineteenth-Century Black Narrative." *Readers in History: Nineteenth-Century American Literature and the Contexts of Response*. Ed. James L. Machor. Baltimore: Johns Hopkins UP, 1993. 180–205.

Heilman, Madeline, et al. "Assumed Incompetent? Stigmatization and Affirmative Action Efforts." *Journal of Applied Psychology* 4 (1992): 536–44.

Henderson, Mae Gwendolyn. "Speaking in Tongues: Dialogics, Dialectics, and the Black Woman Writer's Literary Tradition." *Changing Our Own Words: Essays on Criticism, Theory, and Writing by Black Women*. Ed. Cheryl Wall. New Brunswick: Rutgers UP, 1989. 16–37.

Herbert, Bob. "Cleansing CUNY: Fear and Loathing in New York." *The New York Times*, National ed. (28 May 1988): OPEDA29.

Higginbotham, Elizabeth. *Too Much to Ask: Black Women in the Era of Integration*. Chapel Hill: U of North Carolina P, 2001.

Higginbotham, Evelyn Brooks. "African-American Women's History and the Metalanguage of Race." *Signs: Journal of Women in Culture and Society* 17.2 (Winter 1992): 251–174.

Hill, Mike, ed. *Whiteness: A Critical Reader*. New York: New York UP, 1997.

Hine, Darlene Clark, and Kathleen Thompson, eds. *A Shining Thread of Hope: The History of Black Women in America*. New York: Broadway, 1998.

Holden, Stephen. "Film Review: Within a Florida Civics Lesson, Rich Stories." *New York Times*. 21 June 2002, late ed.: E1.

Holloway, Karla. "Beloved: A Spiritual." *Callaloo* 13 (1990): 516–25.

Holt, Thomas C. *The Problem of Race in the 21st Century*. Cambridge: Harvard UP, 2000.

hooks, bell. *Feminist Theory: From Margin to Center.* Boston: South End P, 1984.

———. *Talking Back: Thinking Feminist, Thinking Black.* Boston: South End P, 1989.

———. *Yearning: Race, Gender, and Cultural Politics.* Boston: South End P, 1990.

———. *Teaching to Transgress: Education as the Practice of Freedom.* New York: Routledge, 1994.

———. *Reel to Real: Race, Sex, and Class at the Movies.* London: Routledge, 1996.

———. *Where We Stand: Class Matters.* New York, Routledge, 2000.

Hopkins, Pauline. *Contending Forces: A Romance Illustrative of Negro Life North and South.* New York: Oxford UP, 1988.

Horner, Winifred Bryan, ed. *The Present State of Scholarship in Historical and Contemporary Rhetoric.* Columbia: U of Missouri P, 1990.

———. *Nineteenth Century Scottish Rhetoric: The American Connection.* Carbondale: Southern UP, 1993.

Howe, Daniel Walker, ed. *Victorian America.* Philadelphia: U of Pennsylvania P, 1976.

Hughes, Langston. *Best of Simple.* New York: Hill and Wang, 1961.

Ignatiev, Noel. *How the Irish Became White.* New York: Routledge, 1995.

Jackson, Helen Hunt. *Ramona.* Boston: Roberts Brothers, 1884.

Jackson, Mattie J. *The Story of Matie J. Jackson: 1866 Six Women's Slave Narratives.* Ed. William L. Andres. New York: Oxford UP. 3rd Facsimile.

Jakobsen and Pellegrini. "World Secularism at the Millenium: Introduction." *Social Text* 64 18.3 (Fall 2000): 1–27.

Jamieson, Kathleen Hall. "Insinuations and Other Pitfalls in Political Ads and News." (3 July 2002). http://www.pressroom.com/-afrimale/jamieson. htm.

Jauss, Hans Robert. *Toward an Aesthetic of Reception.* Trans. Timothy Bahti. Minneapolis: U of Minnesota P, 1982.

Jefferson, Thomas. *Notes on the State of Virginia.* Ed. Frank Shuffelton. New York: Penguin Books, 1999.

Johnson-Bailey, Juanita. *Sistahs in College: Making a Way Out of No Way.* Malabar, FL: Krieger, 2001.

Johnson, Nan. *Gender and Rhetorical Space in American Life, 1866–1910.* Carbondale: Southern Illinois UP, 2002.

Jones, Absolom, and Richard Allen. "A Narrative of the Proceedings of the Black People, During the Late Awful Calamity in Philadelphia, in the Year, 1793." *Negro Protest Pamphlets.* Ed. Dorothy Porter. New York: Arno, 1969.

Jordan, June. *Technical Difficulties.* New York: Pantheon, 1992.

Jordan, Sarah, and Alan Purves. *Issues in the Responses of Students to Culturally Diverse Texts: A Preliminary Study.* Albany: National Research Center on Literature Teaching and Learning, 1993.

Jordan, Winthrop D. *White Over Black: American Attitudes Toward the Negro, 1550–1812.* New York: Norton, 1977.

Kadi, Joanna. *Thinking Class: Sketches from a Cultural Worker.* Boston, South End P, 1996.

Karenga, Maulana. "Nommo, Kawaida, and Communicative Practice: Bringing Good into the World." *Understanding African American Rhetoric: Classical Origins to Contemporary Innovations*. Eds. Ronald L. Jackson and Elaine B. Richardson. New York: Routledge, 2003. 3–22.

Katz, Susan. *Activist Rhetorics and American Higher Education 1885–1937*. Carbondale: Southern Illinois UP, 2001.

Kelley, Robin, D. G. *Yo' Mama's Disfunktional! Fighting the Culture Wars in Urban America*. Boston: Beacon Press, 1997.

———. "Foreword." William Watkins. *The White Architects of Black Education: Ideology and Power in America, 1865–1954*. New York: Teachers College P, 2001. xi–xiii.

———. *Freedom Dreams: The Black Radical Imagination*. Boston: Beacon P, 2002.

Kerber, Linda. "Women and Men: Boredom, Violence, and Political Power." In *Toward an Intellectual History of Women: Essays by Linda Kerber*. Chapel Hill: U of North Carolina P, 1997. 303–18.

Kets de Vries, Manfred F. R. "The Imposter Syndrome: Developmental and Societal Issues." *Human Relations* 43:7 (July 1990): 667–86.

Kidwell, Clara Sue. "Indian Women as Cultural Mediators." *Ethnohistory* 39:2 (1992): 97–107.

King, Julie, and Eileen Cooley. "Achievement Orientation and the Imposter Phenomenon Among College Students." *Contemporary Educational Psychology* 20 (July 1995): 304–12.

Kusz, Kyle W. " 'I Want to Be the Minority': The Politics of Youthful White Masculinities in Sport and Popular Culture in 1990s America." *Journal of Sport and Social Issues* 25 (2001): 390–416.

La Farge, Oliver. *Laughing Boy*. Boston: Houghton Mifflin, 1929.

Labaree, Leonard W., ed. *The Papers of Benjamin Franklin*. 30 volumes to date. Volume 4, 225–34. New Haven: Yale UP, 1861.

LaFromboise, Teresa D., Anneliese M. Heyle, and Emily J. Ozer. "Changing and Diverse Roles of Women in American Indian Cultures." *Sex Roles* 22: 7/8 (1990): 455–76.

Lampe, Gregory P. *Frederick Douglass: Freedom's Voice, 1818–1845*. East Lansing: Michigan State UP, 1998.

Lauter, Paul. "Is Frances Ellen Watkins Harper Good Enough to Teach?" *Legacy: A Journal of Nineteenth-Century American Women* 5:1 (1988): 27–32.

Lee, Valerie. *Granny Midwives and Black Women Writers: Double-Dutched Readings*. New York: Routledge, 1996.

———. "Responses of White Students to Ethnic Literature: One Teacher's Experience." *Essays in Reader Oriented Theory, Criticism and Pedagogy* 15 (Spring 1986): 24–33.

Lefler, Hugh Talmage, and Albert Ray Newsome. *The History of a Southern State: North Carolina*. 3rd. ed. Chapel Hil: U of North Carolina P, 1973.

Lemert, Charles, and Esme Bhan. *The Voice of Anna Julia Cooper*. Lanham, MD: Rowman and Littlefield, 1998.

L'Eplattenier, Barbara. "Finding Ourselves in the Past: An Argument for the Need for Historical Work on Writing Program Administrators." *The Writing*

Program Administrator as Researcher: Inquiry in Action and Reflection. Eds. Shirley Rose and Irwin Weiser. Portsmouth, NH: Boynton/Cook, 1999. 131–40.

Lerner, Gerda, ed. *Black Women in White America: A Documentary History.* New York: Vintage, 1972.

Li, Chenyang. *The Tao Encounters the West: Explorations in Comparative Philosophy.* Albany: State U of New York P, 1999.

Lintin, Daniel Paul. "'Shall It Be A Woman?': A Rhetorical Analysis of the Works of Maria W. Miller Stewart." Master's thesis. U of Minnesota, 1989.

Lipsitz, George. *The Possessive Investment in Whiteness: How White People Profit from Identity Politics.* Philadelphia: Temple UP, 1998.

Liu, Eric. "The Unbearable Being of Whiteness." 16 June 2003. http://www.slate.msn.com/toolbar.aspx?action=print&id=2450.

Logan, Onnie Lee as told to Katherine Clark. *Motherwit: An Alabama Midwife's Story.* New York: E. P. Dutton, 1989.

Logan, Shirley Wilson. *"We Are Coming": The Persuasive Discourse of Nineteenth-Century Black Women.* Carbondale: Southern Illinois UP, 1999.

———. *With Pen and Voice: A Critical Anthology of Nineteenth-Century African-American Women.* Carbondale: Southern Illinois UP, 1995.

Lorde, Audre. *Sister/Outsider.* Freedom, CA: Crossing, 1984.

———. "Foreword." *Wild Women in the Whirlwind: Afra-American Culture and the Contemporary Literary Renaissance.* Eds. Joanne M. Braxton and Andrea Nicola McLaughlin. New Brunswick: Rutgers UP, 1990. xi–xiii.

Lubiano, Wahneema, ed. *The House That Race Built.* New York: Random House, 1997.

Lurie, Nancy Oestreich, ed. *Mountain Wolf Woman, Sister of Crashing Thunder: The Autobiography of a Winnebago Indian.* Ann Arbor: U of Michigan P, 1966.

Luttrell, Wendy. *Schoolsmart and Moterhwise: Working Class Women's Identity and Schooling.* New York: Routledge, 1997.

Lynn, Steven. "A Passage into Critical Theory." *Conversations: Contemporary Critical Theory and the Teaching of Literature.* Eds. Charles Moran and Elizabeth F. Penfield. Urbana: NCTE, 1990. 99–113.

Lyons, Scott. "Rhetorical Sovereignty: What Do American Indians Want from Writing?" *College Composition and Communication* 51:3 (February 2000): 447–68.

Machor, James L. "Introduction: Readers/Texts/Contexts." *Readers in History: Nineteenth-Century American Literature and the Contexts of Response.* Ed. James L. Machor. Baltimore: Johns Hopkins UP, 1993. vii–xxix.

Maher, Frances. "Progressive Education and Feminist Pedagogies: Issues in Gender, Power, and Authority." *Teachers College Record* 101:1 (Fall 1999): 35–59.

Major, Clarence. *Juba to Jive: A Dictionary of Afro-American Slang.* New York: Penguin, 1994.

Marshall, Ian and Wendy Ryden. "Interrogating the Monologue: Making Whiteness Visible." *College Composition and Communication* 52.2 (2000): 240–59.

Marshall, Paule. "The Making of a Writer: From the Poets in the Kitchen." *New York Times Book Review,* 9 (January 1983): 3, 34–35.

Mastrangelo, Lisa. "Learning from the Past: Composition, Rhetoric, and Debate at Mount Holyoke College." *Rhetoric Review* 18 (Fall 1999): 46–64.

Matory, James Lorand. "Religions, African and Afro-Caribbean, in the United States." June 2001. http://www.Africana.com/Articles/tt_496.htm.

Mather, Cotton. *Magnalia Christi Americana.* Ed. Kenneth B. Murdock. Cambridg: Harvard UP, 1977.

Mattingly, Carol. *Well-Tempered Women: Nineteenth-Century Temperance Rhetoric.* Carbondale: Southern Illinois UP, 1998.

———. "Telling Evidence: Rethinking What Counts in Rhetoric." *Rhetoric Society Quarterly* 32 (2002): 99–107.

McAndrew, Donald A. "Ecofeminism and the Teaching of Literacy." *College Composition and Communication* 47:3 (1996): 367–82.

McCombs, H. G. "The Dynamics and Impact of Affirmative Action Processes on Higher Education, Curriculum, and Black Women." *Sex Roles* 21: 1–2 (1989): 127–43.

McHenry, Elizabeth. "Rereading Literacy Legacy: New Considerations of the 19th-Century African-American Reader and Writer." *Callaloo* 22 (1999): 477–82.

McIntosh, Peggy. "White Privilege and Male Privilege: A Personal Account of Coming to See Correspondences through Work in Women's Studies." *Race, Class, and Gender: An Anthology.* Eds. Margaret L. Anderson and Patricia Hill Collins. Belmont, CA: Wadsworth, 1992.

McKay, Nellie Y. "Naming the Problem that Led to the Question 'Who Shall Teach African-American Literature?'; Or, Are We Ready to Disband the Wheatley Court?" *PMLA* 113 (1998): 359–69.

McKee, Patricia. *Producing American Races: Henry James, William Faulkner, Toni Morrison.* Durham: Duke UP, 1999.

McLaurin, Melton. *Celia, A Slave.* Athens: U Georgia P, 1991.

McMurry, Linda O. *To Keep the Waters Troubled: The Life of Ida B. Wells.* New York: Oxford UP, 1998.

Medicine, Beatrice. "North American Indigenous Women and Cultural Domination." *American Indian Culture and Research Journal* 17:3 (1993): 121–30.

Meloney, William Browne, "The Slumming in New York's Chinatown." *Munsey's Magazine* 41:9 (September 1909): 820.

Memoir of Old Elizabeth. Six Women's Slave Narratives. Ed. William L. Andrews. New York: Oxford UP, 1988.

Merians, Linda E. "Hottentot: The Emergence of an Early Modern Racist Epithet." *Shakespeare Studies* 26 (1998): 123–44.

Micciche, Laura. "Male Plight and Feminist Threat in Composition Studies: A Response to 'Teaching and Learning as a Man.' " *Composition Studies* 25: 1 (1997): 21–36.

Middleton, Joyce Irene. " 'Both Print and Oral' and 'Talking about Race': Transforming Toni Morrison's Language Issues into Teaching Issues." *African American Rhetoric(s): Interdisciplinary Perspectives.* Eds. Elaine Richardson and Ronald L. Jackson II. Carbondale: Southern Illinois UP, 2003. 242–58.

———. "Kris, I Hear You." *Journal of Advanced Composition* 22 (2000): 433–41.

Mignolo, Walter. *Local Histories/Global Designs: Coloniality, Subaltern Knowledges and Border Thinking.* Princeton: Princeton UP, 2000.

Mihesuah, Devon A. "Commonality of Difference: American Indian Women and History." *American Indian Quarterly* 20: 1 (1994): 15–27.

Miller, Thomas, and Melody Bowden. "A Rhetorical Stance on the Archives of Civic Action." *College English* 61 (1999): 591–98.

Miner, Valerie. "Writing and Teaching with Class." *Working-Class Women in the Academy: Laborers in the Knowledge Factory.* Eds. Michelle M. Tokarezyk and Elizabeth A. Fay. Amherst: Massachusetts UP, 1993. 73–86.

Modleski, Tania. *Feminism Without Women: Culture and Criticism in a 'Postfeminist' Age.* New York; Routledge, 1991.

Moi, Toril. "Men Against Patriarchy." *Gender and Theory.* Ed. Linda Kaufman. New York: B. Blackwell, 1989. 181–88.

Moore, Jessica Care. "There Are No Asylums for the Real Crazy Women." *The Words Don't Fit in My Mouth.* New York: Moone Black Press, 1997.

Moreno, Renee. "The Politics of Location: Text as Opposition." *College Composition and Communication* 54:2 (2002): 222–42.

Morrison, Toni. *Beloved.* New York: Knopf, 1987.

———. *Playing in the Dark: Whiteness and the American Literary Imagination.* New York: Knopf, 1992.

———. *Playing in the Dark: Whiteness and the Literary Imagination* Cambridge: Harvard UP, 1992.

———, ed. *Race-ing Justice, En-gendering Power.* New York: Pantheon Books, 1992.

———. "Home." *The House That Race Built: Black Americans, U.S. Terrain.* Ed. Wahneema Lubiano. New York: Pantheon, 1997.

Moss, Thylias. *Last Chance for the Tarzan Holler.* New York: Persea Books, 1998.

Mossell, Gertrude. *The Work of the Afro-American Woman.* New York: Oxford UP, 1988.

Mullen, Harryette. "Runaway Tongue: Resistant Orality in Uncle Tom's Cabin, Our Nig, Incidents in the Life of a Slave Girl, and Beloved." *The Culture of Sentiment: Race, Gender, and Sentimentality in Nineteenth-Century America.* Ed. Shirley Samuels. New York: Oxford UP, 1994. 244–64.

Murphy, Patrick D. "Coyote Midwife in the Classroom: Introducing Literature with Feminist Dialogics." *Practicing Theory in Introductory College Literature Courses.* Eds. James M. Calahan and David B. Downing. Urbana: National Council of Teachers of English, 1991. 161–76.

Murray, Donald. "Finding Your Own Voice: Teaching Composition in an Age of Dissent." *College Composition and Communication* 20:2 (Fall 1969): 118–23.

Naylor, Gloria. *Mama Day.* New York: Tickner and Fields, 1988.

Neal, Terry M. "The Ghost of Proposition 187: Identity Politics Is Once Again the Hot Issue in California Politics." 5 September 2003. (http://www.calatinonet.org/eWebpages/news-1062860563.html).

Neely, Barbara. *Commonwealth Journal 2001-49.* Interviews with Ellen Dunlap, President of the American Antiquarian Society, and Jocyce [*sic*] Bermann, Director of Valley "Herstory." CD. 2001.

New York Times. "141 Men and Girls Die in Waist Factory Fire; Trapped High Up in Washington Place Building; Street Strewn with Bodies; Piles of Dead

Inside." March 26, 1911. May 31, 2002. http://www.ilr.cornell.edu/trianglefire/texts/newspaper/nyt_032611_5.html.

Niemann, Yolanda Flores. "The Making of a Token: A Case Study of Stereotype Threat, Stigma, Racism, and Tokenism in Academe." *Frontiers: A Journal of Women's Studies* 20:1 (1999): 111–35.

———. "The Psychology of Tokenism: Psychosocial Realities of Faculty of Color." *Handbook of Racial and Ethnic Minority Psychology.* Eds. Guillermo Bernal, et al. Thousand Oaks, CA: Sage Publications, 2003. 100–18.

Okin, Susan Moller. "Feminism, Women's Human Rights, and Cultural Differences." *Hypatia* 13:2 (Spring 1998): 32–52.

Olson, Gary, and Elizabeth Hirsch. *Women Writing Culture.* Albany: State U of New York P, 1995.

Oxendine, Clifton. "Pembroke State College for Indians: Historical Sketch." *North Carolina Historical Review* 22:1 (January 1945): 22–33.

Painter, Nell I. "Representing Truth: Sojourner Truth's Knowing and Becoming Known." *Journal of American History* 81:2 (September 1994): 461–91.

Park, You-me and Rajeswari Sunder Rajan, eds. *The Post-Colonial Jane Austin.* New York: Routledge, 2000.

Pavel, D. Michael, Rebecca Rak Skinner, Elizabeth Farris, Margaret Cahalan, John Tippeconnic, and Wayne Stein. "American Indians and Alaska Natives in Postsecondary Education." *Education Statistics Quarterly* 1:1 (1999): 67–74.

Payne, Elizabeth Ann. *Reform, Labor, and Feminism: Margaret Dreier Robins and the Women's Trade Union League.* Urbana: U of Illinois P, 1998.

Perelman, Chaim, and L. Olbrechts-Tyteca. *The New Rhetoric.* London: U of Notre Dame P, 1969.

Peterson, Carla. *Doers of the Word: African-American Speakers and Writers in the North (1830–1880).* New York: Oxford UP, 1995.

Phillips, Christopher. *Freedom's Port: The African-American Community of Baltimore, 1790–1860.* Urbana: U of Illinois P, 1997.

Phillips, Layli and Barbara McCaskill. "Who's Schooling Who? Black Women and the Bringing of the Everyday into Academe, or Why We Started *The Womanist.*" *Signs* 20.41, 1007–18.

Porter, James E. *Audience and Rhetoric.* Englewood Cliffs: Prentice-Hall, 1992.

Powell, Malea. "Rhetorics of Survivance: How American Indians Use Writing." *College Composition and Communication* 53:3 (February 2002): 396–434.

Prendergast, Catherine. "Race: the Absent Presence in Composition Studies." *College Composition and Communication* 50:1 (1998): 36–53.

A Quarter Century of Visiting Fellowships at the American Antiquarian Society, 1972–97. Rpt. Proceedings of the American Antiquarian Society, 1997 107:2. Worcester: American Antiquarian Society, 1998.

Raboteau, Albert J. *Slave Religion: The "Invisible Institution" in the Antebellum South.* New York: Oxford UP, 1980.

Randall, Alice. *The Wind Done Gone.* New York: Houghton Mifflin, 2001.

Raphals, Lisa. "Gender Virtue Reconsidered: Notes from the Warring States and Han." *The Sage and Second Sex: Confucianism, Ethics, and Gender.* Ed. Chenyang Li. Chicago: Open Court, 2000. 223–47.

Rasmussen, Birgit Brander, et al., eds. *The Making and Unmaking of Whiteness.* Durham: Duke UP, 2001.

Ratcliffe, Krista. "Eavesdropping as Rhetorical Tactic: History, Whiteness, and Rhetoric." *Journal of Advanced Composition* 20 (2000): 87–119.

Reis, Sally M. "Internal Barriers, Personal Issues, and Decisions Faced by Gifted and Talented Females." *Gifted Child Today* 25:1 (Winter 2002): 14–28.

Rhodes, Jane. *Mary Ann Shadd Cary: The Black Press and Protest in the Nineteenth Century.* Bloomington: Indiana UP, 1998.

Richardson, Marilyn, ed. *Maria W. Stewart: America's First Black Woman Political Writer.* Bloomington: Indiana UP, 1987.

Rickford, John Russell. *Spoken Soul: The Story of Black English.* New York: John Wiley and Sons, 2000.

Riddell-Dixon, Elizabeth. "Mainstreaming Women's Rights: Problems and Prospects within the Center for Human Rights." *Global Governance* 5 (1999): 149–71.

Rilke, Rainer Maria. *Letters to a Young Poet.* Trans. Stephen Mitchell. New York: Modern Library, 2001.

Ripley, Peter, ed. *The Black Abolitionist Papers: Volume III, The United States, 1830–1846.* Chapel Hill: U of North Carolina P, 1991.

Roediger, David. *The Wages of Whiteness: Race and the Making of the American Working Class.* Boston: Routledge, 1991.

Rosenblatt, Louise M. *Literature as Exploration.* 5th ed. New York: MLA, 1995.

Roskelly, Hephzibah. "Telling Tales in School: A Redneck Daughter in the Academy." *Working-class Women in the Academy: Laborers in the Knowledge Factory.* Eds. Michelle M. Tokarezyk and Elizabeth A. Fay. Amherst: Massachusetts UP, 1993. 292–307.

Rowlandson, Mary. *The Captive.* Tucson: American Eagle, 1990.

Royster, Jacqueline Jones. "When the First Voice You Hear Is Not Your Own." *College Composition and Communication* 47:1 (1996): 29–40.

———. *Traces of a Stream: Literacy and Social Change Among African American Women.* Pittsburgh: U of Pittsburgh P, 2000.

———. "Disciplinary Landscaping, or Contemporary Challenges in the History of Rhetoric." *Philosophy and Rhetoric* 36:2 (2003): 148–67.

———, and Jean C. Williams. "History in the Spaces Left: African American Presence and Narratives of Composition Studies." *College Composition and Communication* 50:4 (June 1999): 563–84.

Ryan, Mary P. *Women in Public: Between Banners and Ballots, 1825–1880.* Baltimore: Johns Hopkins UP, 1990.

Sadker, David, and Myra Sadker. *Failing at Fairness: How America's Schools Cheat Girls.* New York: Scribners, 1994.

Sassen, Saskia. "Toward a Feminist Analytics of the Global Economy." *Global Legal Studies Journal* 4.70 (1996): 7–40.

———. "Spatialities and Temporalities of the Global: Elements of a Theorization. *Public Culture* 12.1 (2000): 215–32.

Saxton, Alexander. *The Rise and Fall of the White Republic: Class Politics and Mass Culture in Nineteenth Century America.* London: Verso, 1990.

Schneiderman, Rose, with Lucy Goldthwaite. *All for One.* New York: Paul S. Eriksson, 1967.

———. "Reply to New York Senators on Delicacy and Charm of Women." Available at http://womhist.binghamton.edu/law/doc25.htm. 21 June 2002.

———. "Rose Schneiderman's Story." Course website of Dr. Jeffrey R. Young. <http://www2.gasou.edu/facstaff/jryount/2110doc8.html>. Retrieved 31 May 2002.

Schultz, Lucille M. *The Young Composers: Composition's Beginnings in Nineteenth-Century Schools.* Carbondale: Southern Illinois UP, 1999.

Scruggs, L[awson]. A. *Women of Distinction: Remarkable in Works and Invincible in Character.* Raleigh, NC: 1893.

Sears, David O., and Nicholas A. Valentino. "Race, Religion, and Sectional Conflict in Contemporary Partisanship." Paper delivered at the American Political Science Association, San Francisco, 1 September 2001. www.igs.berkeley.edu/research_programs/racepapers/Searspaper.doc~.

Shadd, Mary A. *Notes of Canada West.* Detroit: George W. Pattison, 1852. University of Maine Archives.

——— to George Whipple, 27 October 1851. American Missionary Association Archives. Amistad Research Center, New Orleans.

——— to George Whipple, 27 November 1851. American Missionary Association Archives. Amestad Research Center, New Orleans.

Shaffer, Pamela. "Using Reader Response Techniques to Teach Multicultural Writings in the Composition Classroom." Paper presented at the Annual Meeting of the Conference on College Composition and Communication, March 31–April 3 1993, San Diego.

Shor, Ira. *When Students Have Power: Negotiating Authority in a Critical Pedagogy.* Chicago: U of Chicago P, 1996.

Slote, Walter H. "Psychocultural Dynamics within the Confucian Family." *Confucianism and the Family.* Eds. Walter H. Slote and George A. DeVos. Albany: State U of New York P, 1998. 37–51.

Slotkin, Richard. *Regeneration Through Violence: The Mythology of the American Frontier, 1600–1860.* Middletown, CT: Wesleyan, 1973.

Smith, Anna Deavere. *Talk to Me: Listening Between the Lines.* New York: Random House, 2000.

Smith, Rochelle. "Walking on Eggshells: The Experience of a Black Woman Professor." *ADE Bulletin* 102 (Spring 1999): 68–72.

Smitherman, Geneva. *Talkin and Testifyin: The Language of Black America.* Detroit: Wayne State UP, 1977.

———. *Black Talk: Words and Phrases from the Hood to the Amen Corner.* Boston: Houghton Mifflin, 1994.

Sosnoski, James J. "A Mindless Man-driven Theory Machine: Intellectuality, Sexuality, and the Institution of Criticism." *Feminisms: An Anthology of Literary Theory and Criticism.* Eds. Robyn R. Warhol and Diane Price Herndl. New Brunswick: Rutgers UP, 1997. 33–50.

Spivak, Gayatri Chakravorty. "Can the Subaltern Speak: Speculations on Widow Sacrifice." *Wedge* 7.8 (Winter/Spring 1985): 120–30.

———. *In Other Worlds: Essays in Cultural Politics*. London: Methuen, 1987.

———. *Outside in the Teaching Machine*. New York: Routledge, 1993.

Standing Bear, Luther. *Land of the Spotted Eagle*. Boston: Houghton Mifflin, 1933.

———. *My People the Sioux*. Lincoln: U of Nebraska P, 1975.

Stanton, William. *The Leopard's Spots: Scientific Attitudes Toward Race in America 1815–59*. Chicago: U of Chicago P, 1960.

Stark, Ryan John. "Margaret Cavendish and Composition Style." *Rhetoric Review* 17 (Spring 1999): 264–81.

"The State of Research on the United States Latino Population." Presentation to Pew Charitable Trusts. Institute for Latino Studies, University of Notre Dame. May 2000.

Stepto, Robert. *From Behind the Veil: A Study of Afro-American Narrative*. Chicago: U of Illinois P, 1991.

Sterling, Dorothy, ed. *We are Your Sisters: Black Women in the Nineteenth Century*. New York: Norton, 1984.

Stewart, Maria W. "Address Delivered to the Afric-American Female Intelligence Society of America." *Maria W. Stewart, America's First Black woman Political Writer: Essays and Speeches*. Ed. Marilyn Richardson. Bloomington: Indiana UP, 1997. 50–55.

———. "Mrs. Stewart's Farewell Address Delivered to Her Friends in the City of Boston. *Maria W. Stewart, America's First Black woman Political Writer: Essays and Speeches*. Ed. Marilyn Richardson. Bloomington: Indiana UP, 1997. 65–74.

Still, William. *The Underground Rail Road*. Philadelphia: Porter and Coates, 1872. Reprinted Chicago: Johnson Publishing, 1970. 355–60.

Stokes, Mason. *The Color of Sex: Whiteness, Heterosexuality, and the Fictions of White Supremacy*. Durham: Duke UP, 2001.

Stuckey, Sterling. *Slave Culture: Nationalist Theory and the Foundations of Black America*. New York: Oxford UP, 1987.

Sundiata, Sekou. "City Suite: Bombs from Bullshit." On *The Blue Oneness of Dreams* [CD]. New York: Mercury Records, 1997.

Sunder Rajan, Rajeswari Sunder, ed. *The Lie of the Land: English Literary Studeies in India*. Delhi: Oxford UP, 1992.

———. *Real and Imagined Women: Gender, Culture and Postcolonialism*. New York: Routledge, 1993.

———. "The Third World Academic in Other Places: The Postcolonial Intellectual Revisited." *Critical Inquiry* 33.3 (Spring 1997): 596–616.

———. "Women Between Community and State; Some Implications of the Uniform Civil Code Debates in India." *Social Text* 18.4 (2000): 55–82.

———, ed. *Signposts: Gender Issues in Post-Independence India*. New Brunswick: 2001.

———. *Scandal of the State: Women, Law and Citizenship in Postcolonial India*. Durham: Duke UP, 2003.

Sutherland, Christine M. "Aspiring to the Rhetorical Tradition: A Study of Margaret Cavendish." *Listening to Their Voices: The Rhetorical Activities of*

Historical Women. Ed. Molly Meijer Wertheimer. Columbia: U of South Carolina P, 1997. 255–71.

Tax, Merideth. *The Rising of Women: Feminist Solidarity and Class Conflict, 1880–1917.* Urbana: U of Illinois P, 2001.

Thompson, Dr. L. S. "The Story of Mattie J. Jackson. 1866." Volume 3. *Six Women's Slave Narratives.* Ed. William L. Andrews. New York: Oxford UP, 1988.

Tokarczyk, Michelle M., and Elizabeth A. Fay. *Working-Class Women in the Academy: Laborers in the Knowledge Factory.* Amherst: Massachusetts UP, 1993.

Toni Morrison Uncensored. Dir. Gary Deans. Princeton, NJ: Films for the Humanities and Sciences, 1999.

Tsosie, Rebecca. "Changing Women: The Cross-Currents of American Indian Feminine Identity." *American Indian Culture and Research Journal* 12:1 (1988): 1–37.

Tyrrell, Henry. "The Theatre of New York's Chinatown." *The Theatre Magazine* 3:29 (July 1903): 170.

Villagra, Hector. Testimony before Senate Select Committee on College and University Admissions and Outreach. Manuscript in author's possession, MALDEF (8 November 2001).

Villanueva, Victor, Jr. *Bootstraps: From an American Academic of Color.* Urbana: NCTE, 1993.

———. "Maybe a Colony: And Still Another Critique of the Comp Community." *Journal of Advanced Composition* 17:2 (1997): 183–90.

———. "The Tree and the Woods: Racism in Multiculturalism." Chair's Address, Opening General Session, Conference on College Composition and Communication. 25 March 1999.

Viswanathan, Gauri. *Mask of Conquest: Literary Study and British Rule in India.* New York: Columbia UP, 1989.

Walker, Alice. "Everyday Use." *In Love and Trouble.* New York: Harcourt Brace Jovanovich, 1974.

———. "For My Sister Molly Who in the Fifties." *Revolutionary Petunias and Other Poems.* New York: Harcourt Brace Jovanovich, 1973.

Walker, David. "Appeal to the Coloured Citizens of the World." *Negro Social and Political Thought.* Ed. Charles M. Wiltse. New York: Hill and Wang, 1965.

Wang, Zheng. "Three Interviews: Wang Anyi, Zhu Lin, and Dai Qing." *Gender Politics in Modern China: Writing and Feminism.* Ed. Tani Barlow. Durham: Duke UP, 1993. 158–208.

Watkins, William. *The White Architects of Black Education: Ideology and Power in America, 1865–1954.* New York: Teachers College P, 2001.

Welter, Barbara. "The Cult of True Womanhood: 1820–1860." *American Quarterly* 18 (Summer 1966): 151–74.

West, Cornel. *Race Matters.* New York: Vintage Books, 1993.

West, Thomas. "The Racist Other." *Journal of Advanced Composition Online* 17:2: 1–16. http://jac.gsu/jac/17.2/Articles/5.htm.

Westbrook, Alonzo. *The Hip Hoptionary: The Dictionary of Hip-Hop Terminology.* New York: Harlem Moon, 2002.

Williams, Daniel. *Pillars of Salt: An Anthology of Early American Criminal Narratives.* Madison, WI: Madison House, 1993.

Williams, Patricia A. *Seeing a Color-Blind Future: the Paradox of Race.* New York: Noonday, 1997.

Williams, Sherley Anne. *Dessa Rose.* New York: William Morrow, 1986.

Willis, Sharon. *High Contrast: Race and Gender in Contemporary Hollywood Film.* Durham: Duke UP, 1997.

Wilson, Gilbert L. *Buffalo Bird Woman's Garden.* St. Paul: Minnesota Historical Society P, 1987, Reprint, 1917.

Winterowd, W. Ross. *Contemporary Rhetoric: A Conceptual Background with Readings.* San Diego: Harcourt Brace Jovanovich, 1973.

Wolf, Margaret. "Beyond the Patrilineal Self: Constructing Gender in China." *Self as Person in Asian Theory and Practice.* Ed. Roger T. Ames with Wimal Dissaayake and Thomas P. Kasulis. Albany: State U of New York P, 1994. 251–67.

Wright, Richard. "The Ethics of Living Jim Crow." *Uncle Tom's Children: Five Long Stories.* New York: Harper, 1938.

Wu, Hui. "Alternative Feminist Discourse of Post-Mao Chinese Writers: A Perspective from the Rhetorical Situation." *Alternative Rhetorics: Challenges to the Rhetorical Tradition.* Eds. Laura Gray-Rosendale and Sibylle Gruber. Albany: State U of New York P, 2001. 219–34.

———. "Historical Studies of Rhetorical Women Here and There: Methodological Challenges to Dominant Interpretative Frameworks." *Rhetoric Society Quarterly* 31 (Winter 2002): 81–97.

Young, John. "Toni Morrison, Oprah Winfrey, and Postmodern Popular Audiences." *African American Review* 35 (2001): 181–204.

Zandy, Janet, ed. *Calling Home: Working-Class Women's Writings, An Anthology.* New Brunswick: Rutgers UP, 1990.

Zhang, Kangkang. *ni dui ming yun shuo bu* (Say "No" to Your Fate). Shanghai: Shanghai Knowledge P, 1994.

Zhong, Xueping, Wang Zheng, and Bai Di. eds. *Some of Us: Chinese Women Growing up in the Mao Era.* New Brunswick: Rutgers UP, 2001.

Contributors

VALERIE BABB is professor of English and African American Studies at the University of Georgia and the editor of the Langston Hughes Review. Her published works include *Whiteness Visible: The Meaning of Whiteness in American Literature and Culture* (1998), *Black Georgetown Remembered,* which has just entered its second printing (1991), *Ernest Gaines* (1991), and numerous articles.

PATRICK BIZZARO is editor of *Dream Garden: The Poetic Vision of Fred Chappell* (LSU 1997). His books of poetry include *Fear of the Coming Drought* (Mount Olive College Press 2001), the forthcoming *Every Insomniac Has a Story to Tell,* and six chapbooks. His pedagogical work includes *Responding to Student Poems: Applications of Critical Theory* (NCTE 1993). A professor of English at East Carolina University, he teaches creative writing and literature and currently serves as Director of University Writing Programs. He is a University of North Carolina Board of Governor's Distinguished Professor for Teaching and for his poetry has won *NYQ's* Madeline Sadin Award and *Four Quarters'* Poetry Prize.

RESA CRANE BIZZARO (Meherrin/Cherokee) is the president of the CCCC Caucus for American Indian Scholars and Scholarship. Her research interests include Native American and Identity rhetorics, Native American Literature, and contemporary creative writing. Her most recent publications focus on the history of postsecondary education provided for Native Americans in this country. She also publishes essays on contemporary American writers. A fixed-term faculty member in the English Department at East Carolina University, she co-directs the Writers Reading Series of Eastern North Carolina and directs the Professional Writing Program at the Brody School of Medicine.

JAMI L. CARLACIO teaches writing in the English department at Cornell University. She has published work on antebellum Anglo- and African

American women's rhetorics in *Rhetoric Review* and in *Rhetorical Democracy: Discursive Practices of Civic Engagement* (2004) and on African American women's autobiography (forthcoming). She has also published essays on ethical citizenship and on the rhetoric of democracy and is currently writing a book on women's rhetorical practices during the 1830s.

AMANDA ESPINOSA-AGUILAR, an assistant professor of English at Washington State University, teaches classes in rhetorical theory, composition, and ethnic American literature. Her publications include "Linking Assignment Design to Paper Grading in Classes About Diversity," in *Contested Terrain* (2001) and "Analyzing the Rhetoric of the English Only Movement," in *Language Ideologies: Critical Perspectives on the Official English Movement* (2001). In 1999 Professor Espinosa-Aguilar was elected to the Executive Committee of the Conference on College Composition and Communication and served as the co-chair of the Scholars for the Dream Award Committee in 2002.

ANN E. GREEN is an associate professor of English at Saint Joseph's University in Philadelphia, Pennsylvania, where she regularly teaches service-learning courses such as Writing through Race, Class, and Gender, and Literacy as a Social Practice. She has published in *College Composition and Communication, Reflections: A Journal of Writing, Service-Learning, and Community Literacy,* and *Writing on the Edge.*

DAVID G. HOLMES, associate professor of English and Director of English Composition at Pepperdine University, is a former secondary school teacher whose articles have appeared in the *Journal of Teaching Writing* and in *Race, Rhetoric and Composition,* edited by Keith Gilyard. He has also authored *Revisiting Racialized Voice: African American Ethos in Language and Literature* (2004). His current research projects include civil rights rhetoric and the racialized aesthetics and rhetoric of Carl Van Vechten's writings.

SUSAN APPLEGATE KROUSE (Oklahoma Cherokee) is assistant professor of Anthropology at Michigan State University, where she is also on the faculty of the American Indian Studies Program. Her research focuses on urban American Indian communities, particularly on women's leadership. Recent publications include, "What Came Out of the Takeovers: Women's Activism and the Indian Community School of Milwaukee" (*American Indian Quarterly* 2004) and "Kinship and Identity: Mixed Bloods in Urban Indian Communities" (*American Indian Culture and Research Journal* 1999).

VALERIE LEE is professor of English and Women's Studies. She is the author of numerous articles on feminist theory, African American Literature, folklore, and multiculturalism. Among her books are *Granny Midwives and Black Women Writers: Double-Dutched Readings* (1996) and *The Prentice Hall Anthology of African American Women Writers* (forthcoming). Professor Lee teaches such courses as Critical Race Feminisms, Women Writers of the Harlem Renaissance, Theorizing Gender Representations, Women Writing the Civil Rights Movement, and The Oral Tradition and African American Narratives. Currently, Professor Lee is chair of the Department of English at Ohio State.

BARBARA E. L'EPLATTENIER is an assistant professor in the Department of Rhetoric and Writing at the University of Arkansas—Little Rock, where she teaches in professional writing track. Her historical research focuses on the rhetoric of Progressive Era women, professional writing, and gender/queer studies. With Lisa Mastrangelo, she co-edited the collection, *Historical Studies of Writing Program Administration: Individuals, Communities, and the Formation of a Discipline.* She has published in *IEEE Transactions on Professional Communication* and *The Writing Program Administrator as Researcher: Inquiry in Action and Reflection.*

SHIRLEY WILSON LOGAN, associate professor of English at the University of Maryland, has published *With Pen and Voice: A Critical Anthology of Nineteenth-Century African-American Women* (1995), *We Are Coming: The Persuasive Discourse of Nineteenth-Century Black Women* (1999), and a number of articles on various aspects of African American women, rhetoric, and composition. She is series coeditor of Studies in Rhetorics and Feminisms and has served as chair of the Conference on College Composition and Communication, chair of the MLA Division on the History and Theory of Rhetoric and Composition, and director of Maryland's Professional Writing Program. She is a 2003–2004 recipient of the AAUW Postdoctoral Research Leave Fellowship to explore black sites of rhetorical education.

JOYCE IRENE MIDDLETON, associate professor of English at St. John Fisher College, is editor of *Of Color: African American Literature* (forthcoming). She has published essays on rhetorical memory; orality and literacy; pedagogy, race, and gender, and works by Toni Morrison and Zora Neale Hurston in *Innovations in African-American Rhetoric* (forthcoming), *College English, Cultural Studies, Journal of Advanced Composition, New Essays on Song of Solomon,* and the *Women's Review of Books.* She has served on the Executive Committee and is chair of the Diversity

Committee of the Conference on College Composition and Communication, and she is president of the Coalition of Women Scholars in the History of Rhetoric. Currently, she is writing about visual rhetoric in film, film as a pedagogy, and a rhetoric of race and whiteness.

JOYCELYN MOODY is author of *Sentimental Confessions: Spiritual Narratives of 19th-Century African American Women* and of numerous articles on African American autobiography, spirituality, and pedagogy. She teaches courses in American literature as an associate professor of English at the University of Washington in Seattle, where she is also adjunct professor of American Ethnic Studies and Women Studies.

RENEE M. MORENO is an assistant professor at the California State University, Northridge, and a former faculty fellow at the Institute for Latino Studies, University of Notre Dame. She received an NCTE Grant-in-Aid fellowship to fund her research and is serving on that organization's College Section Steering Committee. Professor Moreno's research interest is on storytelling and U.S. Latino/a literature, composition, and basic writing.

AKHILA RAMNARAYAN is a doctoral student at The Ohio State University and the assistant coordinator of the university writing center. Her dissertation, "Postcolonial Studies and the Indigenous Writer: the Case of Kalki," challenges a postcolonial critical model based on English only by focusing on the serialized historical romance written in India during the late colonial period and in her native language of Tamil. Her interests include postcolonial theory and criticism, twentieth-century and Anglophone literatures, world literatures in translation, postcolonial and transnational feminisms, ethnography, South Asian studies, composition studies and writing center theory and practice.

JACQUELINE JONES ROYSTER, professor of English at The Ohio State University, is the author, editor, or co-editor of five books, including *Traces of a Stream: Literacy and Social Change among African American Women* (2000), which was awarded the MLA Mina P. Shaughnessy Prize, and *Profiles of Ohio Women: 1803-2003* (2003); the consulting author or consulting co-editor of two school textbook series, *Writer's Choice* and *Glencoe Literature: The Reader's Choice*; and the author of numerous articles in rhetorical studies, literacy studies, and women's studies. She has also served as the chair of the Conference on College Composition and Communication and the chair of the Teaching of Writing Division of the Modern Language Association. Currently, she is working on a project focused on literacy in the rural South.

ANN MARIE MANN SIMPKINS is an assistant professor of English at The Ohio State University. Her works in progress include completing a book-length manuscript entitled *The Nineteenth-Century Rhetorical Practices of Black Women Publishers* and preparing a critical edition of Mary Shadd Cary's *Notes of Canada West.*

HUI WU, assistant professor of Rhetoric and Writing at the University of Central Arkansas, has published numerous articles in *Rhetoric Society Quarterly* and *College English,* as well as in scholarly anthologies, to address theoretical and methodological issues in the historical and comparative studies of women's rhetoric. Her Chinese translation of C. Jan Swearingen's *Rhetoric and Irony: Western Literacy and Western Lies* (Oxford University Press, 1990) is forthcoming in December 2003 in China. She has also written the introduction, and co-edited and translated, *Once Iron Girls: Selected Essays by Post-Mao Chinese Literary Women.* Professor Wu's research interests encompass theory of rhetoric, comparative studies of rhetoric and literacy, Asian rhetorical traditions, and women's rhetoric.

Index